TANKS
AMONG THE

Tulips

Stories of Bennebroek,
a small Dutch town during World War II

WILLIAM AND
ARDITH HEEMSKERK

ISBN: 978-1-4834-2114-8 (sc)
ISBN: 978-1-4834-2113-1 (e)

Lulu Publishing Services rev. date: 12/26/2014

BENNEBROEK, HOLLAND

*Dedicated to Bart and Maria Heeemskerk.
With gratitude for their courage and devotion to God,
their family and their country.*

Contents

Foreword

These are Bill's stories about things that happened during the German Occupation of the Netherlands in World War II, many years ago. Some details have been forgotten. Names of students, athletes and names of streets and some towns are fictitious. Dates are approximate. This is a memoir; not a history book.

We also asked Bill's relatives for their memories. His sister Alice gave us her diary. Sisters Jo and Jet wrote letters about those times and we added the girl's diaries and letters at the end of the book. But this letter, written when it happened, conveys the feelings of helplessness during the time so well that I decided to use it as an introduction, not in chronological order.

The paper is old and the ink is faded. Here is an English translation:

February 10, 1942

Beste Jos and Trudie,

You'll be surprised to get such a strange letter addressed to you both. That is because I have to tell you about a shocking event that happened yesterday morning at 5:45.

There was a loud knocking on the door. The man who was at the door kept on knocking because we didn't answer. We expected something that was not good.

Therefore, Dad stuck his head out of the bathroom window and asked, "Who's there?"

"—Police!"

Dad opened the door. A police detective ran upstairs. "I came to arrest two young men, aged 21 and 24 years. Where are they?"

So he arrested my two brothers, Wim and John.

After half an hour they were dressed and taken away. They were allowed to take two blankets with them. That was all.

Wim needed to go to the basement to get his shoes. But the policeman did not allow him to go by himself for fear he might escape.

After an emotional farewell, they were driven to police headquarters and from there to the Railway Station in Haarlem.

Twelve boys were taken from Heemstede, all from the same area. Around 10 P.M. we had a phone call from someone who did not give his name. He wanted to remain anonymous. He told us to take a suitcase with clothing and some bread and we would be allowed to leave that for the boys.

At that time I was living at school. But that didn't matter any more. When I was told about my brothers being taken, I came home. When I got there, Mother was packing suitcases and I helped. Then I got on my bike and went to the store to buy some caramels and two breakfast cakes.

Then as fast as I could I went to the Railroad Station. Ten minutes later I bought three platform tickets for Mother and Aunt Mimi and me.

But it took too long before the others came so I went upstairs in the station and found the boys in the third class waiting room. It was dark because of the blackout and we couldn't see each other. They were well guarded and could not escape. I went back outside and waited for Mother and Aunt Mimi to come.

About 15 minutes later Mother and Aunt Mimi arrived. We were not allowed in the waiting room, but we left the suitcases with the guards.

When the guard opened the door we saw Wim and he saw us, too.

Then he told the guards he needed to go to the restroom. He came out between two guards. That gave us a chance to talk to him and give him cigarettes. This was allowed. We asked Wim if John could come outside. But others wanted to come out and use the restroom and John had to wait his turn. Anyway, it was very cold and too long for us to wait outside.

Mother and Aunt Mimi heard from the inspector the train wouldn't leave until 3 A.M. Since it was 12:30, they went home and came back later.

When they were gone, I called Leni Smit, John's friend, to come and talk to him at the station.

She came quickly and we waited about five minutes before John came out. Leni gave him two packs of cigarettes. Then he had to go back inside. At 2:30 A.M. Mother and Aunt Mimi came again.

Ten minutes later, Jan van der Putten came out. I also talked with a boy from my school. Suddenly a boy emerged from the waiting room with two blankets under his arm. He said "Hurrah! I am too young—only fifteen years."

The boy from my school was seventeen. They let him go a little later.

In the meantime, Dad found out where the train was going—to Vught. The Germans had built a new concentration camp there for 15,000 prisoners.

When the boys finally came outside at 3:45 and got on the train, John yelled "We are going to Vught."

A little later the train took off. John leaned out of the window. Mother wanted to put some money in his hand but he wouldn't take it. He yelled again "We are going to Vught."

We missed seeing Wim again but we knew he was on the train because this afternoon we got a postcard he wrote on the train and threw out of the train window when they were going through Amsterdam. Somebody we did not know picked it up and put it in the mail.

For the rest we know nothing. Frans (Harry's older brother) doesn't sleep at home any more. If they arrest more young men, I will disappear.

The stockings from Leni have arrived. Please knit another pair from the wool Mother sent you.

Regards for everybody, especially Aunt Mimi.

Harry

Written by Harry Meyer, who married Jo Heemskerk after the war. Their daughter Monique Nachtegeller gave us this letter to be included in these stories of the Occupation of the Netherlands from May 10, 1940 to May 5, 1945.

Chapter 1

The Blitzkrieg Comes to Holland

May 10, 1940

In Holland, nights are quiet. But last night we heard the roar of many planes flying overhead. We thought it was the German Air Force, the Luftwaffe, on its way to bomb London. It was terrifying to think of the destruction raining down on the English people. The war between the Allies and Germany has begun.

On September 1, 1939, Germany had invaded Poland. Great Britain and France had signed a mutual defense pact with Poland and they declared war against Germany. But before the Allies could bring their armies to help the courageous country, it was overrun on both sides—the German blitzkrieg came from the West and the Russian army attacked from the East. The double attack forced their surrender. Hitler and Stalin had signed a secret pact to divide Poland between them.

After Poland fell, Europe held its breath, waiting for war to start. Neither France nor England was prepared to attack. For a while nothing happened.

The Dutch government considered their course of action. They had only a small peacetime army without modern equipment so there was little they could do. Adolf Hitler, the German Fuehrer, promised to respect our neutrality. He told us he would not cross our border as long as we did not threaten him or join the British and French Alliance. So the Dutch leaders declared to remain neutral and did not join Britain and France.

But at dawn we were awakened by an ear-splitting noise like the continuous crashing of thunder. I ran to the window to look out. It was not a storm but the sound of a thousand planes that filled the sky. Men were parachuting down from them. The anti-aircraft guns in nearby Haarlem were booming. The planes flew so low their wings almost scraped the rooftops.

We realized that Hitler had lied once again. We had been careful not to provoke Der Feuhrer, but in spite of his promises, which he repeated often, and without any warning, he attacked!

When the German bombers flew west last night, we thought they were going toward Great Britain, but they flew over the North Sea for a few hours and then turned around and came back to strike Holland. The reason for this strange maneuver was that they had seen our anti-aircraft guns were pointed east—toward the German border, where an attack would be expected to come. The German Generals saw our guns pointing east toward Germany and believed we couldn't shoot planes that came from the west. But our soldiers were able to turn the guns around and bring many planes crashing down.

The sound of the anti-aircraft guns from nearby Haarlem hurt my ears. I covered them with my hands but I couldn't shut out the sound.

The *blitzkrieg*, the lightning war, has come to Holland. Hitler has already taken over Austria, Czechoslovakia and Poland. And last week his armies attacked Norway and marched into Denmark.

My name is William, but they call me Pim. I go to Hageveld, a Catholic boarding school in Heemstede, North Holland. When the sound of explosions awakened us, the headmaster came to the dormitory. "Hurry!" he yelled. "Get dressed and come to the dining hall."

There, cooks were pouring tea and setting platters of buttered bread and cheese on the tables. While we ate, the headmaster spoke. "The Germans are attacking Holland, Belgium, Luxemburg and France. Everybody must leave and go home. Our school is a big building. Its roof is a tempting target. If the Luftwaffe bombs our school, we could all be killed."

He was right. But I think he sent us home because he did not want to be responsible for four hundred boys and the teachers and all the workers. If we went home, we might be killed there, too just as easily. However, I was glad to go home and be with my family in Bennebroek.

I went to my cell, stuffed my clothes into my suitcase and then went outside to the tram stop in front of school. The boom of guns and the roar of planes were louder outside. Waiting in the noisy open space with planes flying overhead felt unreal. With the war going on, I wondered if the trams would be running now. But after waiting a few minutes a car stopped for the boys going to our town and farther down the line. I paid the conductor a *quartje* (quarter) and dropped into an empty seat by a window. The passengers were silent, looking stunned. Nobody could believe this was happening. Why were the Germans bombing Holland? What did Hitler want with so small a country?

Through the window I could see two different scenes; in the sky there were many bombers, planes towing gliders, and big parachutes with men hanging from them, dropping through the air.

On the ground, things looked more normal. A milkman with a milk can on his bicycle platform stood by a kitchen door pouring milk while a woman held out her pitcher to be filled, swarms of bikers on their way to work, a man walking a little gray keeshond that was running along on short legs, holding its curly tail over its back. In the little home gardens, flowers bloomed.

Tulips and hyacinths painted the bulb fields red, yellow, pink, blue and white. It was May, tulip time. The landscape resembled a painting by Van Gogh. In the distance, a windmill was turning broad sails in the cool wind.

In the sky a plane plunged, trailing smoke and flames across the sky. I was horrified—the pilot could not survive a fall from that height. And if the plane landed on the tracks it could collide with our tram. But none of the pieces came close.

While I sat on the tram going toward home, I remembered Mother's birthday party last August. There Uncle Eddie had shocked and amazed us when he announced, "We're leaving the country. I feel sure the Germans are going to invade Holland and I don't want to be here when they come. So I bought tickets on a ship and I'm taking my wife, Bep, and our little son, Paul and going to America."

"Bart," he added speaking to Dad, "You should take your family and go to the States, too. It will be safe there. The other side of the Atlantic is too far away for Hitler's planes to reach."

Dad is always diplomatic, too polite to argue. But he definitely did not agree with his younger brother. "Bennebroek is our home and Holland is our country," he told Eddie. "I'm not going to hand over my country without a fight. Our ancestors made this country by building dikes around the lowlands and pumping the sea out. If we leave, Hitler will take it and turn it into a German state. We'll have to speak German and live by Hitler's rules. Once the Germans take it, we'll never get it back. I'm not going to run away. I'll stay here even if I have to fight."

Uncle Eddie said "But what good will it do if you end up dead? It's your choice. Go to America and be safe or stay in Bennebroek and risk being killed. Bep and I are leaving. Because if Hitler could take a big strong country like Poland, how can a tiny country like Holland fight him? We don't have tanks, planes or enough weapons. We have no air force and not much of an army."

When Hitler invaded Poland, the Polish army was well equipped and ready to fight. The Poles defended their country courageously. They thought they could hold off the German army for the time it would take for France and Britain to come and help them. In World War I, France and Britain had fought against Germany and defeated the Kaiser's army. We thought they could do it again!

But Hitler had made a secret alliance with Josef Stalin, the Russian dictator. The two agreed to divide Poland between them. So Germany attacked Poland from the West. At the same time, Russia surprised the world by invading Poland from the East. Overrun by both the Russian and German armies, surrounded by enemies, Poland had to surrender.

England and France had a mutual defense pact with Poland, agreeing to help each other if any of their countries were attacked. So they declared war on Germany. But when Poland was already conquered, there was nothing the Allies could do. The war became a stalemate.

Holland, Belgium and Luxemburg are little countries with small armies. They could not fight Hitler's humongous forces. They decided to remain neutral. They trusted Hitler and hoped he would keep his promise to leave them alone.

In World War I, the Kaiser invaded Belgium, but left the Netherlands, or Holland, alone. The Dutch government declared neutrality in 1939 just as they had in the first war. Hitler has tens of thousands of planes and tanks and millions of soldiers. Our air force has only a few fighter planes. Our army has no tanks. We have only a tiny defense force.

But we had a plan. Much of the land of Holland is below sea level, protected from the ocean by sand dunes and man-made dikes. If we open our dikes, the North Sea will rush in and flood our lowlands. Tanks are heavy, made of iron and steel; they can't float. A few feet of water will stop them. So if we were threatened we would open the dikes. Hitler's tanks could not come in.

Last week Germany attacked Norway and Denmark. The Danish King surrendered at once. He saw resistance would only get Danes killed and destroy their country.

Norway, on the other hand, is mountainous. Mountains, like fortresses protect defenders. The Norwegians fought back and the British Navy went to help them. They sank the Nazi cruiser *Blucher* in the Oslo Fjord. King Haakon left Norway and went to England to set up a government in exile. The Norwegian fighters fled to the mountains in the north and are still resisting.

I'm very sure Holland will not give in. Many big rivers cross our country and if we defend our bridges, we can keep the German Army from getting into the Western part where most people live, long enough for the French Army to come north through Belgium and help us. At least that is what the Dutch people believe.

When the tram reached Bennebroekerlaan, (the main street in Bennebroek) I got off and walked a few blocks to Schoollaan, (School Street) and down the long path to our house. My two white geese came out to meet me, flapping their wings in a mock attack. My dog, Tiberius, was tied but he jumped up and down in welcome, barking enthusiastically. His mouth was open but it was so noisy I could barely hear him.

Dad and Jan were digging a trench beside our house, making big piles of wet sand on the green grass. Gerard and Ton, the *tweeling*, saw me and came to help carry my suitcase and books.

The sky was filled with planes—troop transports and gliders over the airfields in the west. To the north, bombers were attacking Schiphol, the big Amsterdam Airport. Some planes flew so low they almost scraped the rooftops. If there were any Dutch planes flying, I didn't see them. We have so few. Maybe the Germans shot them down already or bombed the runways to prevent takeoffs.

I walked in through the kitchen door. Mother, Annie, Alice, Jo, and Jet, my youngest sister, were sitting around the dining room table drinking black coffee. It was late breakfast or early coffee time. The children like Jet and the boys had milk. Dad and Jan and the *tweeling* (my twin brothers) came in, too.

"Pim, what are you doing home?" Jan asked. "Did you come to help us dig?"

"The Dean sent us home," I said. "Why are you making a hole in the yard?"

"The announcer told everyone to build a bomb shelter on the radio," Jan said.

"You can't build a bomb shelter on a radio," Gerard pointed out, correcting him.

"The radio's not big enough," said Ton, smiling at their joke.

"It's a little late to build a shelter," I said. "If they told us to build one earlier, it would be ready now so we could use it."

The bomb shelter Jan and Dad are making is only a rectangular trench about two and a half meters long and a meter wide. They are digging now to make it deep enough to stand in. Shoveling sandy soil is back-breaking work in the sun. And they are only half done.

The radio was on and the announcer said Queen Wilhelmina had protested "this flagrant breach of conduct, against the behavior of civilized nations."

A speaker also warned soldiers manning the anti-aircraft guns not to shoot at Allied planes. But no Allied planes were visible. The only planes we saw were German.

After finishing the coffee and cake, Dad, Jan, the twins and I went out to work on the shelter. I asked Dad how I could help.

He said "Pim, you and Ton and Gerard can get some bags from the warehouse and fill them with sand."

Dad and Jan are tall, strong men. They kept on digging for a while. The twins and I filled sandbags. Then Dad put down his shovel and said, "That's big enough; it will have to do."

"Sounds good to me," Jan said and left off digging. They were tired. It doesn't seem very hard to fill bags with sand but the twins and I were tired, too and glad to quit.

We went in to dinner of meat, potatoes and gravy with *snijbonen* (snipped beans) and pudding for dessert. Afterward we sat listening to the news on the radio interspersed with marching songs and warnings about German parachutists and disguised spies. We didn't see any strangers around. I guess there aren't any in Bennebroek.

After dinner, Dad told the twins and me, "Get those old wood planks out of the barn. We need to make a roof over the shelter."

I hated touching the dirty boards. There were spiders on them and beetles crawling on the ground underneath. But Ton and Gerard and I picked them up and carried them to Dad and John. They laid them across the trench, leaving one end open so a person could get in. We dragged the heavy sandbags across the boards to cover the roof. This was our shelter.

Dad found a ladder in the barn and leaned it inside against the sandy wall. The twins and I climbed down. It's awfully dark. We'll need a lantern to see and some kind of a floor to stand on. When it rains the bottom will be wet. It rains a lot in Holland.

Our bomb shelter is just an empty hole. There's no room for a bed or a chair or even a shelf to sit on. I wouldn't want to stay there very long.

We got back to work; we filled more bags with the rest of the sand until we got rid of the whole pile. We put them outside the front door to protect the glass. Then we went inside to clean up and made a mess of the towels and the bathroom. The tub is so big that Gerard and Ton can get in together. The man who installed it must have had bathing a baby elephant in mind when he chose that bathtub.

After I cleaned up, I went outside. Mother, Jo, Alice, Henrietta and Annie were all standing around looking doubtfully at the shelter. Mother didn't like it. She stated her objections to Dad, "What if it's hit? What if it collapses? What if a bomb falls when we're in it? We'd be buried alive. I don't want to go down there. I feel safer in the house."

Dad said, "But if a bomb falls on the house, do you think our tile roof will protect us?"

"If a bomb lands on the shelter, sand bags won't protect us, either," Mother said.

It looks like we wasted our time building the shelter. If Mother won't use it, nobody will.

There are ten people living in our house, my Mother, Marie, and my Father, Bart, and seven children living at home. Jan is the oldest, almost 17. There are three sisters, Jo, 15, Alice, 12, and Henrietta, called Jet, is 8. The twins, Ton and Gerard, are 10. Annie is mother's helper. She's been here a long time and she's like an older sister.

I'm Willem but they call me Pim. I'm 13 and go to Hageveld, a boarding school. I'm only home for vacations. Our brother Frans is 16 and he goes to a boarding school down south on the Belgian border.

We live in a white brick house with a blue tile roof. Attached to the back of the house is the big warehouse Dad built for his business. He grows tulips and sells flower bulbs to growers in Europe and America. Now, with a war going on, he won't be able to sell them to customers in England and the States.

There are several other buildings on our ten acre farm—a barn, the glass house Dad uses to develop new tulips, a chicken house, and a toolshed. And there is a summer house that turns on wheels. It has a deck where we take our coffee in nice weather. Jo keeps her sewing machine in the summer house, and the seamstress, Gre Niewenhuis, uses it to make our clothes. In back of us are fields and woods. On one side a canal flows by and on the other side is an orchard that belongs to the nuns—but they can't eat it all so they share the fruit.

In front of the house a long path goes to Schoollaan. The canal on the side of our farm runs into a bigger canal, called the Ringvaart that goes around Haarlemmermeer Polder* and flows into the huge North Sea Canal that carries the water to the sea.

I asked Dad if I could go to the soccer field, where we heard on the radio that a machine gun nest was set up to shoot down low-flying planes. I could bring coffee and sandwiches to the soldiers. But Dad told me to stay home. I would just be in the way.

There isn't much to do. It isn't safe outdoors with the planes fighting over our heads. I looked at 'Tim Tyler,' the comic strip and listened to our big Philips radio.

Holland, Belgium, France and Luxemburg have been invaded. They are all fighting back. Our army is assembled at the bridges over the big rivers, the Maas, the Waal, and the Rhine, to keep the Germans out of the Western part of the country, where our big cities like Amsterdam, Rotterdam Den Hague, Haarlem, Delft and Eindhoven are. We call it "Fortress Holland."

The Germans already occupy the Rhineland***, Czechoslovakia, Austria, Poland, and Denmark and are fighting in Norway. We couldn't see why Hitler would want to attack us. He said he would respect our neutrality. Only last week he told us he had nothing but friendly intentions toward Holland. He said we are his 'Nordic cousins' and invited us to join his Third Reich*—the name he invented for Germany. He brags his kingdom will last a thousand years.

Bombing Holland is an odd way to deliver an invitation. It won't win friends and influence people. Diplomacy might have better results.

*We live near the Haarlemmermeer Polder, a broad stretch of land made by draining a lake between Haarlem and Leiden. Engineers built dikes to enclose the lake and pumped out the water to create farmland. This is how Holland was built—enclosing low land with dikes and pumping the water out. In the past, they used windmills, but Haarlemmermeer Lake was drained with oil-fueled pumps. It was more efficient than building so many more windmills to drain the whole lake would have been.

** Reich means kingdom. Hitler named his regime the Third Reich because there were two German kingdoms before this. He says it will last a thousand years. Even Methusaleh didn't live that long.

***The Rhineland was taken from Germany after WWI in the Versailles Treaty and given to France. Hitler marched in and took it back in 1936. The French could have halted the German Army then but they just ignored the takeover. If France and England stopped Hitler before he built such an enormous army, they wouldn't have to fight him now.

May 11, 1940

Hitler is such a liar. He says his army isn't attacking us; It's Britain and France who are the real aggressors. He says the Allies were planning to invade us and attack the Ruhr, Germany's industrial region which would threaten Germany. So his army is 'protecting' Holland, Belgium and Luxemburg against this mythical threat. In Holland, nobody believes him.

The Luftwaffe, the German Air Force, is bombing the airfields around The Hague, at Waalhaven*, and Moerdijk*, Ypenburg*, Valkenburg* and Ockenburg* (Dutch airports). They landed paratroopers. We knew they would bring in tanks but we weren't expecting an air attack. If planes fly over and drop bombs on us from the sky, how can we defend ourselves?

On the radio, we heard some good news. The Dutch Army has taken many German prisoners and loaded them on ships to sail to England.

Before the invasion, people said we could keep the Germans out by flooding our lowlands, or 'polders.' If we open our dikes the sea will flood the land and German tanks can not come in. This plan is called the 'Water-line Defense.' But it's not happening here. We haven't heard about any flooding yet. Apparently the engineers have not opened the dikes.

Our army is fighting to defend the western part of the country—the land between the rivers, close to the North Sea. This is where most of our big cities are—Amsterdam, Rotterdam, Haarlem, Delft and Den Hague— 'Fortress Holland.' We must keep the invaders out long enough for the French Army to come and help us.

We don't have a big army or enough equipment. Hitler has millions of soldiers. They have deadly Panzer tanks and fleets of airplanes and huge guns. Our government should have spent more money to keep us safe. But they believed we could be neutral and stay out of the war. Hitler had a plan for winning. It was 'Divide and Conquer.' By taking one small country at a time he had gained almost all of Europe.

When the German planes attacked, our anti-aircraft guns were aimed east—toward the German border. Our gunners had never fired them before, but they were able to turn the guns around, learn how to use them to shoot many planes down.

German planes are flying higher today because soldiers in machine-gun nests shot down some low-flying planes.

Hitler did not expect Holland to fight. He thought we would surrender immediately. In the Bible, Goliath did not expect David to give him any trouble but David beat Goliath with a stone from his sling. Our weapons are like sling shots against his enormous guns. I wish we could use them to bring his army down.

The planes dropped millions of leaflets. "Lay down our arms! Surrender!" they say. "Resistance is useless. We will treat you well if you obey! But if you fight, we will wipe you off the map."

Before the bombing started, Dad and Rinus, his foreman, were working at 'tulpen koppen'—cutting blossoms off tulips to let the bulbs grow bigger. We didn't work outside today—it's not safe in the fields.

Mother tried calling Frans, but all connections to the South are cut. Dad tells her not to worry but she can't help worrying. We are glued to the radio. On the Hilversum station, they tell us the French Army is coming up through Belgium. It's a long way. Can they reach us in time?

After dinner we usually say a short rosary but today mother kept us on our knees to say the whole Rosary. We are praying for a miracle!

May 12, 1940

Yesterday Anton Lommerse was killed. He is the son of a close neighbor—so close we can see the roof of their house through the trees. Everybody is shocked. We know soldiers may be killed but we didn't expect someone we knew to be a casualty. Anton was a soldier but he was so young, too young to die.

His funeral will be held in St. Joseph's Church, a block from here. The church will be crowded. Everybody liked him and they will all come.

Jan and I are listening to the radio. Mother and Jo are cooking dinner. Alice is practicing on the piano. Dad went to a meeting of the town council on his bicycle. My little sister, Jet, is reading a book. The twins are playing outside. Planes are still flying over. The guns from Haarlem are booming. German tanks coming in from the east are attacking the bridges. Our soldiers are still fighting, keeping them out.

"They said they were going to open the water gates and flood the polders. Why didn't they?" I asked Jan. "A few feet of water are all that would be needed to stop the tanks."

"Dutch Nazis control the water gates and they won't let them be opened."

"How they can stop them? There aren't many Dutch Nazis. How can so few Nazis control the gates?"

Jan said, "It doesn't take many—just a few engineers who hold key jobs."

In 1914, when the First World War began, the Kaiser invaded Belgium but left Holland alone. The Kaiser lost the war. Afterward he was granted asylum in the Netherlands, where he is still living out his life. I wonder where he would have gone if Holland hadn't let him in.

They called World War I, 'The war to end wars'. In 1918, when Germany was defeated, the Versailles Treaty* made strict rules to keep Germany from arming again. But Hitler has not kept the provisions. And France and England did not enforce them.

In the 1930's, all of Europe saw Hitler building his army. When he marched into the Rhineland, the other countries did nothing. They thought England and France would stop him.

Hitler justified his war by the loss of former German land and the terrible economy. He spoke to cheering crowds about the superiority of the Germans and promised to bring back prosperity.

Most of the Dutch did not take him seriously—just laughed at his ravings. While the rest of Europe ignored him, he built a huge army and marched it into the Rhineland. France could have stopped him, but they felt safe behind their Maginot Line and were not ready for war.

England and France trusted their alliance. Hitler demanded territory. To satisfy him, Neville Chamberlain, the British Prime Minister, gave it to him. When Hitler took over Austria in what was called the *Anschluss***—the English and French did not protest. They said Austria was German anyway because Austrians speak German. All the Austrian people didn't agree but they could not do anything to stop it.

Then Hitler demanded the Sudetenland*** from Czechoslovakia, Chamberlain said he could have it. It did not belong to the British but Chamberlain gave it away because he believed Czechoslovakia would satisfy Hitler. Adolf said it was his last territorial demand—he wouldn't ask for anything more.

Dad said Chamberlain was too trusting if he believed Hitler would keep his promise. But after his meeting with Hitler, Chamberlain waved the treaty he signed and announced proudly he had won "Peace in our time."

France had created a wonderful fortification with concrete living quarters underground. There the French army could be safe while they protected their country. They set huge guns in concrete pointed toward Germany. This was their famous Maginot Line****.

In 1939, France and England had a mutual defense agreement with Poland but it did not save Poland from the Germans. The Allies declared war but when Poland fell they did not attack Germany.

Hitler promised Holland he would not attack if we didn't join or help the Allies—France and England. Dad didn't believe anything Hitler said. He took his promises with a ton of salt. But, Holland had a plan. Western Holland is very low, with dunes and dikes to keep out the sea. If we opened the water gates we could flood the land and stop the invasion.

Dad didn't think that was a good idea because salt water might keep the tanks out, but it would kill people and animals, destroy crops and buildings and ruin the farmland. Nobody tried it so we don't know what would have happened if they had used the 'Water-line Defense.' But at least we're not under water.

On the radio, they tell us the French Army is coming up through Belgium to help us. We listen tensely to find out how far they have come.

Our big cities are in the Western part of the country. That is what we call 'Fortress Holland.' It is crossed by two big rivers, the Rhine and the Maas, too wide for the German to get across without using our bridges. Obstacles are erected on the bridges to keep tanks off.

When a pro-German officer tried to remove the tank protectors from a bridge, his fellow officers shot him. If the bridge had been taken, tanks would overrun the West Country. The Germans have already taken over the eastern provinces.

*The Versailles Treaty ended World War I. Its provisions against rearming Germany were intended to keep Germany from starting another war.

***The annexation of Austria by Germany was called the Anschluss.

***The Sudetenland was part of Czechoslovakia. Hitler said it belonged to Germany because many Germans lived there. He claimed it was his last territorial demand. He fooled the British Premier, Chamberlain into giving it to him. After he got the Sudetenland, he took all of Czechoslovakia.

****The Maginot Line is the fortified line between Germany and France. The French thought it was so strong the Germans couldn't penetrate it. But the German Army came around the end of it, through Belgium and attacked France from the other side.

Chapter 2

❧

The Destruction of Rotterdam

May 14, 1940

Things are so terrible. I can hardly bear to write it. Holland has surrendered to the Germans. We lost. Now we are a conquered land.

The Dutch army defended the bridges and kept the Germans out of 'Fortress Holland,' the western part of the country, where our big cities are. The French army was coming up through Belgium as fast as they could to help us. They used everything available—they even seized civilian cars and trucks—anything they could ride on to come and defend us.

But the Luftwaffe bombed Rotterdam and obliterated the ancient city. The buildings are gone. The people are gone. Even the streets can not be identified. Rotterdam, our great city, our greatest port, is now a pile of broken bricks and smoldering rubble.

The Luftwaffe didn't bomb the port or any military targets. They bombed the houses, where civilians lived. Some people escaped by running through fiery streets. We can't tell how many died.

The sky over Rotterdam is dark with clouds of black and yellow smoke. Tobacco is burning in the warehouses of the port and winds from the south carry the odor of burning cigars.

This morning, the Mayor knocked on the kitchen door. Mother was surprised to see him. She asked "Would you like a cup of coffee?"

"Thank you, Marie," he said. "I'd like one. I was too busy to eat breakfast. I came to talk to Bart."

Dad and the Mayor went in the living room, next to the dining room. Annie and Jo brought them coffee and cookies. The rest of us stayed in the dining room, listening to the radio tell the story of the attack on Rotterdam. But we wanted to hear what the Mayor had to say.

"The soldiers threw their guns into the canals to keep them out of German hands," the radio announcer reported.

I turned the volume down so we could hear the men in the other room. The Mayor told Dad, "I had a call from a friend in The Hague."

The announcer reported, "We kept the German army out of Western Holland. The army held our bridges so they could not cross."

Jan turned the radio down farther until it was almost off. The Mayor said, "When Hitler attacked our country, he thought such a little country wouldn't give him any trouble. He expected us to surrender immediately. When the Dutch army resisted, he was in a rage because we held him up and delayed his schedule.

He had General Schmidt send an ultimatum. "Surrender within two hours or German bombers will destroy Rotterdam."

General Scharroo got the message and passed it on to General Winkelman, in charge of the Netherlands Armies. The ultimatum was unsigned so General Winkelman sent it back and asked for a signature. General Schmidt wrote a new one, signed it and changed the expiration time to 4:20 PM. He told General Winkelman to light flares on Norder Island in the Scheldt River to show that we surrendered. The planes that came to bomb us would see the flares and fly back to Germany. The city would be spared.

General Winkelman agreed to surrender. He had to give in to save the people of Rotterdam.

The Mayor continued, "But before the expiration time, the bombers took off from Bremen. The Germans told us to light flares to signal that the bombing was cancelled. So flares were lit. When the pilots of the bombers in the left wing saw the flares, they turned back to Germany. But the rest of the planes ignored the flares and flew on to attack Rotterdam."

"When the bombs started falling, the people crowded into shelters. The planes flew low. They bombed Rotterdam's center. The homes were crowded together on narrow streets so when one building burned, the one next to it caught fire. The flames spread with incredible speed and caused a fire storm that sucked the air out of the city.

Gas mains exploded. Water mains broke. Without water, firemen could not fight the fires. The whole city was on fire. Some people escaped running through the streets between burning buildings. Many died in bomb shelters under the buildings.

Rotterdam is gone, buildings and landmarks and everything. Even the streets are unrecognizable. The only thing left standing in the center of Rotterdam is a broken off church tower still pointing a finger to the sky."

Dad said "We must gather as much as we can and go to help the survivors."

The Mayor said "We'll ask people to bring food and supplies to the churches and assemble it there.

Mother was crying. "Oh, those poor people," she said. "We have plenty of food in the pantry. They can have it all." Then she sent the twins for boxes from the warehouse and she and Jo went to the pantry to fill the boxes.

The announcer repeated the news, "Rotterdam is in ruins. The sky is full of yellow smoke."

The Mayor and Dad left to organize help for Rotterdam's refugees.

Jan and I stayed in the dining room to listen to the radio from Hilversum. Then we turned to a German station to hear what they had to say. They had bombed helpless civilians but the German announcer did not apologize.

Instead, he praised the pilots saying "The attack showed the 'invincible strength' of the Luftwaffe."

Jan said "Invincible strength? It was like shooting fish in a barrel. We didn't even fire our guns at them because we surrendered!"

May 15, 1940

You'd think it would be quiet now. But early this morning we heard a huge explosion. Something was hit, something nearby. I opened the shutter and looked out, but it was still too dark to see much. From what I could make out, our barn and outbuildings were not damaged.

A minute later the phone rang. Jo answered. A neighbor's home was hit and the side of their house was damaged. The caller asked Dad and Mother to come and help.

Dad, Mother, Jan and I went to see what we could do. Jo and Alice stayed with the twins and Jet. From the street, except for broken windows, the house looked intact. But when we walked around it, we saw one wall was gone, leaving a heap of bricks, wood beams and shattered glass.

The bomb completely destroyed the side, but the roof and the floor were still there. It looked like a doll house that you can see inside. Where the wall was missing, there was only empty space. The upstairs bedroom was open to the sky.

The neighbors heard the blast and knocked on the door but nobody answered. They were afraid the family was hurt. They went around and climbed in through the missing wall. "Is everything all right?" they called.

The shocked parents answered "Lisa and Marie—our daughters. They are dead."

Lisa and Marie were gone but their parents, Joanna and Dirk, were not hurt. The neighbors were helpless. We wondered how it happened. It must have been a stray bomb. Jan heard a plane fly over before the explosion. He said it sounded like a German plane. It could have been an accident. Maybe a pilot had a bomb stuck in the bomb door. The Luftwaffe would not waste a bomb on an ordinary home in a farming community.

We heard a siren. Someone had called an ambulance. The medics came and looked at the sisters, covered them with a blanket over their faces and put them on stretchers to take them away.

Mother put her arms around Joanna and said, "Come. The men will take care of the house. I will make breakfast for you and Dirk." Mother and I took them home. Dad and Jan and the rest of the men stayed to see how they could close the gap in the wall.

The shock of the bombed house and the memories of Lisa and Marie are too much. Only last Sunday, after church, Lisa and I were talking. I'd asked what she was going to do when she graduated.

"I want to attend a conservatory," Lisa said. She had a beautiful voice and often sang solos with the choir.

"Where do you want to go to—Amsterdam or Haarlem?" I asked.

"Haarlem is closer but I want to visit them both before I decide. You have to take an entrance examination to be admitted. There's no hurry. I'm only fourteen."

That was only last Sunday. But Lisa will never attend the conservatory. We'll never hear her voice again. Her sister, Marie was twelve. They had no time to live, no chance to have a life—to pursue their dreams.

Why did this happen? The girls were their parents' pride and joy. Now their lives are over. It is too soon.

I remember Lisa riding her bicycle, her dark hair blowing in the wind, a smile crinkling the corners of her eyes.

Thousands die every day, but it's only a number. The deaths of a million strangers do not touch your heart as much as the death of one friend.

May 16, 1940

I fed my dog, Tiberius, my fan-tailed pigeons, the rabbits and the noisy geese. I feel so hopeless and angry. I want to blame somebody, but who is to blame?

The Dutch government who believed Holland could stay neutral in this war? They had stayed out of the First World War. Did they think they could stay out of this one? Did our Prime Minister, Mr. de Geer, believe Hitler's promises? Could the attack have been avoided if we joined the Allies? Would the water line defense have worked if we tried it? There are no answers.

The war was over. Our defense lasted only five days.

May 17, 1940

Misery loves company. France and Belgium are still fighting the Germans. Norway and Denmark were attacked even before Holland. Norway fought longer, but they have mountains to protect them. Denmark was defenseless. They had to surrender. The king did not want to fight a battle their country could not win.

Sweden remains neutral. Hitler didn't attack Sweden. He needs their steel for his war machine. Switzerland is neutral. It is a mountainous country and hard to invade. Mountain passes are easier to defend than broad straight highways. Austria ruled Switzerland once. Since the Swiss kicked the Austrians out, they are dedicated to protecting their country. Hitler did not even try to invade Switzerland.

Austria was betrayed by the country's own traitors. Poland was sandwiched between Germany and Russia. Germany attacked from the

West and Russia from the East. Poland, in spite of their strong resistance and brave soldiers was flattened by a steam roller.

The Dutch managed to fight for five days before we surrendered. We had to give in to save our cities from destruction. But in spite of Hitler's conquest of our country, he did not get our navy. Our ships have been given to the Allies. Our soldiers threw their guns into canals to keep them from the Nazis.

Queen Wilhelmina and the Dutch royal family are in London. The Dutch government wanted to send them south to the Province of Zeeland, but there was too much fighting there so they took them to Britain. We feel abandoned without Queen Wilhelmina, but our government felt it was better to keep her out of Hitler's reach. If he captured the Queen, he would make her a hostage to force Holland to do whatever he wanted.

The King of Denmark did not resist. He surrendered to save his people, like General Winkelman ordered our armed forces to lay down their arms to save Rotterdam. Then the Luftwaffe bombed it to smithereens. But the surrender kept the Luftwaffe from bombing other cities like Utrecht, Amsterdam, Haarlem and Den Hague.

May 18, 1940

Today was the funeral for Lisa and Marie. I know people die. My grandmother and grandfather Lommerse and my grandfather Heemskerk died. But they were old. They had lived a long time.

In wars, soldiers die to protect their country. But Lisa and Marie should not have died. They were sleeping, not fighting. They were their parent's only children.

We went to St. Joseph's for the funeral. Rain and a cold wind wailed in the trees. Bent against the wind, we waited outside the church, watching the hearse pulled by two black horses, carrying the caskets. The driver wore a black coat and a hat with a brim. The horses had black plumes. Other carriages with black horses followed bringing more mourners.

The church was crowded. People dressed in black clothes. There was only one priest. Pall bearers carried the black-covered caskets into the back of the church. The funeral was short. The organ played. The choir sang the Latin Mass. Even though it was a weekday, the whole choir attended because the girls' father was a member of the choir.

Four acolytes assisted the priest. When the mass was done and the prayers were spoken, the music sung and the incense and holy water sprinkled, the procession began, led by the cross bearer. On each side, acolytes carried lighted candles. The choir followed and then the pall bearers, four of them carried each casket. After them two more acolytes brought incense and holy water. The priest and parents were next, followed by the rest of the mourners.

The choir sang as they walked. No flowers were brought inside the church. They were placed on the stone cover at the grave.

It was windy and threatened to rain so the graveside ceremony was short. Both caskets were placed in the same grave. Lisa's was lowered first and Marie's was placed on top. Their bodies lie together, shut away from the sunlight forever.

A low-income housing development overlooks the cemetery. The residents watched from their windows, like an audience watching a play. A few planes flew high overhead. Although Holland has surrendered, the war goes on. Nothing can interrupt the war.

Yesterday Anton Lommerse was buried close by in the same cemetery. We had to pass his grave. His helmet rests on the stone cover to show he was a soldier who died for his country. This is the second day young people were buried in St. Joseph's cemetery. How many more funerals will there be?

Are the sisters sleeping under the stone slab that covers their resting place? No. They are in heaven. They look down and see us weep. But they do not cry. In heaven, there is nothing but gladness. .

Jesus said: *"In my father's house are many mansions. I go to prepare a place for you.... And if I go, I will come again and receive you unto myself, that where I am, there may you be also."*

Chapter 3

German Soldiers in Bennebroek

May 19, 1940

German soldiers swarm all over town. There must be a million in the country. They are *Wehrmacht*, regular army men in gray-green uniforms with shiny black boots. They don't goose step like they do in newsreels, but their heel plates are noisy on brick paving.

For barracks, they took over St. Franciscus School for boys. That's the school Ton and Gerard went to before the invasion. It was a new modern school but now the Church must find another place for the boys' school.

The officers do not stay in the barracks. They are quartered in private homes. With so many people living in our house, there's no room for an officer. That's lucky. Dad couldn't stand having a German officer living with us. He hates Hitler and the Nazi regime.

Dad has friends in Germany, growers he's known for years, but the men are not Nazis. He thinks men who joined the NSB (National Socialist Bund) are crazy.

The soldiers moved in last night. This morning they descended on the stores. They cleaned out the bakeries and meat markets of bread, cake, cookies, sausages, cheese and ham like a plague of locusts. They were so hungry they sat right down on the sidewalks, cut up their food with their bayonets and polished it off.

In Holland shops are well stocked; in Germany the stores are almost empty. The soldiers are buying things they can no longer find at home. A little joke is going around. An English spy in a German uniform looked exactly like the other soldiers but he wasn't carrying anything. The Germans could tell right away he was an Englishman; the real German soldiers had packages.

At least the men paid for what they bought—with Dutch guilders, too. The storekeepers were afraid the soldiers would just take whatever they wanted or pay with German marks, useless in Holland.

In 1939, when the Germans invaded Poland, the soldiers were stealing, killing, looting and burning. They don't do that here. They act civil and polite, but we are careful not to provoke them, stepping off sidewalks to let them go by.

Gerard asked Dad "How should we act around them?"

"Just go about your business. They won't bother children."

Ton asked, "What if they ask us questions?"

"Answer them if they want directions. But if they ask you things you don't want to tell, say *Ik weet't niet.*" (I don't know.)

Gerard said. "They only speak German. So how can we talk to them?"

Jo said, "That's no problem. Just answer in Dutch."

"They don't speak Dutch. They won't understand."

"I know some German," Ton said

"I'd rather speak Dutch," Gerard said. "And confuse them."

Mother said "I was in the bakery when some soldiers came in and yelled 'Heil Hitler' at each other. I turned around to see where Hitler was. I thought maybe he was right behind me."

We laughed to think of *der Fuehrer* in Bennebroek. They can yell 'Heil Hitler' until their faces turn blue, but he won't come here.

May 20, 1940

In Hilversum, where our radio stations are, the first thing the Germans did was take them over. The announcers still speak Dutch but their news is propaganda, straight from Germany. We don't believe what they say. We tune in to the BBC and listen to the British.

The Germans made new rules—announced them on the radio, printed them in the papers and posted them in government offices.

Moses gave the people Ten Commandments but the Germans have given us more, mostly prohibitions:

1. **Flying Dutch flags is *verboten*.**
2. **Our national anthem is *verboten*. So are patriotic songs.**
3. **Celebrating royal birthdays is *verboten*.**
4. **Wearing orange is *verboten*.** (The House of Orange is our Royal family.)
5. **The Queen's pictures are *verboten*.** (But her pictures are still on Dutch coins.)
6. **Carrier pigeons must be killed by the end of the week.**
7. **Boy Scouts have been abolished. It's a British organization.**
8. **Restaurant menus may not be printed in French or English— just Dutch or German.** (But Italian and Chinese restaurants may use their languages.)
9. **No ships may leave Dutch harbors, even from neutral countries.**
10. **Newspapers must be authorized by the Germans before printing.**
11. **German laws replace Dutch ones when they are different.**
12. **The legislature has been suspended. They are not needed.**
13. **The courts are German. Dutch lawyers may not defend the accused.**
14. **We must register for identification cards and carry them all the time.**
15. **It is illegal for more than three people to congregate in public. If four people are together, one has to go.**

May 21, 1940

The twins, Ton and Gerard, and I worked in the fields today, clipping blossoms off tulips. When the flowers are cut off, the energy of the plant goes into making the bulb. We put the flowers we cut off in baskets to keep them off the ground so they won't spread tulip viruses.

Afterward, my friend Lou came over and we walked to town. A big red, white and black swastika hangs over town hall. This reminds me of a story I heard on the BBC (British Broadcasting Company):

In Copenhagen, Denmark, the Germans hung a swastika over the king's castle. The King of Denmark told the German commandant he was going to take it down. The official said it would stay because the Germans would shoot the soldier who took it down. The Danish King said, "No, you won't. I will be the soldier who takes it down." The administrator didn't want to shoot the king so they let him take down the Swastika and put back the Danish flag.

In Bennebroek, German soldiers guard the train station, checking peoples' papers to see who is traveling and if the trip is legal. You have to apply for permission to travel on the train.

There are big German cars on our old streets. On a narrow street, two staff cars met with flags flying from their fenders. They stopped facing each other. There was no room for them to pass but neither one would back up to let the other go by.

"Which one will give way?" Lou asked.

"The officer with the highest rank must have the right of way," I said. But only chauffeurs were in the long black cars and must have been in a staring contest. We watched until the drivers got out facing each other. It wasn't a good idea to hang around. They'd think we were making fun of them. We were, but we didn't want them to notice.

We stepped into a bookstore so close to the street that you had to look before you came out the door or you might be hit by a passing car. Lou bought a notebook. I saw a navy blue diary. I wanted to write a journal so I bought it.

"That's a neat book," Lou said. "I started to write a diary in a history class once. But then I got too busy so I quit."

"I wrote everything in my notebook since I came home. I'm going to keep a record of the war."

"That's a good idea. I might start writing in my diary again."

May 22, 1940

Dad's foreman, Rinus, rides through town on his bike on his way here. So he sees what's going on in town. This morning there was a big commotion. The body of a German soldier was floating in a canal. Nobody knows what happened.

Mother noted, "Canals have steep sides. It's hard to get out if you fall in."

"He could have been drunk," Jan said.

"They can't blame us if it happened after eleven. That's curfew. We can't be out after curfew," Jo said.

"Was he alone? Didn't anybody see him fall?" I asked.

"Who would push a German soldier in a canal?" Gerard asked.

"It would pollute the water," Jan said.

Alice said, "On the other hand, the canals aren't very clean anyway."

"In the blackout maybe he didn't see where he was going," Annie guessed. "What canal was he in?"

"The Ringvaart," said Rinus.

That's the big canal that goes around the town. The small canals empty into it.

"He probably tripped and fell. He must have been alone. If there was anybody with him, they would have pulled him out," Alice said.

"Poor man, coming all the way to Holland and drowning in a canal," Mother said.

I'd be sorrier for the poor German soldier if I didn't remember the way the Germans bombed Rotterdam."

Chapter 4

❧

Mistakes

May 23, 1940

The sun was shining this morning so Mother and Annie brought our coffee out on the summerhouse deck. Crows and magpies chattered in the beech trees. My white geese were walking around making themselves heard. They think everything is their territory, not only our farm; they even think they own the street.

Ton and Gerard are playing ball. They don't mind missing school now it's a barracks, but Mother does. She wants them to have a good education.

She asked Dad what the school committee is going to do about setting up a new boys' school.

"We're looking," Dad said. "But we haven't found any empty rooms. If we can't find anything, we'll have to borrow classrooms from the Brotherhouse." That's where the Catholic teachers live.

"It won't be nearly as nice as St. Franciscus," Ton said.

The Germans have taken over our modern boys' school and there's nothing we can do about it.

"We'll just have to count our blessings," Mother said. "Frans is safe in his school. And our house wasn't hit."

"And they let the Dutch soldiers go home. They didn't put them in Prisoner of War camps," I said.

"They claim it's out of kindness," Jan said. "But it's really because they don't have prisons to put them in."

27

Jo said, "And they're keeping Dutch officials. The offices will be almost the same."

Hitler says he's being generous. He has 'forgiven' us for fighting and resisting his takeover. But we haven't forgotten what his army did—invaded our country and killed people, destroyed and stole everything not nailed down.

Alice said, "Maybe Hitler thinks we'll be so grateful that he's kind to us so we'll join Germany."

"You vill do vat ve say," I said giving my impression of a German accent. "Ve have Vays to make you obey."

Before the war we made fun of Hitler, a ridiculous little man, screaming and yelling, making ridiculous gestures. But crowds in Germany love him and cheer his speeches. He promised so much. Some politicians will do anything to get elected and gullible people want to believe them.

At least France and England are still fighting. We're praying for their armies. If the Allies win they'll throw the Nazis out. That's what they should have done. But the German army got around in back of the Maginot Line and the French are fighting against the tide.

Belgium has a great fort, Eban Emael.* Its guns can fire in every direction but up. If that fort was still in Belgian hands, the German Army couldn't have gotten behind the French Lines. But they didn't figure on an attack from the sky, and that's what happened. The Luftwaffe flew over, dropped parachutists on the fort who overpowered the defenders.

And when the French Army went north to help Belgium it weakened their defense and the German Generals marched in.

"Did our side make all the mistakes? I asked Dad. "Didn't the German generals make any?"

"He's made a big one if he thinks bombing will make the British give in, he's has another think coming. He's not dealing with Chamberlain, anymore. Now he has Churchill to deal with. He's an English bulldog. He won't give in. He'll fight till the last man's dead. Hitler has to bring his blitzkrieg across the channel to defeat the British. Without an invasion, he can't defeat England."

We were enjoying the sun. But all of a sudden the wind shifted, dark clouds filled the sky and rain pelted down. We went inside and listened to the progress of the war on the radio.

May 27, 1940

More than 340,000 Allied troops from all over—Britain and France and Belgium, even some from Poland and Holland are stranded on the coast at Dunkirk, Belgium, hemmed in by the troops and tanks of General von Rundstedt.

The Luftwaffe's planes are flying over, strafing the soldiers on the beach. The tanks are holding back to let Goering finish them off. The Allies had no place to go, no escape.

Then the British Admiralty broadcast an appeal to every Briton who has a motorboat from 30 feet to 100 feet long to come and rescue the troops. The water by the coast is too shallow for big ships of the British Navy to come to shore. Thousands of boats responded. The soldiers stand on the beach and the fleet of ferries, fishing boats, tugs, yachts and every imaginable seagoing vessel is coming to rescue them and bring them to England.

They have to leave their equipment behind. But men are being saved by these little boats while RAF planes are shooting German planes. Dunkirk is the scene of a terrifying battle to save Britain's armies.

The troops are nearer to Britain than they are to Germany so the soldiers waiting on the shore are being taken off. The Straits of Dover are hundreds of miles from the Luftwaffe's base. German planes don't have enough fuel to stay over the channel as long as the British planes do. They have to go back to refuel. The RAF bases are nearby. Their planes can stay over the channel to protect the boats and escaping men. Many men have been killed and many boats sunk. The Germans and the British are losing many planes. But the mass escape is being called the 'Dunkirk Miracle.'

The Germans are astonished. They thought they had won the battle, but now their enemy is escaping. Everything was going their way—they won their battles by marching into small countries, picking them off one at a time.

They thought they could drown the Allied troops in the sea, but the Royal Air Force is protecting them. General von Rundstedt kept his tanks back expecting the Luftwaffe to finish them off.

"Wars are not won by retreating" is an old saying, but another adage points out that "He who fights and runs away—lives to fight another day."

God, please help us. Defend the Allies. Help them defeat the Nazis!

May 30, 1940

School is opening again. We'll have to cram to make up for everything we missed and finish the school year. I've been home enjoying life, not opening my books. Too much is going on. And it's too noisy to study.

At Hageveld, life will be the same—the same teachers, the same rules and school food. I should be grateful for the privilege of going to such a good school. Tuition isn't free. And now that Dad won't be able to sell his bulbs, he won't have as much money. He might not be able to afford it.

But Dad helped to build the school. He's proud to have me going there. He'll keep paying my tuition as long as he can. I've always wanted to be a priest and Mother and Dad would like that, too.

But Dad is worried. He said "The Germans might take over the buildings for their headquarters. It's big and modern and in a good location—close to Haarlem and The Hague."

Jan said, "Well, they will if they want to. We can't stop them."

Dad said "The one thing that makes them hesitate before taking over the seminary might be that most Germans are Catholics. The Nazis won't want to offend them."

Jan said, "It didn't stop them taking the boys' school."

Unless the army takes it over by tomorrow, I have to go back to Hageveld. Jo is ironing my clothes and packing my suitcase. She's Mother's best helper and she does a lot for me.

The twins are playing checkers, arguing about whose turn it is. They are having fun, enjoying fighting. Arguments and wrestling with each other are the way they play.

I went in the kitchen to see what Mother's cooking for dinner—pot roast, my favorite. She browns the beef in butter in an iron pot. When it's tender she adds potatoes and onions. The cooks at school don't make food half as good.

I went to say goodbye to my pets. I feed Tiberius and the rabbits and the silly geese. When I'm gone the twins feed them. But I'll miss my pets.

The twins tease Tiberius by hitting the fence around his yard with a stick. The clattering makes him bark and jump up at the fence. Once he got over the fence and tore the shirt off Gerard's back. Tiberius was going to teach Gerard a lesson, but he didn't hurt him.

Dad said if the twins don't stop aggravating the dog, he will give Tiberius to somebody else—someone who will take care of him.

I asked "Why punish Tiberius? It's not his fault. That's what dogs do."

Tiberius is a black and tan German shepherd, a good watchdog. Dad says we don't need a watchdog; the geese make enough noise. Alice and Jo want to get rid of the geese because they attack their friends when they come over, running toward them, waving their wings and gabbling. But the geese never hurt anybody; they're just pretending.

I got the geese from Mr. van Maris, a neighbor. When the little yellow goslings were just hatched, they were so cute. He saw me admiring them and said I could take a pair. I climbed over the fence to get them but the mother goose rushed at me with her wings spread out, gabbling to make me leave. I scrambled back over the fence so fast that Mr. van Maris and everybody else who was standing around laughed out loud. When he stopped laughing, he gave me two fluffy yellow birds. I've had them a long time but they haven't laid any eggs—they must both be males.

I have more pets—four little Holland rabbits and three big Belgian rabbits. My favorite pets, after Tiberius, are the flock of white fan-tailed doves. Mr. Peters, the caretaker for the convent gave me the first pair, but our dog, caught one when it landed on his doghouse and Mr. Peters gave me another pair. They laid eggs that hatched. Now there are seven.

I'm glad they're not carrier pigeons. The Germans ordered all carrier pigeons killed, for fear we might send messages. I can't see what difference it would make. Who would we send them to? Churchill? What good would that do? He's already fighting and nothing we say could help him.

The Germans made many rules and kindly bestowed them on us. For example, a family can only raise two pigs. If a mother pig has a lot of little piglets, the farmer has to get rid of the extras. With all the hungry soldiers here, you'd think they'd want us to raise all the pigs we could.

May 31, 1940

Today we heard a speech by Hitler's Reichscommissar, Arthur Seyss-Inquart. He's a traitor who betrayed poor Chancellor Schussnig in Austria. He engineered the German takeover. As a reward for his treachery in Austria, Hitler made him the ruler of Holland.

Seyss-Inquart spoke at the Knight's Hall in Den Hague where the Queen used to come every year to open Parliament, riding in her golden carriage.

Seyss repeated what Hitler says—the Germans and Dutch are cousins, related by our 'common blood'. It's true that we are related—and so are many Europeans if you go back in history, but the German government is a dictatorship and living under a dictator like Hitler doesn't appeal to us.

German rule may be accepted by Austria, but our country has been independent since the Dutch defeated the Spanish in 1572. We fought for over eighty years to get rid of the Spanish. Now Holland is a democracy and we'd like to keep it that way. Being ruled by Germany is against our tradition.

We listened to Seyss Inquart to see if he had anything new to say. But he just chewed the same old cabbage. He was a lawyer in Vienna. Lawyers should be clever and witty, but he's dull and boring and uninspiring. He says he won't force Nazi ideas down our throats. He will respect our own laws and let us live by them."

Mother asked, "Then why did they attack us? We weren't bothering the Nazis."

Hitler thinks he's the greatest conqueror ever—greater than Napoleon. He says Holland is German because the Dutch and the Germans are cousins, but what kind of relative takes tanks and planes and goes to kill his cousins?

Dad said, "Seyss Inquart won't keep his word. I give him ten days, two weeks at the most before he tries to turn us all into Nazis."

Mother said, "He's not a German. He's an Austrian. That might not be as bad as a German."

"It's not the nationality of the man, it's his ideas. Napoleon was a Corsican. Alexander was a Greek. Julius Caesar was a Roman and Hitler is an Austrian," Dad said. "Dictators are madmen. All they want is power."

Mother said, "I'm afraid he'll bring the Gestapo."

"It's here already," Dad said. "Rauter is their leader."

The twins put on old hats and boots and marched like German soldiers, kicking out their legs and imitating a goose step. They were comical. Dad wanted to hear the radio. He told the boys "Go outside if you want to play."

I asked "What makes the Germans follow Hitler? Why do they worship him?"

Jan said "They're used to it. They don't mind following leaders. The Kaiser led them into the First World War and ruined the country. But they didn't learn anything. They're doing it again!"

At last Seyss-Inquart ran out of breath. The radio played martial music and we heard applause. Why were they clapping? Because the speech was over?

Old Seyss was tired of talking. We were tired of listening.

One thing I remember from the speech was Seyss-Inquart saying "Officials, Judges, and Civil Servants must obey the German regime!"

That was not a surprise—they make new rules every day.

Jan said, "I could have made a better speech myself. Anybody could. Even Pim."

Chapter 5

Back to Hageveld

June 5, 1940

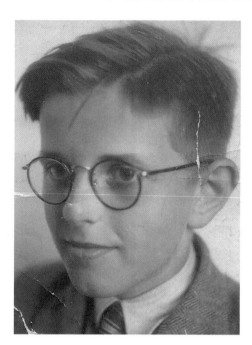

Today started early. It's back to school for me. I looked at the newspaper but there was nothing new and interesting. I like to read our comic strip, Tim Tyler. But that wasn't in there. Maybe the Germans wouldn't give the paper permission to print it because it's too English.

Alice said, "I'll miss you, Pim. I'm sorry you have to go back to school."

"No you won't. You'll be too busy playing tennis, riding your bike, visiting friends and fixing your hair. I don't know how you do it all."

"I do some work, too but you didn't mention it."

"You do a lot of work. Mother cooks, Annie cleans and Jo does everything else. What's left for you?"

Alice doesn't do much housework. Mother and Jo cook the meals. Annie cleans the dishes. Alice practices her piano lessons and studies. She plays tennis with her friends. But she's only 12, There's time enough to work when she grows up.

Henrietta, called Jet is our littlest sister. She's cute. She likes to help mother with cooking and drying dishes.

The twins and I weed the garden and plant things and clean bulbs in the warehouse. Girls work indoors. Boys work outdoors. That's the way it is, the way it always has been in Holland.

Jo offered me a ride so I don't have to walk to town and wait for the tram. And it saves me a quarter. She likes to give me a ride because it gets her outdoors. I'd rather take my own bike but there's not enough room at school for everybody to park their bikes.

Mother smiled when we said goodbye but she had tears in her eyes. She is a Lommerse. They are emotional.

Dad shook my hand and handed me the envelope with tuition money. I wonder how he can spare it. Since the war started, they won't be able to ship bulbs so he won't have much income from selling bulbs.

Jo dropped me off at Hageveld. It was early. I was not in a hurry to go in. A boy named Steve was leaning on the bridge looking down at a barge moving slowly through the canal.

"Pim Heemskerk, what are you doing? Waiting for the bell to ring and go in at the last minute?"

"Steve van den Berg," I said in surprise. "How did you know my name?" He's a senior and I'm only a first year student so we don't have classes together.

"Simple. I know Jo and when she brought you, I could tell she was your sister by your Heemskerk eyes."

Steve is tall and slim. He stood on one leg with the other bent like a stork. They call him 'Legs' because his are so long.

"Cheer up," he said. "It's only two months till vacation."

"I get tired thinking about it," I told him. "Dull subjects, lousy food, no sports."

"That reminds me of the fellow who joined the Trappist Monks," Steve said. "It's a silent order. He was only allowed to say two words a year. After he was there a year, the Abbott asked him what he would like to say.

He said, "Bad food." That did not go over well but it was what he had been thinking.

Another year went by and he could say two more words. He said "Hard bed."

On the third year, when it was time to speak he said "I quit."

The Abbott said, "I knew you were going to say that. Ever since you got here, all you've done is to complain."

"That's an old joke," I said. "But I know how he felt."

June 6, 1940

After dinner tonight I went to my room and got out my diary. So far I wrote about the invasion. Now I'm going to write about our boarding school, Hageveld.

Hageveld is a seminary for boys who are studying to be priests. You have to be recommended by your parish priest and pass an exam to get in. Since I wanted to study for the priesthood I applied. When I was summoned by Bishop Huibers to hear my fate, I cried because I was so afraid he would tell me I failed.

The Bishop told me, "You passed. Why are you crying?"

I was elated—happy to be accepted at Hageveld.

There are six grades. I started in September, 1939. The first year class had over a hundred boys. Since then, many have left although the year will not be over until the end of July. August is summer vacation. When I come back after vacation, I will be a second year student.

The building is big and grand. It resembles a medieval castle set in broad fields, surrounded by thick woods. The Meerweg Canal runs in front of the school. It looks like a moat surrounding a castle. A bridge over the canal leads to the entrance.

The main building has a chapel, a library, administration offices and dining rooms. On each side are wings, two stories high. The classrooms, recreation rooms, art rooms and barbershops are on the first floor of each wing. The dormitories are on the second floor. First and second year students are in the right wing; the third, fourth, fifth and sixth year classes are in the left wing. There are fewer students in the upper classes, because some drop out each year.

There are two hundred small rooms on the second floor on each side. The rooms or 'cells' are about two by three meters, or 8 by 10 feet. A bed, a desk, a chair and a closet furnish each room.

My bed is narrow, the width of a cot. The floor is light cream colored linoleum. The bedspread and curtains are white. There are no pictures on the walls, only a cross. It is clean and hygienic but without character, like a hospital. Every room has a sink with a cold water faucet. And a pot is tucked under every bed because we can't go down the hall to the bathroom at night. In the morning, a man wearing a yoke with two pails hanging from it comes around. The students nicknamed him 'Potiphar,' because he empties the pots. But they don't call him that to his face.

There are big bathrooms with eight cubicles where we shower on Saturdays. A priest stands by the shutoff valve and controls the water. When he thinks we've had enough time, he turns the water off. If you don't hurry and rinse, you end up with soapy hair.

We wear robes to the showers, close the curtains, take our robes off and wash. When we finish drying, we put on the robes and open the curtains. The priest watches to keep us from talking.

There is no laundry. Every week Jo brings me a suitcase with clean clothes and sheets for my bed. All my clothes have name tags.

I put my dirty laundry in the case and write a letter home to go with it. When Jo brings clean clothes, there's a letter from mother and a treat— usually gingerbread. I wish it was cookies. I divide the gingerbread in three pieces and throw a piece to the boys in the cells on either side. The partitions between the cells are about 7 or eight feet high so we can throw things over them. We can't visit each other's rooms. Probably we aren't supposed to throw things over the walls, either—but nobody said not to.

A sign in the corridor says '*Silentium*' in big gold letters. It reminds us not to talk. Talking is against the rules.

To save Hageveld having to furnish silverware for four hundred boys, we each bring a place setting, engraved with our initials. But since it's too much work to sort the silverware, we get odd pieces, whatever they put at your place. A fork monogrammed for one kid, a knife for another, and a different spoon. You never get your own.

It looks ridiculous. I think the school should furnish the silverware. It lasts forever so after buying it in the first place, it wouldn't cost anything. But it would be nice if everything was the same pattern.

At meals, the rule is you must eat everything you are served. Sometimes you don't like the food or you're not hungry. Regardless of how you feel, you have to clean your plate.

Dessert is fruit or pudding. A friend from my class, Pieter de Wit said "There was a big pile of apples on the end of a table with a big sign, "Take only one apple. God is watching."

At the other end of the table was a tray with cookies. And a sign there said, 'Take as many cookies as you want. God is watching the apples."

June 7, 1940

Here is our schedule. There are rules for everything. It's like the army.

5:30—Rise, wash, and dress.
6:00—Morning prayers and Mass,
7:00—Breakfast,
7:30—Free time. We go outside if it's not raining.
8:00—The bell rings for class.

We sit at desks made for two. The students stay in the same room all the time and the teachers come to us. This cuts down on the commotion we would make if we had to change rooms. I'd rather walk from one room to another—we could get up and move a little, have a new scene.

Mathematics is our first subject. This year it's Algebra. I hate it.

Next year we'll study Geometry. I know I'll hate that, too. Why do I have to study math? I'm never going to be a mathematician.

After math we have two languages, one modern and the other ancient. One right after the other—French and Latin one day, Greek and German the next day. I like languages best.

We won't have English until next year. That will be easy for me because I understand it already from hearing Dad. He is fluent in English because he sells tulips to buyers from England and America. He knows French and German, too. Holland is surrounded by big countries—Germany, France and England. We have to learn their languages to trade with them. They don't learn ours.

Lunch is at noon. Afterward we have Bible study, Geography, World History and Church History, depending on the day. On Thursday afternoons you can choose Art or music or you can have free time. I have choir practice.

At 4:00 we have tea and sandwiches. Then we go to Chapel for a short service and study till dinner at 7:00. After that we're free until bed time. I write in my journal and get ready for bed. Lights out at 8:30.

On Sunday if it doesn't rain, we play volleyball or walk around the campus for exercise. Sometimes we line up and take a walk around town. We can talk all we want when we're outdoors.

There's a strange old woman living across the canal. We pass her on our walks. When she sees the priests who walk along, she gets angry. She waves her arms and yells. The priests don't pay her any attention.

I feel sorry for her. She wears dark clothes and her long gray hair makes her look like a witch. I'd like to know what the matter with her is, but we can't hear her because she's too far away. I smile to show I'm friendly. She never smiles.

June 12, 1940

In History class today, we talked about the war. There are no radios in our dorms so we don't know what is going on. By the time we hear the news, it should be called 'olds'.

We talked about the stranded Allied troops they evacuated from Dunkirk on the Belgian coast. The British rescued more than 300,000 men off the beach.

The French army is trying to keep on fighting but we know they've lost the war.

After Dunkirk, when the British Expeditionary Forces left, there was a big air raid over Paris. Refugees poured out of the city into the country. They remembered the firestorm when the Luftwaffe bombed Rotterdam and they were afraid Paris would soon be burning.

The French General, Weygand, pulled back and set up a new line, south of the Somme River. The brave French troops fought but troops can't win against tanks. They withdrew across the Marne. As they retreated, they were strafed by the Luftwaffe. France's mighty army crumbled. The French Government left Paris and went to southern France.

We wondered what the Germans will do now. Someone asked "Will they destroy Paris?"

The teacher said, "I don't think so. The whole world is watching."

Pieter said, "Hitler wants his picture taken in front of the Eiffel Tower. He needs the buildings standing to prove he's in Paris."

Carl said, "The Germans won't destroy Paris because of the outrage when they wiped out Rotterdam."

The French declared Paris an open city. According to the Geneva Convention, the German army can come in, but not attack it.

When Hitler is opposed, he goes into a frenzy, screams with rage and waves his arms. The Germans should beware of their crazy leader. Mother used to ask, "If your friends all jumped off the bridge, would you jump, too?" And we would answer, "Of course not."

If Hitler asks his followers to do anything, they say, "Yes, Mein Fuehrer, we will do whatever you say. If you ask us to, we will die for you... Whatever you tell us to do—even kill everybody, we'll obey."

How can people be so dumb?

The lights blinked. In five minutes someone will come and fling the sheets that serve as doors to our separate cells aside to see if we are in bed.

June 13, 1940

I wonder where to put my diary. I don't want everybody to read it. If I put it under the mattress, it looks like I'm hiding it. So I guess I'll leave it in a desk drawer with study papers and a book over it.

This morning, in Greek class, three German soldiers came in. They wore gray-green uniforms. Their tall black boots clattered on the tiles. Two of the men were tall and husky looking, the supermen Hitler likes. The third man was shorter and older. He looked like a professor with steel-rimmed glasses.

A young priest showed them our classroom. They didn't smile at us or say anything, but the priest said "These officers want to see the size of the rooms," to Mr. Nolet. So we naturally quit working and watched them look around. One soldier wrote on his clipboard and after a few minutes they left.

After lunch, the Dean spoke to us. "You may think Hageveld is a long way from the new administration, but remember, Holland is an occupied country. The Germans are in command. We must obey them. If you have any pictures or papers they might object to, get rid of them. If they search the school and find any illegal things, they have strict penalties and they will enforce them."

He didn't say the 'legal authorities' want our modern buildings for offices. Our school has a lot of space and it's in a handy location between Haarlem and The Hague.

I don't have anything illegal, except a cartoon of Hitler that Ari drew. I slid it under the paper cover of my Latin book. Nobody takes off school book covers. Besides, if they want Hageveld, they will just take it—like they took over the boys' school in Bennebroek. Like they walked in and stole our country.

I have to be careful what I say. But I'm writing in English. German soldiers probably don't read English.

June 14, 1940
The Chapel

It is taking a long time to write all the things I want to remember about Hageveld.

We have a beautiful chapel with room for over 400 students and all the teachers. There's a big pipe organ and a choir loft. The music director and two students are organists. I'm in choir and sit in the loft when we sing. The students sit with their classes and the priests sit together in the back.

I don't mind singing but hate to give up my free time to practice. So I told the director I had to quit because my voice was changing.

He just laughed and said, "Don't worry, Pim. I'll tell you when your voice changes."

The sanctuary is in front of the chapel. From the altar, steps go down to the communion rail. There are two beautiful wooden statues in front—Mary holding the baby Jesus on the left. Joseph is on the right. They are just carved from wood and left unpainted.

We go to chapel three times every weekday—before breakfast, after tea and for evening prayer. The chapel is nice and services are short. But once or twice a day would be enough for me.

On Sunday there is Morning Prayer, High Mass and breakfast. After that we are free till lunch at noon. Then we have free time until Vespers at three. Dinner is at six. Then we have study hour, and chapel before getting ready for bed.

Ari complained once when we were playing a game "We do everything by the clock. We're too regulated."

"Way too much," I agreed. "I wonder how they regulated people before there were clocks—by sundial?"

June 16, 1940
Lisa

Last night I dreamed I saw Lisa, but when I woke she was gone. My dream was so real I remembered it all day. I was in a place I've never seen before, like an auditorium or a huge classroom with light pouring in from tall windows.

Outdoors the sun splashed through branches of chestnut trees on grass and flowers and a wide river ran between its banks lined with reeds. In the distance there were bells chiming. People in beautiful clothes were all around.

Lisa and her sister were there. I went to the windows that separated us and the glass melted and I could pass through. I was so happy. I ran toward them but the girls disappeared before I could reach them.

Thinking about Lisa makes me cry. I've known her for years. When I was learning to ride a bike once I bumped her and almost knocked her over. I was afraid she would tell me to look where I was going. But she just smiled and said it was all right, she wasn't hurt.

When the war is over, I will forget the terrible things that happened in Holland. But I won't forget Lisa ever—not in a hundred years.

Chapter 6

The Fall of France

June 23, 1940

Jo brought my laundry today and put a newspaper in the suitcase. What surprise! We never get newspapers here. Maybe they don't want us to read them, but as far as I know, there's no rule against it. I wondered why she brought it until I saw the bold headline:

'FRANCE SURRENDERS!'

Below in smaller type was "Petain surrendered!" It is an unconditional surrender. German troops entered Paris. The French Army collapsed. It was bound to happen when the British Expeditionary Force left Dunkirk. But this catastrophe is overwhelming, the end of our hopes to be free.

Before the war France was the strongest European country. The French had a magnificent army and along their border they built impregnable fortifications with guns facing Germany—the Maginot Line. Everyone believed the French Army could not only defend their country but was strong enough to save the Low Countries—Holland and Belgium.

France and England together would defeat the German army and make Hitler beg for mercy! The Allies would wipe the Huns from the continent of Europe. The Allies would be victorious.

When Holland was invaded we fought as hard as we could and watched for the French to come and help us. But the German generals were diabolically clever. They saw they couldn't attack the French guns head on. Instead they attacked the Low Countries to the North of France. When the French went to the aid of Belgium, the Germans came around the end of the Maginot Line and surrounded the French fortification from the back.

France's big guns were fixed in place and aimed at Germany. But the French could not turn them around and shoot at the attackers behind the Line. When the Germans got behind their line, the guns were useless.

The brave French soldiers faced German tanks. They could not fight against the armored Panzers. Petain was forced to surrender to save Paris and the French people. So he agreed to an unconditional surrender.

Hitler conquered France without losing too many troops. And when Benito Mussolini, the Italian dictator, saw the Germans winning, he wanted to share their victory and in the surrender, grab some French colonies. So he joined Hitler. The countries of Italy and Germany are called the Axis. I don't know why—maybe to distinguish that alliance from France and Great Britain, who are called the Allies.

When the American President, Franklin Roosevelt, heard Italy attacked France, he said "The hand that held the dagger has plunged it into the back of its neighbor." Roosevelt was strongly anti-Nazi, but the United States did not declare war against the Axis.

Petain and Hitler met to sign their surrender in the same forest and even in the same railroad car where Germany surrendered in 1918. This makes 'der Fuehrer' happy, positively gloating, thinking the war is almost over.

His victory is not complete; the British will not quit. The RAF planes still fly. The Luftwaffe lost many planes and they see that they can't defeat the British by air raids alone. To finish the war, Hitler must cross the English Channel and defeat the British on the ground.

But Hitler does not have enough ships to bring the Blitzkrieg to England. In Dutch ports, ship builders are adapting barges to make thousands of landing craft. It can't be done overnight.

And to put an end to the war, he must defeat the British Navy.

Germany is a landlocked country. It doesn't have the ships to compete with Great Britain's Navy. There's always something!

June 24, 1940

Everybody is talking about France's defeat. The Dean talked about it at lunch. But there is nothing we can do.

Hitler screams and raves to get his way. But when people give in to him, he acts as polite as a gentleman and a diplomat. He was mighty pleased with the French surrender and told General Petain he "did not want to cast aspersions on such a courageous enemy." He explained he was "only trying to keep Germany safe from the English and repair the 'injustice' suffered by the German Reich."

In France, a million refugees wander across their devastated land. What does he care? He swallowed Europe a bite at a time—Austria, Czechoslovakia, Poland, Norway, Denmark, Holland, Luxembourg, Belgium and France.

Europe is quiet. Italy joined Germany. Now Mussolini is Hitler's ally. Spain, after their civil war, is too weak to fight. Portugal is neutral, too. Switzerland is Hitler's banker so it is neutral. Sweden supplies steel for his war machine and it is neutral.

Stalin signed a non-aggression pact with Germany so Hitler is not afraid Russia will attack. Every country in Europe is where he wants them, except Britain. He piously offered the British 'an honorable peace' if they choose to take it'—on his terms, of course. He thinks it a generous offer.

England's new Prime Minister, Winston Churchill, is a fighter, quite different from Chamberlain, the appeaser, who gave in to Hitler because he thought it would bring peace. But it only encouraged him to ask for more.

Churchill is the Prime Minister of Great Britain. His speeches inspire the British. Once he said he had "nothing to offer the British people but blood, sweat, toil and tears."

In another speech he said "We will wage war by land, sea and air, with all the strength God can give against a monstrous tyranny never surpassed in the catalogue of human crime."

When I was home we listened to him on the British radio. But we don't have radios at Hageveld. It is a crime to listen to the broadcasts from London. If you listen, you must do it secretly or risk being shot, the penalty for hearing Our Queen on 'Radio Orange' or any other English station. We have a hidden radio in the ventilator on top of our warehouse. Someone has to climb up there to listen to it. Then they come down and tell us what was said.

During study hour I was reading the newspaper and the teacher said, "Where did you get the newspaper?"

"From my suitcase. It was in with my laundry from home."

I was afraid he'd say I shouldn't have it. Maybe punish me for reading it when I was supposed to be studying.

But he surprised me, "When you are finished, I'd like to see it."

Everybody wanted to see it. When I tell Jo, she'll be pleased. She likes to do everybody favors.

June 24, 1940

Last night I felt gloomy. I couldn't sleep for thinking of all the troubles in Holland. Since France fell, it seems Hitler's Third Reich might really last a long time, if not a lifetime.

Europe is under Hitler's rule. He has conquered more territory than Napoleon, the Germans brag.

The terms of surrender divide France into 'Free' and 'Occupied' France. Hitler will let General Petain run 'Free France' as a puppet government as a reward for his collaboration.

Hitler shook hands with the defeated French leader. Petain justified his decision when he told his country, "In the spirit of honor, to maintain the unity of France, I enter on the path of collaboration. I speak as your leader. We must collaborate. We must be sincere. History will judge."

In 1939, Poland fell because the Germans attacked them in the West and the Russians in the East. Edouard Daladier was the French premier. Britain and France declared war on Germany but didn't attack. They might have stopped the German army if they did then.

France waited behind its strong fortifications, like a lion in his lair. England waited while they built up their defense. The Allies did not want to take on Germany's army.

France and England were too late. In 1936 when he marched into the Rhineland, Hitler would have backed down because France had the biggest and strongest army.

Instead of fighting, the Allies gave in and Hitler got what he wanted. Hitler wanted the Sudetenland from Czechoslovakia. It never had been part of Germany. It was part of the Austro-Hungarian Empire. Hitler said it was his last territorial demand. He liked that phrase and repeated it a lot. Every time he wanted something, he said it was his last territorial demand.

The Allies acted like they believed him. He was good at making promises though he wasn't good at keeping them. He signed treaties but couldn't remember what they were about. They were just pieces of paper and he forgot about them as soon as he got what he wanted.

When Hitler marched into Austria. England and France did not try to stop him. They thought since the Austrians spoke German, they might as well be part of Germany. They never called for a vote on it to see what the Austrian people wanted.

Hitler wanted the Sudetenland, part of Czechoslovakia; he said it was his 'last territorial demand.' Chamberlain agreed to give it to him. That was terrible. It belonged to Czechoslovakia, and Chamberlain had no right to give it to Germany. But he agreed with Hitler. President Benes was a sick old man. They put pressure on him to sign a treaty giving it to Germany. After Hitler got the Sudetenland, he took over the rest of the country.

Chamberlain didn't interfere. He just waved the treaty and announced proudly we would have "peace in our time."

But in 1939 Hitler invaded Poland. Then France and England declared war because they had a mutual defense treaty with Poland. That was too little and too late.

While leaders were negotiating, Hitler built an army of millions, greater than any army before. He equipped it with all the planes and tanks and artillery he bought from Krupp* and gobbled up Europe.

June 26, 1940

The Germans occupy Paris and the northern and western part of France. But the southern part, 'Free France' is ruled from Vichy by Pierre Laval. This works to Hitler's advantage as he doesn't need as large an occupation army as he would need if he had to supply soldiers to govern all of France.

Hitler took over the French colonies in Africa, too and seized the ships he could get from the French Navy.

The British took over French ships in their harbors, but French commanders in North Africa refused to give their ships to the British. So the

British sank them. This satisfied Churchill but it didn't make Hitler happy. You can't please everybody.

One French General, Charles DeGaulle did not surrender. He said they lost a battle, not the war. So he went to Britain to lead the remnants of the French Army. He calls his troops the 'Free French'. These are troops that escaped and went to Great Britain to fight alongside the British.

This gets confusing. 'Free France' is the name of the part of the country ruled by the Vichy government. But the 'Free French' are soldiers who escaped to Britain and are commanded by General DeGaulle.

When Queen Wilhelmina went into exile, we gave the Duch ships to the British. Hitler's army occupied Holland but they didn't get her ships or her colonies. The Dutch Navy is helping Great Britain command the seas.

Queen Wilhelmina did not surrender. Holland is occupied but when the Queen escaped to England, she set up a government in exile there. Some people felt betrayed. They thought she left us and saved herself. But if she didn't go, Hitler would have taken her hostage. Then he could force us to do anything he wants. She still speaks to us from England and we listen on our radios. The Nazis have a rule against it. But they can't check on what we are listening to on our radios.

June 29, 1940

The occupation government has made many new laws. Now they have made a new one. They have forbidden us to pray for the Queen.

The Reformed Churches say they will not obey, but they added a prayer for the Germans. They don't mean it when they pray for the enemy; it's only 'lip service'.

The Catholics love the queen, too. We sing "Lord, Safeguard our Queen" in our church every Sunday. And there's not a lot they can do about that.

Do they think they can tell us who to pray for? Well, they are doing it so I suppose they can try, but how can they enforce that rule?

They might as well tell the wind to quit its eternal blowing or the waves to stop washing the sand.

June 30, 1940

Yesterday was Prince Bernhard's birthday. He isn't here and we can't fly his orange, white and blue flag. So we wore orange carnations for the House of Orange.

Some brave people went to the palace and signed his birthday book. It's the custom in The Hague.

At Hageveld we got orange candy sprinkles on our rusk** and sang the birthday song in his honor.

> *Long shall he live,*
> *Long shall he live,*
> *Long shall he live,*
>   *In the Gloria.*
> *Hiep, hiep, hoera!*

Pieter said, "Wouldn't you like to go to The Hague and see what's happening?"

"If I had my bicycle and they would let me leave Hageveld, I would," Carl said. "It's a long way to the Hague."

"I can see the crowds lining up to sign his birthday book," Ari said.

"Celebrating Royal birthdays won't do any good," I said. "It will only make them mad."

The Prince was a German before he married Princess Juliana and became a Dutch citizen. Hitler hates him. The feeling goes both ways.

Wilhelmina is Queen and Juliana is her heir. There is no male heir to the Dutch throne so Princess Juliana will be the next Queen. Her husband, the Prince can't inherit the throne.

They have a daughter, Beatrix. Someday the Germans will go back to their own country. Holland will be free. And if there are no boys in the family, Juliana will be Queen and Beatrix will follow her.

* Krupp is the German munitions maker who armed Hitler's Army.

**Rusk is a crisp round Dutch toast. We sprinkle it with orange candies when we celebrate royal birthdays.

Chapter 7

❧

Dutch Officials Fired

July 3, 1940

Ari is my best friend. We agree most of the time. Pieter and I do, too. Carl doesn't. He'll argue with anybody about anything.

Yesterday was a nice day so we could walk on the path outdoors. Ari and I were talking about school.

"I wish we could go home weekends," Ari said.

"Or we didn't have so many rules. The only time they let us talk is when we're outdoors."

"The food here isn't great. Not like mother makes."

"And there's not enough time for sports."

"It wouldn't be bad if we could go home every night—like getting out of prison."

"It would be great if we could play afterward."

Carl came up. "Did you hear about Mayor de Monchy?" he asked. "They kicked him out of office because he signed the Prince's Birthday Book."

"He might have known they would," Ari said. "He's lucky they didn't put him in jail."

"Taking his job away is bad enough," I said. "It was just an excuse so they can put a Dutch Nazi in his place."

De Monchy is the Mayor of Den Hague, the 'Seat of Government' where they make laws. Every year Queen Wilhelmina used to ride in a golden coach from her palace in Den Hague to open Parliament.

51

Amsterdam is the Capital, but Den Hague is the 'Seat of Government.' Both Amsterdam and Den Hague once claimed to be the Capital of the Netherlands. In 1806, when Louis Bonaparte was king of Holland he settled the dispute. He named Den Hague the 'Seat of Government' and made Amsterdam the Capital. This satisfied both cities.

And it's been like that ever since. The Royal Palace is in Den Hague where Parliament meets to make laws. So The Hague is the real Capital. But Amsterdam is the official Capital. This is a Dutch situation. It makes no sense, but they can't change it without starting a fight between the two cities.

In the new regime, Dutch Nazis are plucking plummy jobs. A Dutch Nazi named Jan applied to become mayor of a tidy little Dutch town, but the job was given to Kees. Jan complained to Anton Mussert, the Dutch Nazi in charge of appointments.

Mussert said, "I'm sorry, Jan. I would have liked to make you the mayor but I had to give the job to Kees because he is more qualified. He can read and write."

July 4, 1940
General Winkelman Arrested

Ari and Carl and I stood watching storks on a nest on the roof of a house across the canal. Pieter joined us, wearing a navy blue jacket. I noticed his sleeves are a little short for his arms.

He had shocking news.

"The Germans arrested General Winkelman and made him a prisoner of war!"

General Winkelman was the Commander of the Army and head of the Dutch Government when our government left. The German Occupation Government made him demobilize the army. Now, since there is no Dutch Army any more they don't need him. A Dutch patriot has no place in their government so they want him to disappear.

"I understand why they let him go," I said "But why put him under arrest? He only did what they told him to."

Peter said, "Because he told the truth. General Winkelman said the bombing of Rotterdam after we surrendered was deliberate. Hitler claims it was merely an oversight."

On May 14, the Germans told the Dutch Army to surrender or Rotterdam would be wiped off the map. But the German bombers set out from Bremen before the Dutch could answer. Luftwaffe bombers were already flying to Holland when the Dutch agreed to surrender. The German General told the Dutch to light flares to tell the planes to turn around. The flares were lighted and the first squadron turned back. But the other one flew on and destroyed Rotterdam.

Ari said "That's ridiculous. How could one squadron see the flares and the other one, setting out from the same city and going to the same target at the same time didn't?"

General Winkelman said he didn't believe that. But the German government wants to cover it up. They lie in their teeth but one thing liars can't stand is being accused of lying.

Pieter looked up, squinting, at a plane flying over. "One squadron was not ordered to turn back. They bombed Rotterdam to punish us because we didn't obey Hitler's command to surrender. He expected us to lay down our arms, but our army fought back and that slowed him down."

"Bombing civilians is against the Geneva Convention," Carl said.

Seyss-Inquart used Winkelman to make him demobilize the army. Now they put him in prison for telling the truth.

The Nazis don't want us to think. It might lead us to doubt their intentions. Who knows where that could go?

July 5, 1940

After dinner I asked Pieter. "Did you hear where they took General Winkelman?"

"Nobody in Holland knows. The Germans haven't said a word."

"What's next?" I asked "Will the rest of the Dutch officials resign now to protest?"

"They should. Dutch officials make things seem normal. But this isn't Holland any more. It's a police state," Pieter said.

"Maybe Dutch officials think they are helping by staying."

"But they don't have any power. They are only window dressing. To keep their offices, they have to swear, "I pledge to you, Adolf Hitler...."

"So they promise to obey him. No man can serve two masters—they have to choose one or the other."

"Maybe they're pretending to work for the Germans but they are really working against them."

"It might work in a spy story," Pieter said. "But it's too risky. The Nazis are a suspicious lot. They would be hard to fool."

July 6, 1940

They say the only sure things are death and taxes. But students have tests, too at the end of the school year. We sit at our desks and the teachers sit in theirs, watching us so we don't copy.

The teachers grade us; but we can't grade them. But we give them nicknames. Father Verschure's nickname is 'Pa'. I wonder if he knows we call him that. We call Father Verbeem 'Kikker'. That's Dutch for 'frog' because of his long legs and bouncy steps. Father Nolet's nickname is 'Monkey'. We call Father van Deursen 'Doos' which means 'box'. The way we pronounce deurs, it sounds like 'doos'. He is tall and nice looking with wavy hair and nothing like a box.

The nicknames were there when we came. We don't use them where they can hear us. But everybody in Holland has a nickname. They might not know what it is but they all have one.

I got a nine on my French test—a good grade—ten is excellent, six is passing. Languages are my best subject. I always do well on them. Except for Greek. The Greek alphabet is confusing. If it was written in our alphabet, Greek would be a lot easier.

Mathematics is another hard subject. No matter how hard I work, I still can't get a nine. Once Dad hired a tutor to help me learn math. After he gave me a lesson, the tutor asked me to bring a note home. So I brought a note in an envelope and gave it to Dad.

The note told Dad not to waste his money on tutoring me. And he added a piece of advice for me—I should avoid any career based on mathematics.

Math, they say, is based on logic. I guess I was behind the door the day they passed out logic.

It's Greek to me.

Chapter 8

❧

Waiting Time

July 12, 1940

A new teacher, Father Straathof, came to Hageveld today. He's a tall drink of water and just graduated from Seminary. We were eating breakfast when he walked through the dining room, smiling and waving. We're delighted to see him because when we get a new teacher we have a 'free' day. Classes are canceled, except first period.

We sing a Latin song. "*Io vivat, Io vivat, Professoris sanitas. Dolores antidotum.*" It means 'a little love, an antidote to sorrow.' After we sang he waved a skinny arm and left.

Math is the first subject. After that we talked, played games like checkers and ping-pong or went outside for volley ball or a walk. We were noisy but anything is better than silence. If school was play, we'd be happy *jongens**.

At lunch things changed.

There are forty tables in the dining hall. As you enter, the tables for the lower classes are on the left and the upper classes' tables are on the right. In between is an open space where Dean Starrenburg presides. He says grace before we eat. Then he reads from the Bible or a classic book. We can't talk.

The stew was terrible. A hunk of glistening gristle shone on my plate. I couldn't stand to look at it, let alone put it between my lips. But we have to eat everything on our plate. I turned over my spoon to hide it. The Dean was watching me. He thinks I am a 'picky eater' and feels called on to change that. He came up behind my chair, picked up the spoon and pointed at the grisly gristle, pierced me with his stern eye and said, "EAT IT!"

I could not believe what I heard. Everybody saw the Dean of the school standing over me to make me eat the disgusting mess. This was an outrage! Nobody eats gristle! My mother wouldn't have it in her kitchen! Who made him the judge of my diet? I wanted to be a priest, not a garbage pail. Did the Pope decree that students had to eat garbage?

I wanted to say, 'EAT IT YOURSELF' but he was too big and too close. He glared. I put it in my mouth and started to chew. It tasted like a bicycle tire. The more I chewed on it, the bigger it became. I had to drink two glasses of water before I could swallow the first piece. I grimaced, wrinkling up my mouth. He thought I was smiling.

"Do you think this is funny?" he asked. My mouth had gristle in it, even after swallowing some. I didn't answer. I could only keep chewing, clenching and unclenching my jaws on the grisly, gruesome, greasy gristle. I hope it made him happy.

Finally I got it all down. Then my stomach rebelled. It wouldn't tolerate the ghastly mess. I threw up. The Dean backed up to avoid it but he got some on his clothes. I ran for the W.C. and did not return to my seat in the dining room.

July 13, 1940

I'm still trying to understand why the Dean made me eat the disgusting gristle. Everybody's laughing. Boys I don't know stopped and asked how I liked my lunch. They thought it was hilarious. But they didn't have to eat it. I thought it might be something I could make a skit from. But then I thought again. It was too far out. If I ever wrote the scene and acted it out at a party, nobody would believe me. They'd think I made it up.

July 14, 1940

I passed 'Pa' Verschure's office and he said "Come in a minute, Pim." I wondered what was coming. The teachers don't eat with us so he wasn't there when I ate the gristle. Somebody told him about it—but who? The Dean?

'Pa' Verschure is a friendly man. His dark hair is beginning to turn silver at his temple. His smiles reach into the corners of his blue eyes and light up his face. He is about my father's age, older than the rest of the teachers. But when the students play volley ball against the faculty every year, he's the best player.

"Now that you've been here a while, Pim, how do you like our seminary?"

"It's fine. But I'd like it better if there weren't so many rules."

"I guess there are a lot of them. But we need them with so many boys. Which rules don't you like?"

"Not talking at meals and eating everything the cooks put on your plate."

"Well, if four hundred boys were all talking at the same time, it would be so noisy you couldn't hear yourself think.

But having to eat everything on your plate is quite strict. It seems like you could leave *something* for the mice. But if so many boys each left half a cup of food at every meal, we'd have a mountain of garbage."

"I had to eat gristle. It was disgusting."

"I wouldn't like that myself."

"It made me throw up."

"Other than that, how do you feel about school? Do you still want to be a priest?"

"Gristle has nothing to do with my vocation. So, yes, I do."

"When did you decide you wanted to be a priest?"

"I always wanted to be as far back as I can remember. When I was four, my grandmother gave me priest's vestments. I'd dress up in them and say Mass."

"What do you like about being a priest?" asked Pa.

"Everything—the people singing, the liturgy, and the light streaming through church windows. I wanted to help people and be kind like a priest."

"Keep your faith, Pim. And you will reach your goal."

"I want to but it doesn't seem like I do very well. No matter how hard I try, something always goes wrong."

"You're very young to make a decision for your whole life. But if this is the path God wants you to take you will be successful. Come and talk to me if you have questions. I'll try to answer them."

July 16, 1940

Today Pieter and I were walking down the hall to the office. We could hear "Pa" talking to the new teacher. We stopped before we were in front of the open door where they would see us.

We couldn't resist listening. It was eavesdropping, but the door was open and they weren't keeping their voices down. I don't think they cared if anybody heard.

Father Straathof said, "Do you think they can get the new party going?"

'Pa' said, "It won't work. The Nazis won't allow it. They certainly don't want us to have any power. They won't let more than three people talk together in town. They're afraid if we get together; we'll make demands and find ways to resist them."

"But wouldn't it be easier for them to govern Holland if we cooperate? If they let us have some say in administering the country; it would be easier for them to rule. Nederlanders are reasonable people; if we cooperated, it would be to their advantage."

"They don't want us to have any voice in things. They would rather deal with us one at a time, as individuals."

"And the different groups would not always agree. The Protestants won't join unless the new party recognizes the House of Orange."

"There you are, then. Hitler hates the House of Orange. He can't bear even to hear their name spoken."

The talk about a forming a new party was a surprise. I would have liked to hear more about it, but we had to move on. Everybody in Holland probably knows about this. It must be on the news. We don't have a radio here. At home we listen to the radio all day.

Only ten more days before we go home for a whole month. August is summer vacation!

July 20, 1940

The bombers of the Luftwaffe fly over Holland on their way to England. When the sound wakes me, I listen as long as I hear them. I can't go back to sleep until they pass and it's quiet again.

Those air raids are awful for the Brits, sleeping underground in bomb shelters. The children must be frightened in the dark without their own beds. It's chilly and drafty in the subway where they sleep. They worry and wonder if their houses are still there.

Bombing and killing people who haven't done anything to you is insane. The Luftwaffe Heinkels are bombing the people of London repeatedly, to try to make them surrender.

The Germans talk about an invasion but they still haven't tried that. Invading isn't easy. They need to bring a million or more soldiers with their tanks and guns across the sea to attack the English. Since that is too hard, they are trying to scare them into giving up, but they can't scare Churchill. His speeches keep up their courage.

The British bomb Holland, too, trying to destroy railroad bridges. The bombs always miss the target and land alongside the tracks, hitting houses imstead. When people's homes are blown up, they have to move into any building they can find—a barn, a warehouse, a cottage or a shed. People are living in anything with a roof over to keep the rain off their heads.

The Nazis put up posters saying the English don't care about the Dutch. We tear them down. We laugh at their anti-British slogans. The Nazis bombed Rotterdam to rubble. If anybody cares about the Dutch, we know it's not the Germans. They showed how they care for us when they sent us the Luftwaffe.

July 25, 1940

Mother wrote that Oma Heemskerk (Grandmother) is coming to live with us. The directors of her retirement place are closing it for cleaning and painting. She will have my bedroom and I will sleep in the twins' room when I'm home. They wrestle and fight so much it's hard to sleep but it's worth it having her.

Oma could live with one of her other children, but she likes it with us best. We love to have her to stay. She's our only grandparent now.

Some of Dad's brothers and sisters have bigger houses, but Dad is like the head of the family. He takes care of the Heemskerk clan.

We're lucky to have a house and a field for growing crops. Dad looks ahead. He says the German Army lives off the land in occupied countries. Their multi-million army eats everything in sight. He planted fruit and vegetables now because you can't depend on markets.

Oma likes living with us but it's hard for her to climb the stairs. Our stairway is wide and has no railings. The steps are narrow and as steep as rungs on a ladder. Each one is only deep enough to put the front of your foot down on it. It was built a long time ago when Dutch builders didn't waste room for deeper steps. They didn't think about people carrying things up and down. Mother can climb them with a basket of clothes. When the twins were little she went up and down with both children—one on each arm.

I have to help Oma climb the stairs. She asks me to carry her big purse because it's too heavy. She tells me she loves me and I know it's true. I tell her she's my favorite grandmother. And she says that's because she's the only one.

Before we lived here this was her house. After Opa died, Oma bought a smaller place. Mother and Dad needed more room for our family so we moved here from our home in Hillegom.

When Oma grew old she moved to the retirement home she lives in now. She doesn't have to do any work. And there are people to make her meals and people to look after her, I think she'll like living with us better.

July 31, 1940

This morning we cleaned our rooms and packed our suitcases to take home. When we return in September we'll be the second year class and have new rooms. The beginning class will take our rooms.

It will all be different—books, subjects, classrooms, and teachers. I made up a silly rhyme:

> The school year is finished
> Don't try to find us, Jack
> We're going on vacation and
> We'll see you when we're back!

Everybody has a nickname here. Jack is the name they gave Father Straathof, our new teacher because he's so tall and thin—like Jack Sprat in the English nursery rhyme who 'ate no fat.' But we don't use nicknames to people's faces. We only use nicknames when the person is not around.

Tomorrow I'm going home to see my family. I passed! I believe in miracles because I thought my math scores were so low they were in the basement.

Now I'm thinking what I'll do when I'm home for a whole month!

Chapter 9

Summer Vacation

August 1, 1940

Hurray! Today is the first day of vacation. For the whole month I can do what I like. I left school with my suitcase and all my books. When I come back I'll have a new room. Riding home on the tram, I listened to the tram wheels and they seemed to say 'Bennebroek'!

On May 10 when I came home, anti-aircraft guns around Haarlem were booming, planes were roaring, the sky was filled with parachutes and gliders and broken planes.

Today was quieter. The wind was blowing, turning the windmills, lifting the water into the canals. Each one raising the water a little until it is high enough to flow into canals and rivers that take the water to the North Sea. The dikes are the hills that keep water from flowing over the land. The canals are higher than the fields. When you are in the fields and look up you can see boats going by above your head.

The windmills make a thumping sound. On holidays, millers used to fly Dutch flags on the windmills. But now that Holland is occupied, our flags are forbidden.

The windmills are tall and can be seen a long way off. When they are still, their sails give us the news. Traditionally, the miller places the sails like the hands of the clock at just before 12 and 6 o'clock to announce a birth. Sails are set just after 12 and 6 to announce a death. The sails are set at a 45 degree angle when the mill is not ready to work. When one sail is vertical and the other one is horizontal, the mill is about to start. The Dutch know what the sails mean but Germans have no clue. Windmills could be used to send messages the Germans wouldn't even notice.

On the road to Lisse, an old stone tower peers over the trees. I asked Dad about it. He said it was an ancient windmill.

"Did you ever see it working?"

"No, it was just an old stone tower as long as I remember."

"Why don't the owners take it down?"

"It would be too much work to break it up. And where would they put the stones?"

I want to look inside to see what's there. Maybe the miller left something behind. The miller lived there, close to his work, which is keeping the machinery working and adjusting the sails.

The wind blows all the time. When it shifts direction, the miller has to turn the sails to the wind if he wants it to work. In recent times, steam engines are replacing the old windmills. Steam engines are more efficient but not as beautiful.

August 2, 1940

When I came home yesterday, Tiberius barked a welcome. My two silly white geese gabbled and ran at me flapping their wings. They must have missed me. Or maybe they thought my pockets were full of grain.

I'm happy they are still here. They annoy the girls by mock attacks on their friends. Jo and Alice would like to get rid of them. But they can be useful, too. They warn us when somebody comes.

The twins were playing ball when I came down the path with my suitcase and my books. It was a blg load and they helped me carry it.

Gerard said "Jo made a cake!"

"For vacation!" Ton said.

"Where's Jan?" I asked.

"Working on Gijs's farm." Gijs is a tulip grower on *de Tol* in Hillegom, a piece of land once connected by a bridge over a canal. I think at one time it must have been a toll bridge, but it isn't now.

Gijs has the same last name as we but we're not related. Heemskerk is the name of a town in North Holland. Our ancestors and Gijs's must have both come from there. Long ago people in Holland didn't have last names. But there were too many people with the same first name. To tell them apart they might add the word 'van' and the place they were from. Or sometimes they would add a characteristic like the color of their hair or their trade. Van means 'from'. There are many people with 'van' in front of their name so when we alphabetize, we disregard the 'van' and keep names in order by what comes after. Our name used to be 'van Heemskerk' but our family dropped the 'van' to shorten it.

When I came home, Mother smiled and hugged me. Her eyes were shining. She cries when she's sad and she cries when she's happy. She is a Lommerse and that's the way the Lommerses are.

Dad came in from the greenhouse where he was pollinating tulips to develop new varieties. When he is working there he doesn't want us to come in. A bee might come in with pollen on its legs and do some unwanted pollination.

He was glad to see me and to hear that I passed. He's proud that I go to Hageveld, the school he supports.

Jo brought in a cake—a masterpiece, frosted in stripes of red, white and blue to look like a Dutch flag. It tasted as sweet as it looked. We gobbled the cake, drank our coffee, listened to the radio and talked. Dad was angry because of the new rules the Germans made. When he was home he wasn't always careful about what he said.

"Seyss Inquart promised we could keep our own laws and live by them. He said he was not going to turn our country into Germany. But they changed the rules. Now Jews are being forbidden to teach or go to school or ride in trams, or shop in our stores."

Jo added. "They even forbid Jews in parks. Why? What is their reason?"

Hitler hates Jews. They are doctors, lawyers, bankers, and business owners. Hitler is jealous of them. He wants to get rid of them but keep their money. Jewish refugees came to Holland because it was a friendly, neutral country where they believed they would be safe. But the occupation government is getting rid of them; sending them to the refugee camp in Westerbork.

Cardinal de Jong, the Archbishop of Utrecht is at the head of the Catholic Church in Holland. He sends letters to be read in Catholic Churches. He tells us we must feed and shelter people who are being persecuted. He tells us we must obey God rather than man. Many Jews are living in hiding and people are finding safe places for them.

When we had to register for identification cards, we had to give our religion. Telling the truth was a big mistake. We should have lied to mislead the Nazis. Now Jews have to wear a yellow Star of David on their sleeves and Germans are looking for them to take them away. There are not many here. I suspect Uncle Frans has a couple living in his attic. I'm not sure because I haven't asked. If the Germans find out they would take them away.

August 3, 1940

This morning Lou came over. He goes to the Ulo* in Haarlem and goes home every night. That's better than living in a boarding school and sleeping in a dormitory.

Jo served us what was left of the cake. Lou said "What is this? Cake? And frosting too, yet?"

We don't get many sweet things any more. Sugar is rationed.

The radio was tuned to Hilversum. The music is good but we don't believe the commentators. They only tell us what they want us to believe. The Nazis are turning somersaults and patting themselves on the back with glee. They can't contain themselves! Germany owns almost all Europe. Everything belongs to the Third Reich!

Hitler hates Queen Wilhelmina and the royal family, especially Prince Bernhard, the German Prince who married Princess Juliana. He was furious that the Queen escaped to London. He planned to take her hostage.

We listen to Dutch and British stations. Listening to the BBC is *verboten* but they can't tell what we are listening to. Every night the British broadcast a program in Dutch called 'Radio Orange'. The Queen speaks to us from London. She always says "We are one day closer to liberation" at the end of her talk.

The BBC plays a song 'Hang up the washing on the Siegfried Line'—this is the border between France and Germany. The Germans reply by playing 'Sailing to England'—as if they're ready to cross the channel.

"Do you think the Nazis will really invade England?" Lou asked.

"Oh, for sure—when they can get a million men across the channel complete with tanks and guns. How many ships would that take?"

"I don't know," Lou said. "How many Panzers can you load on a barge? Ten? Maybe twenty? Tanks are heavy. And how many do they have now?"

We didn't know how many tugs and barges it would take to invade England. But they don't have enough. All they can use to get tanks across the Channel are barges because barges don't need deep water. The shore is too shallow for big ships.

The closest the Germans are to Britain is the Channel Islands. These are English islands on the French side of the English Channel. To reach Britain, the Germans have to cross strong tides and swift currents—before the fall storms. Sailing is risky in the fall and winter.

Shipbuilders in Dutch ports are fitting barges for landing craft, pouring cement floors so they can hold tanks. But they haven't completed many. The Germans are not shipbuilders; it's not a seafaring nation.

When the Allied soldiers left Dunkirk on the fleet of little ships, they left their equipment on the beach. But to mount a blitzkrieg the Germans would need to bring a mountain of tanks and guns and fuel supplies.

*ULO-secondary school

August 4, 1940

Grandmother Lommerse's upright piano stands in our parlor, polished and ready to play—but nobody can play. Mother thought one of us should take lessons. So she asked her friend, Jo Braam, a music teacher, for tea. After we ate, Mother asked her to play our piano. We listened to the beautiful music and Mother asked who wanted to learn. Alice and I both did. Miss Braam made us promise to practice every day before she agreed to teach us.

Alice loves music and practices all the time. I started out well, but I got too busy and decided to quit. Mother said I couldn't quit because I hadn't made an effort. So I had to keep on with the lessons.

I wanted to know which of us played better. I asked Alice if I could listen to her take a lesson. But she said she couldn't play when I was listening. It made her self-conscious. So one day I hid behind the couch while she took her lesson. But after a while, I felt confined and came out. Alice said I was spying. Now she looks behind the couch before her lessons.

The space behind the couch was created when Dad installed central heat. The workmen took out the fireplace to use the chimney for the furnace in the cellar. That left a hole in the wall where the fireplace used to be. Mother told Dad to get a bricklayer to fill it in with bricks and plaster. But Dad said it was a good storage space. He moved the couch in front of the opening. If you didn't know the space was there, you wouldn't see it.

Anyway, when I'm home I can practice. I can play a little but I hate music with more than two flats or sharps. I like the easier pieces.

Once when we had choir practice, our old organist, Martinus van Lierop, didn't show up. The director looked around and said, "Bill, you play the piano, so you can play the organ tonight."

An organ is different from a piano. An organ has stops and different pedals. I didn't know how to play the pedals or how to set the stops. That old organ has only one keyboard but some have more. I tried to play softly when the choir was singing and louder when they didn't, experimented with the different stops to hear the instrumental sounds. I made mistakes, but what can they expect? I never had lessons.

There is a long wooden beam on the side of the organ. In the old days they used it to pump air into the pipes. A person would stand on the beam and move up and down to fill the bellows. Now they've added an electric motor to use instead of the person pumping. But they didn't take the beam away. They thought if the power went off, they could use the beam and the organist could still play.

The director thanked me for my help and gave me what I call a Dutch compliment. That is a little praise, but not too much because they don't want you to get too big headed. "You didn't do too badly, Bill. Why don't you study the organ?"

That made me proud. I like the organ. An organ can imitate a whole orchestra of instruments--a flute or a trumpet an oboe or a clarinet. You can make it play loudly or whisper softly. I'd like to learn to play it.

August 6, 1940

This morning I saw an old friend, Al Borg, waiting for the train to Haarlem. Since I started Hageveld we hadn't talked much. Al was wearing the uniform of the Sons of the NSB, a blue shirt and short black pants. That is what the Dutch Hitler Youth wear. Al and I were in Boy Scouts together. Now the Scouts are *Verboten* because it's a British organization.

"How do you like Hageveld?" Al asked.

"Pretty good. But it's harder than St. Franciscus."

"I thought of going there," Al said. "But Dad wouldn't let me. I'm glad because now I'm in NSB and it's fun! We go camping and hiking, practice shooting and marching. We meet people. They gave us uniforms and we're learning to be troopers. You should join, Pim. You'd like it!"

"But they're Nazis, Al. How can you join them? It's against our religion."

"Well, it's just like the Boy Scouts, only German instead of English. And so what if their philosophy is different? You don't have to agree with everything they say. They want you to be strong and healthy, the same as the Scouts."

"But Nazis are not Christians. They run around saying 'Heil Hitler' all the time. They pledge 'to follow Adolf Hitler—even to death.' How can you do that?"

"The pledge doesn't mean much—it's just something you say at meetings. It's not like I'm in the German army. I'm only fourteen. It will be four years before I'm old enough for that. The war will be over by that time."

"Aren't you being disloyal? Don't you love our country, our Queen, our flag?"

"Of course I do. I love Holland. But I admire Germany, too. There isn't a dime's worth of difference between governments. Face it! Germany rules Europe. We fought a little war. Holland lost and Germany won. The Queen left Holland. She's in London and she's not coming back. But the Germans are here now. They're in control. Since we can't beat them, we might as well join them."

"But this is our country. Someday the war will end and Holland will be liberated. The Germans will go back to Germany."

"It'll never happen. Europe is a united country now, with Hitler at the head. The German Army is the biggest in the whole world. They can't lose.

When things change, they never go back like they were before. You can't drag old cows out of the ditch. You can't bring dead cows back to life. All the little countries are joined together to make the great German Empire. The time is past when all the little countries to have their own rulers."

I was stunned by what he said. Tonight at dinner I talked about what Al said.

Dad said "Too bad. People believe what they like. He made up his mind what he wanted and then thought up reasons to justify himself. Al thinks joining the Germans will help him get ahead."

Jan made a pun, "Well he should get a head—he needs one."

Mother said, "What are his parents thinking?"

"Simple," said Jo. "They think Germany will take over completely and they'll be on the winning side. They believe they'll rule the rest of us. They want power. But Hitler is the ruler. He'll make us all slaves. He wants all the power himself and he isn't giving it to anyone else."

August 10, 1940

When Dad took over our house in Bennebroek, it had a small potting shed attached to the kitchen end of the house. But his bulb business grew and he needed more room. So he built a warehouse two stories high, attached to the house, but bigger. There are shelves for sorting and drying the tulips and hyacinths. He has an office there and a place for his equipment. It is like a barn only instead of a place to store hay, we have boxes and shelves and tables for bulbs. It is an impressive building with two white ventilators sitting on the roof that look like little gables.

He kept the iron bell that used to tell workers it was time to start work in the morning and stop work for dinner. He put it on the roof, but it isn't needed now because there aren't as many workers. Rinus, Dad's foreman is still here. The twins and I stand by the wood plank tables, cleaning the bulbs that were dug in spring. The flower bulbs have dried dirt on them. Their outer skin must be completely removed. Cleaning bulbs isn't fun and it's not easy.

We put the bulbs in paper bags to fill orders. We can't ship them to customers in Britain or America any more. We can still sell them to Germany, France, and the Scandinavian countries though. But not many so we don't get as much money.

There are rules for shipping flower bulbs. Bulbs must be eleven or twelve centimeters to be big enough to be sold. Bulbs that are too small to sell are planted in the fall and grow big enough to be sold the next year.

We were listening to our old radio while we were cleaning bulbs in the warehouse. The announcer was talking about Seyss-Inquart, the man Hitler appointed over the Netherlands. He's an Austrian who helped Hitler by turning Austria over to Germany in the Anschluss. He is supposed to be a Catholic. But Herr Hitler once said "You can be a Nazi or a Catholic, you can't be both."

August 11, 1940

Besides news, the Dutch radio plays marches and classical music. Today they were playing something from Wagner, German music. On our stations they don't play popular songs. They would be too English or American.

"I don't care for Wagner," a helper called Adrian said. "They say Wagner is a great composer. I don't think it's so great. Maybe Wagner's music is better than it sounds." I had to smile. It's not my favorite music either.

Between the music and the news, there were speeches. The radio was playing one by Arthur Seyss-Inquart, the Reichskommissar of the Netherlands. He isn't an inspiring speaker. And he wasn't chosen for his good looks. He wears thick glasses and limps when he walks.

When he first took office at the Knight's Hall in The Hague, on May 30, he said he would respect our laws and govern us according to them. But then he contradicted himself by saying Dutch judges and civil servants have to obey German laws.

Seyss-Inquart brought four deputies to help govern. His chief deputy, Hanns Albin Rauter, is also an Austrian. He is Chief of Police in the Netherlands, in charge of security and has organized a Gestapo. He is supposed to be working for Seyss, but he acts like his superior. He is close to Himmler and that gives him power.

In addition to German deputies, Seyss has a Dutch deputy, Anton Mussert. Mussert is a Dutch Nazi. He helped the Nazis win. He thought he would be appointed to rule Holland.

His brother was a Colonel in the Dutch Army. This was the officer who ordered obstacles removed from a bridge to let German tanks cross. After he gave the order to remove the tank obstacles, his fellow officers shot him.

Dutch and German deputies don't work well together. Mussert started the W.A.,* an organization filled with Dutch hoodlums. They stir up trouble by harassing Jews. Mussert is disappointed he isn't in charge of Holland, like Quisling in Norway.

Hitler made Quisling the ruler of Norway. But it didn't work. The Norwegians hate him because he's a turncoat and use his name as a synonym for *traitor.*

Weer Afdeling. A paramilitary organization or Defense Division. It soon became the Dutch S.S. like the German auxiliary organization. The members then swore allegiance to Hitler, not to Mussert.

Chapter 10

Being Home

August 12, 1940

This morning I slept until 7:30. At Hageveld we can't sleep so late. After breakfast we went to the service at St. Joseph's. Father Schmidt preached a long sermon. A couple of times I thought he was coming to the end but he took a deep breath and kept right on.

He's our parish priest. He is from Germany and doesn't hide his German sympathies. He told Dad that Holland should join Germany. Dad didn't want to argue. So he only said, "I don't think the Queen would agree."

The pastor is big and looks like he eats well. His hair is a mixture of pepper and salt. His eyes are gray. His face is too pale; he needs to get out in the sun. His mouth turns down in the corners and he looks grumpy. But he's always friendly to me. He wrote a nice letter of recommendation when I applied to enter Hageveld.

After church he asked me "How was your first year of school?"

"*Fijn*," I said. "That was a good sermon." My reply was the truth. It was a good sermon. I didn't mention it seemed endless.

He smiled. "I left out a story because people say my sermons are too long." Then he told me the story of Theseus and the Minotaur. I liked hearing it. I like the old Greek and Roman myths.

When I got home, Mother remarked, "I could have said 'Amen' a dozen times."

Alice said she could hardly remember a longer sermon.

So I told them "You're lucky he quit when he did. He had another story he left out because the congregation was restless. Would you like me to tell it?"

The family groaned but I told it anyway. "There was a cave in Greece with an intricate maze. Nobody who went in it was ever seen again.

At the center of the maze a Minotaur lived, a creature—half bull and half man. It devoured everyone who entered. Every year the Greeks brought him 14 young men because they thought it was better to let him kill a few young men than for him come out of his cave and kill everybody.

Theseus vowed to stop the horrible sacrifice. He knew only way to stop the beast was to kill him. So he went into the maze and killed the Minotaur. He might have been stuck in the maze afterward because it was impossible to find the way out.

But Ariadne, a girl who loved Theseus, gave him a spool of red thread and told him to unwind it on his way into the maze. After he killed the beast he followed the red thread to find his way out.

Theseus was a Greek hero. He founded Athens and established Greek civilization. He did a lot of other great things, too.

But he didn't marry Ariadne. She saved his life by giving him the spool of red thread so he could get out of the maze. You would think the end of the story would be: 'Theseus married Ariadne and they lived happily ever after.' She deserved a reward for saving his life. But he married her sister. The story didn't say why he didn't marry Ariadne. Maybe she was lucky. He might not have been a good husband.

But she did the right thing and what was her reward?

August 13, 1940

Today was a day of contrary weather. The sun shone and I went outside. I had only been outside for a few minutes and it started to rain. So I went in and then the sun came out. Seeing it was sunny, I decided to walk over and see Lou. Then the clouds burst open and it rained again.

After that I decided it was not a good day to walk outdoors. Jan was listening to the radio. He works for Gijs, a grower. Gijs is getting out of the bulb business so Jan will lose his job.

"What will you do now?" I asked him.

"I'll stay home and help Dad. There's plenty to do here on the farm."

That doesn't qualify as employment. Unemployed men of eighteen or over must register for the Labor Force. Jan won't be eighteen until June. He still has time to look.

I suggested, "Why not go back to school, Jan, so you won't have to register?"

Jan said. "I'd rather stay around the farm and help Dad. If the Germans come, I'll hide."

"Everybody knows you're here, Jan. What if they catch you? Then you'll be sent to Germany and have to work in a factory."

"It wouldn't be worse than working in a factory here."

"But it is. In Germany it's slave labor. The workers live in unheated buildings with no beds, just wood plank shelves to sleep on. They are kept behind barbed wire. Armed guards with attack dogs keep them from escaping."

Jo said, "And the food isn't so good either."

"If it's so bad, they can't expect the men to work."

"They don't care. If they work men to death they can always get more from the occupied countries. Living conditions are horrible."

But Jan made up his mind and it was set in stone. "I'd rather stay home," Jan said. "If the Germans come, I'll hide in the warehouse. And they won't be able to find me."

August 14, 1940

Hitler is afraid the British will come over and free Europe. The occupied countries will rise in revolt. It must keep him awake nights. So he has a plan to 'protect' his kingdom. He will build an Atlantic Wall around Europe from Norway to the Mediterranean. I don't know how long it will take to get it done—but it will be as long as the Great Wall of China. And that took centuries to build. Hitler can't wait. He wants to start today and finish yesterday.

It will take millions of workers to build the 'Atlantic Wall'. Where will they come from? He can't use German men because they're all in the army. So he'll take men from occupied countries—like Holland and France and

Belgium and Denmark. But he'll need billions of tons of concrete and steel. Where will he get them?

Building a wall around so many miles of coast is crazy. Included in his plan are bunkers in the sand dunes for soldiers' living quarters with guns and tanks to keep out invaders. The workers will set barricades under water to keep the British from landing on the beaches.

Jan said, "They tore down Dad's farmhouse on the coast and set guns in the dunes."

But if they use men from occupied countries, first they have to build camps for the workers and their guards. Hitler will have problems with his Atlantic Wall.

August 15, 1940

Last night around nine we heard an unbelievably loud roar and looked up to see wispy clouds, bright stars, a crescent moon and so many dark shapes of planes we could not count them, flying west to bomb England.

Goering is determined to beat England. He thinks bombing will bring Churchill to his knees, and make him beg for peace.

The glass prisms of the chandelier in the dining room were vibrating. Mother is afraid we'll be killed in our sleep. She made us stay up and sit together in the living room. She won't get in the bomb shelter Dad made the day of the blitzkrieg.

Jan said, "Why are we sitting in the living room? We might as well go to bed."

Mother said, "I want us together so we'll be safe."

Dad said, "Those planes aren't bombing us. But if they do, being awake won't help."

"I'm hungry," Jan said. "Let's get out the cookies." So Jo got the cookie box from the top shelf of the cupboard and we each had two almond cookies with milk. Gerard and Ton fell asleep on the couch. They looked like angels. After the Heinkels passed over, we went to bed. Dad picked up the sleeping twins and carried them upstairs.

The bombers flew over again on their way back to Germany, but Mother didn't wake us. I asked her why she let us sleep when they flew over then.

She said, "Because they dropped their bombs. I don't worry about the planes after they drop their bombs. The planes won't hit us. I'm afraid of bombs hitting the house."

On the radio they said it was a successful raid on England but didn't mention how many German planes they lost. The British said they shot down so many planes, the Germans would have to quit before they were out of bombers. The announcer finished by quoting a line from a speech by Churchill, "We will fight them on the beaches. We will fight them in the streets. We will fight them everywhere. We will **never** give up."

August 16, 1940

This morning Dad went to the Town Council Meeting on his bike. When he got back, he told us Father van Reuven was arrested. They put him in the prison in Haarlem. That prison is called "The Umbrella" because it has a round roof. It was a Dutch prison but the Germans run it now and we hear terrible things about the way they torture prisoners there. They tie prisoner's hands behind their backs and hang them from meat hooks, causing terrible pain because their weight pulls the shoulder joints out of their sockets.

We're praying for Father van Reuven. The Nazis took him because he protested the treatment of the Jews. The Nazis are extremely angry at priests and ministers and anyone who protects the Jews.

Dad wrote a petition to ask them to let Father go. He is asking everybody in every church in Bennebroek and Heemstede to sign it and bring it to Seyss Inquart and ask him to release Father.

August 17, 1940

We were having coffee this morning. Dad brought up the subject of a cow. We have plenty of milk now but he thinks we'll need a cow.

"Where will we keep it?" Ton asked. He works for a dairy farmer after school and weekends so he knows about cows.

"What will we feed it?" Gerard asked.

"There's plenty of hay," Dad said. "We can keep it in the little barn that's filled with bales of straw. If we take it out, there will be room for a cow. The

Germans are killing cows to feed their army. Killing cows will make us short of milk. So if we want milk, we need a cow."

Dad's right. But somebody has to feed the cow and milk it and clean its stall. Keeping a cow is a lot of work.

Our milkman brings milk in a can on his bicycle. Every morning he rings the bell and mother brings out pitchers to fill. He sells milk by the liter. It's always fresh and we always have enough. But if Dad wants a cow, he'll get one.

I like animals for pets. It will be odd having a cow around. I wouldn't like cleaning up after it. I won't be home to help, but the boys will do the chores.

I might think of a name for it.

August 18, 1940

Annie, Mother's helper, was all smiles today, dimpling and twinkling at breakfast.

"What makes you so happy?" I asked.

She held out her right hand to show off her ring. The stone was not large but it sparkled.

"Oh, what a beautiful ring! You must be engaged. When did it happen?"

"Last night," she said. "Piet and I are getting married and you'll all be invited."

"When will that be?"

"At Christmas time. If we find some place to live."

Annie has been living with us and helping mother four years. She bustles around the house like a busy hen. She's like another sister to us. Piet, the man she is going to marry, is tall and dark. Annie is a blond, like a ballerina. When they are together, love beams from their eyes.

I asked Mother what she will do for help when Annie leaves. Mother said, "Annie's sister, Allie will come and work for us."

Annie comes from a family with four girls and no boys. She is older than Jo, but still she seems too young to marry. We'll miss her.

I wonder where they will find an apartment. Many houses and apartment buildings were hit by bombs so there's a shortage of places to live, now.

Chapter 11

The Old Windmill

August 19, 1940

This morning I was reading an English grammar in the dining room while Mother was singing a favorite Dutch song. I listened, substituting English words. "At the wall of an old cemetery, stands a boy crying for his mother to come back." Mother likes sad songs. She has another one about a soldier wounded in a war who dies in the hospital for honor and glory."

Lou came over to see us. He doesn't live on a farm so he has very few chores. There's always some work to do at our place. "Wouldn't it be nice to go to Zandvoort today?" he asked.

Zandvoort is a seaside town a few kilometers from Bennebroek. On warm summer days before the war we often went there to swim. Now we can't go to the sea or the beach because the Germans fenced off the coast.

Jo said, "It would be, Lou, but it's off limits so we'll have to swim in the pool."

"No way! It's too crowded—just wall to wall kids. And the water is ice cold. Let's sneak through the woods. If we get to the sand dunes we can at least see the water and find out what the Germans are doing."

Alice said, "Sneak through the woods? Are you crazy?"

Jo said, "Don't even think about it. There's the wall across the road connected to a fence on both sides. If you got over the fence, the guards would shoot you. They might even have dogs."

Lou didn't want to go to the pool so we thought we'd take a ride down the road instead. We made cheese sandwiches and filled a thermos with milk to share. Then we got on our bikes to see how close we could get to the water.

Jo was right. There was a wall across the road and a funny sign saying 'Mauer Muur'. Mauer is the German word for wall, and Muur is the Dutch word for wall. The Germans didn't want to take a chance we might not know there was a wall. The sign said it was 'verboten' to pass.

Lou laughed. "It says wall, wall."

On both sides of the wall a fence was attached, too high to climb and too wide to go around.

I said, "They didn't label the fence, though. "At least they gave us credit for sense enough to know a fence when we saw one."

"Maybe the painter didn't know how to spell the Dutch word for fence," Lou speculated. "Maybe he ran out of paint."

We wanted to run on the sand, swim in the surf and watch sailboats skim the waves on the North Sea. A strong west wind was blowing with huge waves crashing on shore. These were our dunes and we loved them. What harm would it do the Germans to let us go there? Why do they want to keep us off the beach?

We couldn't get a glimpse of the sea from the road. Since we couldn't be near the water, I had an idea. "Let's look at the old tower," I said. "I've always wanted to see what's inside."

"Let's try." Lou said. "It's probably locked, though. I don't think we can get in."

We turned left and followed the road south. In the distance we saw the top of the old tower above the trees. When we got closer, we got off our bikes and pushed them through the leafy woods. There was no path so we went in the general direction through bushes and under trees.

When we finally reached the stone tower, we were amazed at its size. We walked all around. It had heavy double wooden doors on the front and back. "They made it that way so horses could pull the loaded wagons through," Lou said. We tried the doors and pushed with all our might, but neither one would move a centimeter.

Windmills usually have walkways around their towers where the miller stands to adjust the sails, but the walks were gone and the roof cap where sails should have been fastened had disappeared.

"If we had a crowbar we could pry the doors open."

"Even if we had tools, we couldn't use them. Breaking and entering is a crime."

Higher up on the sides of the tower were openings for windows. But we couldn't reach them without a ladder.

"Entering is against the law, but if we could get to that window we could look in. Looking in a window isn't illegal," Lou said.

"Not if nobody sees us."

It was a lonely place in the deep woods, far from everywhere. The grounds were wild and overgrown with bushes. Since we couldn't get in, we sat down under the trees and ate our sandwiches.

"I'd really like to know what it's like inside," Lou said. "Do you think they left the old machinery?"

"If they did, it wouldn't be any good after so long. The iron would be turned to rust. Squirrels and bats are the only living things that were here for years."

"How long do you think it's been empty?"

"It's been deserted for ages," I said, "because when they build windmills; they give the miller a license to the free use of the wind. Nobody may put anything up around the mill to block the wind. No trees were allowed to grow. These trees grew after it was closed and they weren't planted yesterday."

A Beech tree stood close against the stone wall with one big branch reaching inside, like a gnarled arm of an old man. "Help me climb the tree," I said. Lou bent down. I climbed on his back and stood up to grab the branch. I pulled myself up and crawled along it. The branch tapered down until it reached the wall. I am afraid of heights so I didn't go too far. But I crept close enough to see in.

"What do you see?"

"There's a wooden floor with a hole in the middle and a ladder coming through the hole. We could climb that if it's still strong."

There wasn't much light inside because the window opening was not big. Below the window the floor cut off the view. I was afraid to go too far along the branch where it narrowed. I didn't want to climb in. The floor was probably rotten. If I fell through I would be trapped inside with no way out. I didn't want to take a chance so I jumped down.

Lou said, "Let me try."

"No, the floor might cave in."

"I'll test it. If it doesn't feel solid, I'll climb out."

I helped him jump and grab the branch. He snaked along the same way I had. But he's more reckless. He climbed in through the window. Then he stuck his head out. "The floor is all right. I'm going down the ladder to take a look."

I waited. What if he couldn't get out? I would have to get help. We just wanted to look. That was permissible but we knew we shouldn't enter.

I waited, then the door opened and Lou walked out. "Come on. It's not locked. A beam was leaning against it holding it shut. We should have tried to slide it open instead of pushing it."

The interior was dark and creepy. It smelled damp and moldy. The stones laid on the earth to make the floor were quietly sinking into the ground. Heaps of rotten wood and rusted iron junk were all that was inside. There was nothing else to see, nothing anybody would want.

"It must have been a mill for grinding wheat or cutting lumber." I said. A water mill would be next to a canal. Even if the canal was gone you could still see the banks.

For centuries, Holland depended on windmills for power. When the steam engine was invented, it was more efficient. Gradually, many old windmills were replaced by modern machinery using oil, not wind.

When the miller abandoned the mill, he took off the cap that held the mechanism turned by the sails and covered the top of the stone tower with a flat roof. He didn't clear the tower away. It would be too much work. And where would they put the stones? Besides, they probably thought they might need it someday.

The tower was 30 meters high, I guessed. It would have been taller with its cap intact. It had to be tall enough for the sails to clear the ground when they turned. Windmills need to reach up high where they the winds are stronger.

Lou said, "Let's climb to the top."

I hate heights but I wanted to see the view so I went up the ladder behind him. It was cool and dim even in daylight because the light was at an angle and the sun did not shine directly inside. There was a window opening on every level. There were several floors but I didn't remember to count. In places where the rain had come in the wood was black with mildew. There were piles of dead leaves.

It was a long climb but the ladder was strong enough to bear our weight. In a few places it creaked and here and there a step was missing. But we could take a big step up and reach the next one. When we got to the end of the last ladder, we looked down at the treetops. In the distance we could see the North Sea. We didn't see any white sails—we couldn't see any ships at all. This surprised me.

"Where did all the little boats go that used to be anchored along the shore?"

"The fishing boats and yachts? You can't keep them along the seacoast any more. It would be a way to get across the channel. The Germans took them and keep them in harbors. Maybe they will use them when they invade England.

"Sure, if they ever get around to it. Like the English evacuated Dunkirk," I said. "But I don't think so. The English were only taking soldiers off the beach to the big cruisers. They didn't take tanks or guns or equipment. The Germans would have to bring their tanks and fuel along if they wanted a Blitzkrieg. Just fishing boats and ferries and yachts won't do the job.

We stood there, breathing fresh wind, looking into the far distance— blue-green waves breaking against the sand, white birds flying and hundreds of clouds sailing across the blue sky. The view from the old tower was glorious.

Then the wind blew harder and clouds darkened, moving toward us, covering the blue sky.

On the sand by the shore, we saw five tiny men moving on the dunes.

"Those must be German soldiers," I said, "out for a walk."

"The three grayish ones look like soldiers in uniform," said Lou, "But there are two men in dark clothes, too. They must be workers."

"They are so little and far away, you can hardly see what they are doing," I said. "We need a spyglass."

"The three soldiers are standing holding guns. The workers are digging in the sand."

We could see the men enlarging a hole and the sand pile growing bigger. Lou said, "It looks like an execution. I think the soldiers are going to kill those men and bury them in the hole."

"Why would they?"

"They must be enemies. They don't want a trial or they don't have any evidence. It's the quickest way to get rid of them."

"It's murder. What can we do?"

"We can't call the police. We could yell but nobody could hear us. There's no way to stop it. It's a long way off. Even if we had wings and could fly there we still couldn't do anything. The soldiers have guns."

Then dark clouds blotted out the sky. The wind blew onshore, bringing a thunderstorm. It was too dark to see until a flash of lightning lit the scene. Only the three soldiers were left. Two of them had laid down their guns and were covering the hole with sand.

The sun hid behind the clouds and it rained so hard it was like a bathtub overturned as if water could wash away the scene. I wanted to tell Dad but I knew there was nothing he could do. Nothing anybody could do.

We climbed down the quaky ladders to leave the tower. I was so concerned with getting home I did not even think how far the ground was if I should fall.

Lou said, "What can we do? We aren't supposed to be here."

"We have to tell somebody about the missing men."

"Maybe they can find out who is missing," Lou said "and notify their relatives."

When we reached the ground, we leaned the post against the heavy doors to keep them closed and slid them shut. We did not want to leave anything to show we'd been there. We looked carefully. Our tracks would be erased by the rain.

Streak lightning flashed as we left, pushing our bikes through the woods. Heavy rain kept pouring down as we rode home.

I went to Dad's office in the warehouse to tell him what we saw on the beach at Zandvoort.

Dad said "There is nothing we can do about it now. The Germans don't want us to know they killed the men. If they found out they would take you next.

August 20, 1940

Today Uncle Wim and Aunt Corrie came over. Uncle Wim is *vreemdeling*, an outsider. He is not a bulb grower and not from Bennebroek. He's in our family only because he married Dad's sister Corrie, who grew up here. Uncle Wim is a tall, slim man with unusually large hands and feet. They have a little boy named Robert and live in Amsterdam in a new apartment.

Before the invasion, Uncle Wim was the editor of a woman's fashion magazine called *Libelle*. But the new regime won't let them publish it. You can't print anything unless the Germans approve and they don't approve of anything that doesn't contribute to the war. A fashion magazine is frivolous and unnecessary.

When Uncle Wim lost his editing job, he had to register for work. The Labor Force made him a manager. He wears a green uniform to work, made of a cheap coarse material. He has to wear it to work, but when he gets home he can wear regular clothes. He's lucky he got a desk job. He could have been given a lot worse assignment like digging ditches or making fortifications.

Aunt Corrie said, "It isn't great, but at least he doesn't have to travel."

Dad asked, "What do you do?"

"I assign workers and keep track of their hours so the accountants know what to pay them. It's only five days a week. I have weekends off."

"How are you getting along?" Dad asked.

"It could be worse."

The Germans are obsessed with work. Everybody must work to help the war effort. They don't ask what you like. They don't care. They decide and you do what they say.

Dad is concerned about Aunt Corrie and Uncle Wim because of the troubles in Amsterdam. The W. A. and the Dutch Gestapo are fighting with the labor unions which the Germans abolished because the unions are full of communists.

They are picking on Jews, even Dutch citizens. Immigrants came here to escape the Nazis. They thought it would be safe in a neutral country. But Hitler followed them and he hates Jews. Dutch Jews are scientists, teachers, doctors, lawyers, bankers and business owners. They work everywhere—in stores, in the diamond industry and in the arts. But not many live in rural towns. They live in big cities.

Hitler was born an Austrian but he wants to be German because he thinks the Germans are the greatest nation in Europe. They say he has a Jewish grandparent but he would never admit that. But why does he blame the Jews for Germany's troubles? Is it because he wants their money?

The soldiers stationed here don't work, just march around and drive trucks around and eat. Before the war there was always enough food in Holland. We grew so much we exported tons of food—cheese and milk and meat. Our factories made clothes and shoes and machines and sold them to other countries. But the government steals everything they can get their hands on and carries it away. And they've introduced rationing. You need coupons now—you can only buy things if you have money and coupons. There's a shortage of everything! And you can't sell the food you grow because they call that black marketing. The Germans buy it—at the price they set.

August 22, 1940

Dad is a musician. He sings in the choir and plays a mean violin. But he says there is no money in that, so he works in the bulb business. Now there's no money there, either.

Last night he took us to Saint Bavo's Church to listen to a concert on their famous old pipe organ. We rode on the tram to the church in Haarlem's town square. The tram stops there so we didn't have far to walk. The organ pipes are 30 meters high. The church tower is twice that high. Haarlem is a beautiful city. It's skyline is filled with towers.

The church is huge, but only a small part was furnished with pews. There are boxes around the pillars where important people sit. But we sat on folding chairs because there weren't enough pews.

St. Bavo's was built before the Reformation. Around 1600, Protestants took it over. This is the first Reformed Church I was ever in. Catholics are not supposed to attend Protestant churches, but Dad wanted to hear the concert so he got permission to take us.

"They haven't much of a congregation," Jo said, seeing all the empty space in the auditorium.

After the concert we walked around looking at the church. It was interesting. A sign on a pillar shows where a giant is buried under the church floor. His name was Daniel Cajanus. He was born in Sweden and served in the Polish army. He died in 1749. He was almost ten feet tall. There is a mark high on the pillar to show how tall that is. Farther down on the same pillar is a mark that shows the height of Jane Paap, the dwarf of Zandvoort. She was less than two feet tall. I was thinking about their difference in size. If the giant and the midget walked in church together, it would have been as odd as a giraffe walking with a kitten.

Saint Bavo's has one of the most beautiful pipe organs anywhere. In 1765, Mozart played it. I wonder how he could play it—he was only ten years old. His feet couldn't have reached the pedals.

This church was started in 1370 and finished in 1520. Once there were beautiful stained glass windows, but during the Reformation, it went from Catholic to Reformed. The Reformers don't believe in decorations in their churches. So they broke out the stained glass windows and broke the statues. The only things left are plain wooden pews, the pulpit, the organ and its soaring pipes.

I would like to see the way it looked before they cleared it out. It must have been a sight. But it was a great concert. And it was free, so we didn't even have to pay.

August 23, 1940

I asked Dad about Haarlem and the Grote Kerk where we went yesterday. He told me to look it up in the encyclopedia. When teachers or parents tell me to look it up, I wonder. Do they think it's good for you to look things up or don't they know either?

This is what I found: After the Reformation, Catholicism was outlawed and Catholics could not gather to worship. So they made churches in attics and worshipped in secret.

Later the old rules were changed. So they were allowed to build churches again. In 1645 the Catholics built a new church and called it the Nieuw Kerk. In 1845 they built the new Roman Catholic Basilica and named that St. Bavo's, like the church the Reformers took over. So there are two St. Bavo's churches in Haarlem.

St. Bavo was a knight from the southern Netherlands which is now called Belgium. He is the patron saint of Haarlem.

Holland belonged to Spain. But the Dutch hated the Spanish because they brought the Inquisition. The Dutch didn't like King Philip, their new ruler. He ruled Holland as absolute monarch, just like he ruled Spain. His father, King Charles, had let the Hollanders live by their own laws and manage themselves. They were used to freedom. King Philip's stringent rule made them rebel.

William of Orange was the representative in charge of Holland, Utrecht and Zeeland provinces. He tried to persuade Philip to give the Netherlands the same freedom they had under King Charles. But instead of listening to William, Philip sent the hated Duke of Alva to subdue them. They decided to get rid of the Spaniards.

This began the 'Eighty Years' War.' William of Orange and his followers rebelled against the Spaniards because of their cruelty during the Inquisition. Under William, they drove them out and established the Reformed Church as the official church. This was the church of William of Orange although he was a Catholic before he led the rebellion.

Until 1579, Spain ruled Holland and Belgium. Then the Catholic provinces in the south made peace with Spain and became the Spanish Netherlands, or Belgium as it is now.

The Protestants in the north kept on fighting, and proclaimed a Republic of the Seven United Provinces of the Netherlands—Holland, Utrecht, Zeeland, Gelderland, Overijssel, Friesland and Groningen.)

The war went on. It finally ended after the Spaniards laid siege to Leiden, a walled city. They camped around the low fields and the people in the city were starving. A lady of extremely big proportions lived there. The Dutch lifted her up to the top of the wall to show the Spanish that they still had plenty of food and would not surrender.

Then the Dutch opened the dikes and flooded the polders around Leiden where the Spanish army was camped. When the water rose, the Spaniards had to leave or drown. When they fled the low plain, they left a humongous pot of stew they were cooking for the army. The Dutch call it 'hutspot. The people of Leiden feasted on the stew which saved them from starvation. Every year the Leiden celebrates the end of the siege by eating 'hutspot'.

The Eighty Year's War ended in 1648. Since then Holland has been a free country, a constitutional Monarchy ruled by the House of Orange.

Haarlem's motto, "Vicit Vim Virtus" proudly proclaims "Virtue conquers force." But Hitler acts the opposite. His motto seems to be "Might makes right."

August 25, 1940

The Mayor of Bennebroek, Baron van Hardenbroek, was appointed by Queen Wilhelmina. He is a competent man, but we are afraid he will be replaced by a Dutch Nazi like other Burgomasters have been.

Dad took me to the town hall to see how the Mayor was getting along with the petition to get Father Van Reuven released from 'The Umbrella.'

The Mayor said, "They didn't tell me anything. All I got from the Germans was they said they will look into it."

"We'll have to go higher and speak to more people. Even talk to Mussert, much as I dislike the idea."

"The Bishop of Utrecht asked for his release. If they won't hear him, who will they listen to?"

"The Bishop will put this in one of his letters he sends to the churches. People won't stand for Nazis attacking churches. If enough people write, the Germans will have to let him go because they are afraid the country will turn against them."

August 26, 1940

People who live on the seacoast had to move farther inland. Dad is buying a farm in Koegras on the North Sea and thought he was lucky to find a place he could afford. It's eighty kilometers north of here so he hired a manager to take care of the place.

The German Army took down buildings along the coast they judged were too close to the North Sea. The farmer who manages the place, Jaap Huisman, can still use the back land to grow things, but they took down the house. He and his wife moved their furniture into an old chicken coop when the Germans cleared the buildings and set guns pointed to the west to defend themselves from British invaders.

Dad needs to bring his crops home. But he doesn't have a truck so he has to rent one. And now nobody can get fuel to drive.

"You can't grow your crops, can't move them and can't sell them," Dad *brummed** (complained). "But you still have to pay the taxes on the house they took down. The Germans are crazy. They make rules you can't keep. But if you break them, they send you to prison."

German officials steal everything we have—cars, food, clothes, bicycles, cows, even factories and take it all back to Germany.

Do they think this will make us want to join their *Third Reich*, the kingdom Hitler says will last a thousand years?

Dad says, "The way things are going, Europe won't last too long. When the government collapses it will take a hundred years to get it going again. Hitler needs oil and the Russian Caucuses is an oil rich region. He'd like to march in and take it. But Russia is ten times the size of Germany. And Stalin is watching Hitler. It might not be long before they get into a fight."

"If they fight, who will win?" I asked.

"I don't know. One's Communist, the other's Nazi. And one is as bad as the other. They don't see eye to eye. Sooner or later they'll attack each other and then we'll see the biggest war the world has ever known."

Chapter 12

❧

Mother's Birthday

August 30, 1940

This morning Dad picked big bouquets of dahlias and arranged them in white Delft vases. He picks them every year for mother's birthday because they bloom in August. It makes our house look like a flower shop.

This morning Jo made a three layer cake and frosted it generously. We brought presents for her. Alice gave her a pretty pin. Jo embroidered a white scarf. I painted a picture of a Swiss chalet. Jan is working on the farm in Koegras so he won't come. Frans sent a letter from the Brother House where he attends school. The twins bought a bottle of perfume. We sang the birthday song and Mother's eyes shone with happy tears.

This afternoon relatives came. Aunt Jacoba and Uncle Cor were first. Dad and Cor are brothers. They are both tall but they don't resemble each other. Dad takes after their mother's family. Uncle Cor looks more like his father.

Aunt Jacoba was one of the wealthy Pijnackers and married Cor. They have more money than we do. Uncle Cor doesn't need to work in his fields; he has workers do the planting and harvesting. He supervises. Dad has a foreman and five sons, but he doesn't have as much help. Frans is away in school and the twins are still very young. Jan is the oldest and he does the most for Dad.

At birthday parties, the first thing everybody does is congratulate the birthday person. This takes a while. "Congratulations on your birthday," and

"Congratulations on your mother's birthday" and "Congratulations on your wife's, friend's, sister's birthday" are given according to the relationship of the person speaking. The congratulations are accompanied by everybody shaking hands.

After the congratulations were done, Dad and Cor and Mother and *Tante* (Aunt) Jacoba were drinking their ersatz coffee, Cor said, "It's hard to make any money since we can't reach our markets."

"We should plant less flower bulbs and more food. I have a vegetable garden and some chickens and I think I'll get a cow," Dad said. "You have a big farm. Plant some vegetables and fruit—beans and potatoes, and carrots and cabbages and strawberries."

Uncle Cor did not agree. "I'm a grower, not a farmer," he said. Both farmers and growers own land. Uncle Cor thinks it is better to grow flower bulbs than food.

"If you don't raise your own food, you might not have any," Dad said. "You can't depend on the Germans to feed us. They need everything they can get for their army—and send whatever's left to Germany for their own people."

Uncle Cor said "Now that France surrendered and the British left, things will settle down. When things are normal, I'll need tulips and hyacinths for the market. If the crop is small, prices will be higher."

He added "I still have customers in Germany. And there is Denmark and Sweden. If you have enough money you can buy food."

Soon more relatives came, riding on bicycles—basic transportation in Holland. Everyone went around the room, shaking hands and congratulating Mother and Dad and each other. They don't bring gifts, just good wishes. If everybody bought gifts for all the birthdays, they would soon be broke.

These people came: Uncle Piet and Aunt Riet, Uncle Nick and Aunt Riek, Uncle Gerard and Aunt Lies, Uncle Frans and Aunt An, Uncle Nol and Aunt Annie, Uncle Paul and Aunt To, Uncle Theo and another Aunt To, Uncle Bert and Aunt Corrie, Uncle Dorus and Aunt Agnes.

It was a full house but a few relatives were missing. Uncle Wim and Aunt Corrie didn't come. He works in Amsterdam, too far to come for Mother's birthday. Uncle Eddie and Aunt Bep are in New Jersey. We won't see them until the war is over. Grandmother Heemskerk lives in a retirement home in Hillegom. She doesn't ride a bike any more. Since we don't have a car we can't go and get her. We visit her in Hillegom.

First, there were tiny cups of ersatz coffee and an almond cookie—then another cup of ersatz and another cookie. When everybody drank two cups of coffee and ate two cookies, Mother closed the cookie tin and put it on a high shelf.

Then the party started. Annie and Jo brought the drinks. The men drank little glasses of *jenever** called *borreltjes.*** The women sipped bright colored cordials from sparkling crystal glasses. Annie, Jo and Alice passed canapés on tiny dishes like miniature saucers. When one serving of snacks was eaten, the girls collected the dishes and washed them to use for more treats.

The women sipped cordials and chatted together about the church, their children, clothes, recipes and rationing. Mother looked beautiful in her blue silk.

The men drank *borreltjes* and smoked cigars until the air was hazy. They talked about the weather and the bulb business. After they discussed those subjects, they talked about the war and the changes under the occupation.

We need coupons to buy necessities—food and soap and shoes and clothes. We can't get benzene to drive our cars. Only doctors, nurses and emergency services are allowed coupons. They don't give coupons to civilians, only to firemen and emergency vehicles. You have to give a serious reason to drive. How can we bring crops from our farm up north if there's no transportation—by horse and wagon? A round trip to Koegras would take two days with a horse-drawn wagon.

Uncle Cor is optimistic. He thinks the war will end soon.

Uncle Nick has the opposite view. "Do you think the British will surrender?" he asked. "Hitler won't quit until he defeats them. And if Churchill keeps on fighting, the war will last for years."

Dad is diplomatic. He didn't want any arguments at Mother's party. He doesn't like disagreements. So he said "I'm afraid it will be worse before it gets better."

Mother perched on the edge of the chair, ready to jump up and wait on everybody. She loves parties but she can't relax and let the girls take care of things even on her birthday. The other ladies ate and drank while Annie and Jo and Alice replenished the snacks. The children drank orangeade— sweet orange syrup in cold water.

After a while, the food and drinks created a party mood, like the birthday parties we had before the war. The relatives told old stories and laughed and enjoyed themselves.

The party ended when we heard the roar of planes flying over. Everybody got up and shook hands again to say goodbye. Then they got on their bikes and left. They had to be home before curfew. No bells or sirens warn us but everyone has to be indoors from eleven till seven. Streets are not lighted anymore because of the blackout, but the moonlight was bright enough to guide them home. The Germans turned off our lights, but they can't hide the sun or the moon.

Before the war, birthday parties lasted until two or three in the morning. Children were allowed to stay up until the party ended. We weren't supposed to drink, but when relatives were saying goodbye; we went around and sipped what they left in their glasses.

Jo and I went out to close the heavy blackout shutters. Dad stayed inside and fastened them so no light escaped. When the planes passed over we went to bed.

*Jenever—Dutch gin. It has less alcohol than English gin. Men drink it straight.

** Borreltjes—small drinks of Jenever in a shot glass, about two ounces.

September 1, 1940

"Vacation is over, Pim," Jo said this morning.

"Who told?" I asked accusingly, looking around at the family. They all laughed and Dad said, "Word gets around."

I hate to go back to school. Everything is better at home—I can do what I like, go where I please and see my friends. Since there are no rules about silence I can talk whenever I want.

While I was home, I heard the Queen speak on Radio Oranje. She talks to us more now than when she was in her palace at Soestdijk. We heard Nazi propaganda on the Dutch radio from Hilversum.

Mother took me to school on the back of her bike. When we got to Hageveld, there was coffee and pastry in the refectory. The Regent said he was happy to see us. We sat around talking until the bell rang. Then the parents got up and left in a group. Of course they had to shake hands again before they went. Shaking hands is a necessity unless you a want to be rude. Whenever people meet and leave they shake hands.

We got our room assignments. Our class doesn't have as many boys as we did last September. The new first-year class has more than a hundred boys so they took over our dormitory because it is biggest. We found our new places, made our beds, and put our stuff away. The new rooms are the same size as our old ones—small cells all furnished alike. But there are different boys in the rooms on either side of me than before.

There were no classes today. We had free time in the rec hall and played games, bought and sold our used books, talked freely and went happily to chapel. After dinner we had more free time, went to chapel again and went to bed.

The sub-regent checked to see we were all in our places and pulled the curtains over our doorways to close us in.

September 3, 1940

I enjoyed vacation so much; I hated to come back. There is a night and day difference between home and school. I didn't fit in but I decided to try harder. It is a new beginning. I had finished the first year. I had not failed any subjects, although I just squeaked by in algebra.

There are old friends here and new teachers to listen to. I'll try to pay attention, study hard and keep my mind from wandering.

September 4, 1940

At home I learned things about the country. But we don't talk about them here. All the old political parties have been outlawed. There is only one party now, the NSB, led by Anton Mussert. But this party is split into the radical wing, led by Rost van Tonningen, which wants Holland annexed to Germany like Austria was when Germany took over during the 'Anschluss.'

Mussert has a different view. He doesn't want Holland to be joined to the German Reich. He wants it to be joined with Belgium as it was before the Eighty Years War, the United Netherlands. And he wants to be the grand ruler of the whole country. He wants power so much he can taste it.

Mussert is a traitor who supported Hitler because he thought he would become a leader under the Nazis. Can't he see the Nazis are just using him and they'll dispose of him when he's wrung dry? If he was not blinded by ambition, he'd see the way they treated General Winkelman. He dismantled the Dutch military and turned over the reins to the occupation government. And they put him in prison when they couldn't see what more they could get from him.

Does Mussert see that what happened to General Winkelman could happen to him?

September 6, 1940

Alice and I were both born on September 10, but I'm a year older. This year Alice wanted to have a party. Mother said if Alice had a party, I should have one, too. So I'm escaping Hageveld and going home for my birthday. Dad will get me Saturday and bring me back Sunday so I won't miss any of my classes.

September 10, 1940

It is Alice's thirteenth birthday and my fourteenth birthday. Dad picked me up on his bike. When we got home, Jo was making food for our party. Two of my friends, Louis van der Wal and Lou de Vries came to the party and two of Alice's girl friends are coming. First we'll play games and then have dinner with a beautiful cake for dessert and everybody sings the birthday song, "Long shall he live."

> *Lang zal hij leven*
> *Lang zal hij leven*
> *Lang zal hij leven in de Gloria.*
> *In de Gloria, in de Gloria.*

They sang it twice. For Alice they sang, *Lang zal ze leven,* because 'ze' means 'she'. For me they sang *hij* meaning 'he.'

Afterward we opened presents. Mother knitted us sweaters. Alice's was blue and mine was gray. Jo gave Alice silk stockings she had been saving. Her friends gave her a tiny bottle of French perfume and a red scarf. She's blond and blue eyed and looks good in red.

I got pair of new shoes. My old ones are stretched and their soles are wearing thin. Jo reminded me of the time I was five and had new shoes. I wore them to church for the first time. I was so proud of them but when I came home, I sat on the steps and cried.

"Why are you crying?" Jo asked.

"My shoes are spoiled." I thought if I was careful I could keep them looking like new.

Leather is scarce now and shoes are hard to find. What will we do when there aren't any? *Klompen*, or wooden shoes are *fijn* for wearing in muddy fields, but not for other occasions. They're too noisy, for one thing.

I got two pairs of stockings mother knitted…and some foreign stamps for my stamp collection. We don't get many foreign letters now. They have to come through Spain or Portugal.

The twins gave me a candy bar. Alice and Jo gave me handkerchiefs they initialed. I gave Alice a little box of Belgian chocolates. Alice asked where I got them. I didn't tell her Grandmother Heemskerk gave them to me last Christmas and I hid them in my room. I didn't want her to know how old they were. They still look OK but the chocolate is a little white.

We played records and danced till one. Then we had to go upstairs to bed. All our friends stayed overnight on account of curfew. Lou and Louis and I slept on my bedroom floor in sleeping bags. Alice's and her girl friends put a mattress on the floor in Alice and Jo's room.

Dad is taking Louis and the twins and me to a soccer game Sunday. After a game Dad buys everybody *an ijs* (ice cream sandwich) I hope Bennebroek will beat Hillegom. Our team is not the best. They lose more often than they win, but is it too much to ask them to win for my special day?

Chapter 13

The Soccer Game

September 11, 1940

For my birthday Dad took us to watch a soccer game between Bennebroek and Hillegom. It was a close contest. Near the end, the score was 3 and 2 in favor of Hillegom. We were down a point. Then Henry van Kampen kicked the ball to Jaap Vernooy and the goalie came out to intercept. The ball got free in the scuffle and Henry kicked it right into the unguarded goal, making the score an even 3 and 3. But the game wasn't over. Jaap kicked it in again and scored. We won the game 4 to 3!

The game was brilliant. It happened so fast I could hardly follow the plays. Everybody was yelling and cheering! Bennebroek won! We were thrilled!

Dad bought us each an *ijs*. The ice cream melted and ran down the sides of the cones. We licked the drippings. Some dripped on my new sweater and I tried to wipe it off with my handkerchief. What a mess! But Jo will wash it out.

When we were walking home from the soccer field, Louis said, "Remember we were talking about the little ships? I thought they moved them to Dutch harbors but now nobody sees them."

Dad said, "If Hitler uses them to cross the Channel, he'll start from Belgium or France where the English Channel is narrower."

No crossing is likely now. Fall makes the North Sea too rough. Small boats can hardly survive.

All I could think of was Bennebroek's win! We won the game!

September 14, 1940

Today was too rainy and windy to go out. Arie drew pictures of a dogfight between British and German planes. His drawings are better than photographs.

I told him about the little boats disappearing from the coast and he drew a picture of an invasion fleet of little boats with thirty foot waves on the stormy sea. He drew tanks on barges and sailboats. We had to laugh because it looked too ridiculous. Would Hitler put his tanks on little boats where they would sink in the English Channel? He is audacious but he's far from stupid and he knows he needs tanks to launch a blitzkrieg!

The Luftwaffe bombers, Heinkels, don't fly when the Atlantic is rough and small boats stay in port when the strong wind and high waves would likely sink them.

Is God sending bad weather to help the Allies?

September 15, 1940

When I was home, Dad was planning a trip to the farm in Koegras with his friend Fons Belle. I don't know where Fons got benzine for such a long ride. Maybe he bought it from someone who still had a can hidden in his garage. He can't get coupons to drive because he's no doctor.

I wish I could go with them. Frans and I used to come along. Now we're both in boarding schools. Maybe Dad will take the twins.

Koegras is on the North Sea fifty miles from home. That is the farthest I ever traveled. Whenever Dad went to the farm, he planned the trip several days ahead to be sure he remembered to bring everything he needed along.

He got the farm because we don't have enough land around our house in Bennebroek to raise as many flower bulbs as he wanted and he said our land needed a rest from growing too many of the same crops. When the farm at Koegras came up for sale, and at a price he could afford, he thought he was lucky to find it. Land is scarce and expensive in Holland. Dutch farmers often must go across the German border to find land they need.

Mijnheer Huisman is his manager. When the war came, Dad told him to plant more wheat and vegetables and less flower bulbs. Dad predicts food shortages because the Germans take so much for their enormous army. He decided to raise more vegetables and wheat so we'll have food to eat.

I remember riding in Fons' shiny black Packard. To go to the farm, you have to cross the North Sea Canal. Fons drove onto the ferry but we didn't get out of the car; just kept our seats for the short crossing. It didn't take long; I think it was about fifteen minutes.

When we got to the farm, Mevrouw Huisman welcomed us with milk and cookies. She knew we'd be hungry because we came so far. Dad, Fons and Mr. Huisman walked around the fields to see how things were growing. Afterward Mrs. Huisman served us dinner and *appeltaart* for dessert. We were well fed for the return trip.

Frans and I rode in the back, enjoying the view. When we came to Castricum, Fons parked in front of an old church there. He told us to pull the curtains over the windows. He said he and Dad were going to Confession. That was one big whopper. They really went across the street to a little *kroeg* (pub) and had a drink or two.

They came back after a while and Fons drove us home. Frans and I were naïve but not stupid. When Fons said they were going to Confession, we believed him until we saw them go into the kroeg. Why did he have to tell us a lie? We didn't care where they went.

Tomorrow Dad is going to Koegras to see what the Germans have done to the farm. He knows they took houses down on the coast including the house on his farm where the Huismans lived. He's afraid they will take more buildings down and keep his farm manager off the fields next to the seacoast. The Germans won't let anyone near the sea, not even landowners.

Why are they so worried? Do they think the farmers would help the British if they come? (They probably would.) Or the farmers will escape? (That could happen, too.) Or because they don't want us to see the guns and bunkers they are building in the dunes?

Mr. Huisman works for Dad. The way it is in Holland, Mr. Huisman gets a salary and land to grow his own plants. Dad and he share the harvest. The manager has no problem getting his crop home because he lives there. But Dad has to bring his harvest almost eighty kilometers. He'll take as much food as Fons' car can hold. He needs to find a way to get the rest.

September 16, 1940

The BBC said the RAF shot down 115 German planes. Hitler thought he would win by bombing Britain. He thought the English would beg for peace—but they haven't. 'Winston Churchill is their leader and he will never give in.

His speeches inspire the British people. Once he said "Hitler will have to break us in Britain or lose the war. If we stand up against him, all Europe will be free. If we fail, it will lead to a new dark age. Let us brace ourselves—and do our duty. If the British Commonwealth and Empire lasts for a thousand years, men will still say, 'This was their finest hour'."

September 18, 1940

The weather was sunny this afternoon and our class walked to downtown Heemstede. It is more than twice the size of Bennebroek. We saw the Swastika on the town hall and German soldiers walking around. They say 'Sieg Heil' and 'Heil Hitler' all the time. Why are they here?

An underground newspaper was lying beside the path—just a single sheet, printed on both sides, torn and dirty. I bent to tie my shoe and put it in my pocket. Later, I smoothed it out to read. Then I gave it to Arie. He'll read it and pass it on to somebody else. Underground papers are illegal. You could go to prison for having it, but it was an exciting find. After everybody reads it, they'll get rid of it.

The paper said everyone has been expelled from the coast because Hitler is afraid the Brits will attack. German troops are training on the shore for the coming invasion. The paper also said Dutch men were taken out on the dunes near *Katwijk* and shot.

I told Arie, "That's true. They're buried in the dunes. Nobody may ever find them. I saw it happening from a tower of an old windmill.

Arie agreed. "A man boarding with my aunt disappeared. Two German soldiers came and got him. They claimed they wanted him to do some work. But he didn't come back and nobody's heard where he went. My aunt says they must have killed him. If they took him to prison, they would have told her to pack his clothes."

September 19, 1940

Arie said a fleet of tugs and barges and little ships are crowded in Belgian ports. The RAF is keeping an eye on them to see if the invasion is going to start. If the ships try to cross they'll bomb them. The Luftwaffe planes couldn't stay in the air when the British evacuated Dunkirk because they had to refuel. Their bases were too far from the coast. But the RAF is nearer home so they don't have a problem staying over the Channel.

September 20, 1940

Fr. Langelaar teaches History. Today we studied Napoleon's campaign against Russia. History is always about one war or another. I asked "Why are there so many wars?"

He said "It's the nature of man. There is something in men that makes us want to kill each other. Cain killed Abel. A war is killing on a grand scale. There have been wars since history began."

Carl said, "Wars are terrible. They kill people and destroy the cities. All the countries should join together and keep their rulers from starting one."

Arie said, "Kings and emperors and rulers are greedy for power. They don't care about soldiers being killed. They want to be like Napoleon and Alexander the Great and Genghis Khan."

Fr. Langelaar said. "After the First World War, the Allies thought they would end war. They made disarmament provisions in the Versailles treaty and thought that would make them stop. But they couldn't get all the countries to agree. And they didn't enforce the provisions."

Steve said "I'd rather read newspapers about what is happening now than a history book telling about old wars."

Fr. Langelaar said we could write a newspaper article about war in general. I wrote "Before the war, Neville Chamberlain was the Prime Minister of England. He wanted peace and thought if he gave Hitler what he wanted there would be peace. But his policy of appeasement only delayed the war for a while. Meanwhile Hitler was building up his army and getting ready to fight.

Now Churchill is the Prime Minister of England. He is trying to protect his country. He fights like a bulldog and they don't let go. They don't know how to give up."

Fr. Langelaar said, "Well written, Pim, but we can't say anything like that. Write about the Romans or the Greeks—other times, other places."

September 21, 1940

Fr. Langelaar and Fr. Verschure listen to the radio. They don't usually tell us what they hear. But today in class Fr. Langelaar surprised us by saying, "I heard an interesting story," he said.

"Germany planned to cross the channel. It was a test, not a full scale invasion. They took ferryboats, barges, fishing boats and yachts and got them ready. Then a storm came up and they waited until the weather improved—there wasn't much time before the fall storms set in. So they started across. An RAF pilot saw the boats and warned the British Navy.

The seas were choppy but the British were ready. When the little fleet neared England, they poured fuel on the water and set it on fire.

The wooden boats couldn't go through the flames so they headed back to port. A tug towing a barge carrying tanks rode low. In the high waves it took on water and sank. Now tug and barge are on the ocean floor.

One mistake they made was to use soldiers on the boats, not seasoned sailors. The soldiers got seasick because they weren't used to the rocking boats. The cruise did not go well. They went back to the French side of the channel.

That's what I heard."

Chapter 14

My Crime

September 25, 1940

Today is not my day. Tomorrow won't be either. And I'm not looking forward to the rest of the month.

Today in study hall I looked through a book of paintings. I saw a picture of the Madonna and child that was not like any painting I'd ever seen. The baby didn't have a stitch on! Not even a diaper! And the artist painted every detail of his bare body.

I had to laugh. Carl was sitting beside me and he looked to see what was so funny. He laughed, too.

Later he must have had second thoughts. He told Mr. Nolet I laughed at a picture of Jesus. The priest was horrified. He didn't even look at the picture. He said I committed the sin of blasphemy.

Mr. Nolet is a serious man. He's not the kind of man who tells jokes. I don't think he ever laughs. But I saw him smirk once—at least the corners of his mouth turned up.

Most teachers wouldn't have made a big deal of this. But Nolet climbed on his high horse, condemned me without listening to my side of the story, and punished me by making me copy the Greek dictionary. It's written in the Greek alphabet! I like languages but I'm not crazy about the Greek alphabet. Copying it will take a lifetime!

But the thing I can't understand is Carl telling on me. Why does he want to get me in trouble with Mr. Nolet? He laughed, too.

If laughing is a sin, what is frowning? A virtue?

And why did Nolet give me such an impossible penalty? Why didn't he look at the picture? If he saw it, he would have thought it was funny. He would have laughed, too.

September 26, 1940

There are signs in the halls with big gold letters 'Silentium' telling us not to talk. But everybody was talking about me and what happened. The story went through the school like lightning. Everybody is smiling at me—except Carl. He's afraid I'll tell on him.

Mr. Nolet is tall and dark and has bushy brows. His has a short nose with big nostrils. His nickname is 'monkey'. I realize he can't help the way he looks. But I think he could be kinder.

I used to think priests were always kind like Saint Francis. Mr. Nolet is not kind. He's more like a judge in the Spanish Inquisition.

October 2, 1940

I don't have any time now for playing games, reading, or writing my journal. I have to spend all my free time copying the Greek dictionary.

Arie told me, "Carl is talking about you."

"What is he talking about? The picture in the art book?"

"No. He said your parents got a letter about you smoking and inhaling."

"How does he know that? Somebody said I couldn't inhale when I smoked. He was smoking a cigarette. So I tried it."

"What a bunch of tattle tales! Somebody reported me. That's why Mother got the letter. It said I was smoking through my nose. Mother wasn't upset. She told me about the letter. She said that was a funny way to describe what I was doing."

They have a rule. You can smoke a pipe but you are not allowed to smoke cigarettes. And you can only smoke outdoors. But the day before vacation some boys were smoking cigarettes in the dining hall. That was two rules they broke! And nobody stopped them. The Dean had left the hall. Maybe he didn't hear about it. The rule against cigarettes and smoking indoors is usually strictly enforced, but not that day.

Ari drew a picture of a camel with a cigarette in his mouth and smoke coming out of his nose. It made a halo around his head. I wrote a title for it, 'Vlad, the inhaler.'

I'd tape the picture on the wall in my room, but taping pictures on the wall takes the paint off.

October 3, 1940

Nothing is going right. I got a one on my Math—the lowest mark you can get. Even if you handed in a paper with just your name on it, you would get a one for effort.

At home I play games, study, take care of my pets, and help Dad in his office. But here I am in disgrace because I laughed at a picture. Maybe I wasn't meant to be here. Maybe I should go home and forget about studying to be a priest.

Last night I had a nightmare and yelled so loud I woke up everybody in the dormitory.

'Pa" Verschure talked to me. He is an understanding man. He sympathized with me. He told me "I think being punished for laughing at a picture is out of proportion, Pim. I can't change it because every teacher disciplines his own classes. But what was your nightmare about last night?"

"I dreamed somebody chased me up a stairway to the top of a tower and was going to push me off."

"You had a nightmare. If it happens again; try to tell yourself it's not happening. It's only a dream."

"It seemed real to me until I woke up."

"Do you often have nightmares? They can be caused by worrying. If you want to talk things over, come and see me. When things go badly, it helps to talk about it."

'Pa' Verschure is a good teacher. He cares about the kids. If the teachers were all like 'Pa', school would be easier, more like home.

October 4, 1940

We have one classroom and stay in it for all our classes. The teachers come to us. This keeps the noise down in the hall. But it takes a while for the teachers to get here and when one teacher leaves and the other one hasn't shown up yet, the kids get rowdy.

Before Latin class, I was writing in my journal while we waited for the teacher. Harry wanted to know what I was writing so he came up behind me and grabbed my book and started reading it out loud.

"Give it back," I said. He is taller than I am so he held it over my head.

"Who's going to make me?" he asked.

Then Harry threw it to Carl in back of the room. Carl passed it to Yuri who threw it back. I jumped up to get it from Harry just as Father Verschure came. It looked like I was attacking Harry. He said "Terpstra, Heemskerk, *niet vechten.*" (No fighting.)

Harry handed my journal to me, smiled sweetly and acted like an angel. You would think he never did anything wrong in his life. How does he get away with it? Why did a joker like him decide to be a priest? With his talent for pretense, he could be an actor, a magician, an alligator wrestler or even a circus clown!

October 6, 1940

Today is Saturday. Arie asked "How many pages did you copy?"

I counted the pages of the Greek dictionary I copied so far. "Nineteen!" I said.

"Write small—two lines in the space for one line. That will save paper and make it harder to check," Arie said.

Steve told me "Skip some lines."

"He'll make me do it over if he doesn't like the way it's done."

Confucius said, 'A journey of a thousand miles begins with a single step.' I've only taken the first step. If there are 190 pages in the book and I do 3 pages a day, it takes two months to finish. My fingers will get calluses and I'll run out of paper!

October 7, 1940

Today Father Nolet asked how my Greek copying was coming. I said, "Fine."

He corrected me, saying, "Fine, Mister Nolet."

So I said, "Fine, Mister Nolet, Sir." I thought I might as well do it up brown.

How long will it take to do my assigned copying? There's no point hurrying because if any one of three things happens, I won't have to finish it.

Number one: I might die. I don't think so unless I have an accident.

Number two: the Germans might close Hageveld. But they probably won't since they haven't already.

Number three: Father Nolet might get a pastorate and leave. He is only 26 so I don't think he will, either. Young priests who become teachers usually stay for nine or ten years before they become pastors. Most priests would rather be a *predikant* (preacher). Some of them get tired of teaching the same thing to us over and over and take it out on us.

October 8, 1940

Today we walked from Heemstede to Bennebroek. We came so near our house I could see our blue tile roof and the top of the chestnut trees by our door. I wished I could stop a few minutes and say hello to my family, but of course the priest in charge wouldn't let anyone leave the group. It wouldn't be fair to the rest of them.

We passed my old school, now the German barracks. Soldiers were practicing marching in the school yard and the band was playing. We watched through the fence.

Having German soldiers in Bennebroek is a shame. But here they are and they don't look like leaving. Watching them marching was like watching a newsreel. There was music and the iron plates of their boots were hitting the paving. The band playing sounded wonderful. It gives a military spirit to the troops.

Arie said "The army is irresistible—a machine that can't be stopped."

I asked, "What happens when an irresistible force meets an immovable object?"

Steve said "There's no such thing as an immovable object. When an irresistible force meets an object, it moves!"

"Or there's no such thing as an irresistible force." Arie argued. "It's one or the other. They can't both exist."

October 9, 1940

Bennebroek is next to Heemstede, where we go to school. Yesterday the weather was nice so we walked toward Bennebroek where it's more open country. When we started the sun was shining, but on the way back, the wind blew stormy clouds over our heads and buckets of rain fell. The wind on our wet clothes made us shiver.

When we got back Father Nolet was in the hall. He must have changed his mind about my punishment. He told me I had misunderstood him. He said he hadn't told me to copy the whole Greek dictionary, only the vocabulary in the back of the book.

I'm sure he said I had to copy the Greek dictionary, not just the vocabulary in the back of the book. But I'm too pleased with the new penalty—I'm not going to argue. The vocabulary is a small number of the pages in the dictionary. A big load dropped off my back when he said that. I suspect he talked to 'Pa' and Pa told him to be easy on me.

Some teachers don't seem concerned about the students. They just teach their subjects and couldn't care less how we feel. 'Pa' is different. He's like the Good Samaritan who brought the wounded man to the inn and took care of him. That's the way priests should be.

October 12, 1940

Today is the anniversary of Columbus sighting land on his voyage to the new world. It happened almost five hundred years ago. In the dining hall, the Dean read a story about Columbus and we ate fried cod for dinner. That was appropriate. The sailors must have eaten a lot of fish when they crossed the Atlantic. The cod was cooked in butter. *Heerlijk!**

I copied 30 pages of Greek vocabulary. It won't be long now!

October 14, 1940

The weather was sunny and we played volleyball. We don't choose teams; just play a while. When a player gets tired he drops out and somebody else takes his place. I'd like to do this every day, not just Sunday. When we play games, Hageveld is a blast!

October 15, 1940

Carl asked "How much Greek did you finish?"

"I'm almost done."

"Well, don't worry," he said. "With the way you are going in Algebra, you'll fail math and leave school."

"You know what, Carl? You're a jerk! What did I ever do to you?"

"Don't take it to heart, Pim. It's just a joke—not personal!"

But I'm a person. So if it's about me, it's personal!

October 16, 1940

In the suitcase of clean clothes Jo brought today, there was the front page of a newspaper. I was reading it in the rec room when Arie came in.

"Where did you get that? I didn't think we're supposed to read newspapers," Arie said.

Steve said, "Well, nobody told us not to."

"Besides, who does it hurt?" I asked.

"I'd like to read it when you finish," Arie said.

The newspaper is history but not always true. I wish I could pile up all the papers and save them until the war is over. Then I'd like to get the British papers and compare them with the German papers.

October 21, 1940

We were walking on our path around the school when the German S.A., the Brown Shirts, came marching down the road past school singing. I could hear the melody but couldn't make out the words. I don't know who composed the music but it's beautiful. The soldiers were singing it in German. The lyrics say to raise the flag—the Swastika, high. This is the final call for all men. Hitler is making everything better and setting things right. He will end slavery and provide food for all men. It's empty promises—if the soldiers believe that, they're not too bright. It seems like he's starting slavery, not ending it. Nothing has improved! It's only getting worse wherever he goes.

Heerlijk—delicious

Chapter 15

❧

Changes

November 1, 1940

Looking down from the bridge, the surface of the canal is smooth as glass.
Three swans floated by attached to their mirror twins. The windmill on the
glassy surface turned its sails like the windmill on the dike. A stork flew to
the roof of a house on the bank; an upside down image in the water flew
along. Two old men with long fishing poles sat on the bank of the canal. Their
reflections looked up at me like a painting on the water.

A passing barge broke the picture into a jumble of waves. The bell rang
for class and I went in.

I sat in class and tried to pay attention, but my mind wanders. I think
about the rules the Germans are adding. In the margin of my book I listed
things we didn't have before the war:

Ration coupons, ersatz, shoes, bicycle tires 'uitverkocht' (sold out),
The Atlantic wall around the North Sea Blackouts.
Curfews.
Jewish teachers were fired.
Jews have to wear a yellow star to show they are Jews.
Jewish doctors are forbidden to practice—we need good doctors.
Garages closed. No car repairs. No new cars.
Identification cards to carry everywhere.
No fuel except for emergency vehicles.

110

Broken windows--Lumber and glass unavailable for repairs.
No newspapers printed without permission.
(*But some people print underground newspapers.*)
The Occupation Government controlling our radio stations.
Censorship of British radio programs.
Political parties prohibited,
The NSB.
Labor unions forbidden.
Longer work weeks.
Permits to travel outside your district.
Hitler's pictures.
The swastika replaced our flag.
German Soldiers everywhere.

"What are you writing?" Carl asked, leaning over to see.
"Things to remember," I said and shut the book.
"You'll have to erase them to sell your book," Carl said reasonably. I didn't care. I wanted to write them anyhow.

Before the war we always had plenty of food—food was one of our biggest exports. There is just as much food now, but we don't have as much because the government takes it to feed the troops.

We've been robbed!

November 3, 1940

Today was one of those days when the weather makes it hard to decide what you should do—part sunny and part cloudy and rainy. When you were inside it looked nice but when you went out the cold wind blew. It was a warm jacket day.

Ari and I walked around the building on the short path, close to the building. There are two paths; the upper class uses the long one near the trees. Next year we'll be in the upper class and we can walk on the long one, beside the woods. I'd rather go there.

November 5, 1940

This morning when I looked out the window, I saw a long black car parked in front of school with swastikas on the fenders. Arie asked, "What are you looking at?"

"We have visitors in an official car—it just drove up."

When Arie saw it, he asked, "Are they coming to take over Hageveld?"

"How would I know? I'm not a mind reader."

Three men got out. The driver pulled away from our building. "Maybe the takeover is coming," Arie said.

Steve came up, "They're inside, keeping an eye on us, looking for an excuse to grab our school. They want our school for a bigger administration building but they need an excuse."

"That's simple, they'll say they're protecting us from the English," Arie said.

"Why do we need them to protect us? Is the RAF bombing schools now?"

"If they close Hageveld I'll go to the gymnasium in Haarlem," Arie said.

"Not me," said Steve. "I'll go to England and join the RAF." Steve is a couple of years older than we are.

"That would be a long trip. How would you get there? Swim? Steal a boat?"

"There is a way. Freighters from the chemical factory at Delfzyl bring supplies for Swedish steel mills. Dutch freighters go to Sweden, a neutral country. If you can get on one of those freighters you can get to Stockholm and from there you could fly to England," Steve said.

"Where did you hear that?"

"My uncle works in Delfzyl," Steve said. "He said some students from the University of Leiden escaped that way."

November 5, 1940

There's no radio in the dormitory, but when I took a message to the office today the radio was tuned to the BBC.

The announcer said Germany lost the Battle of Britain. Repeated bombing of London did not break their spirit. Churchill walked right through the rubble waving 'V for victory'. There were more than twenty air raids by the Luftwaffe, causing terrible destruction. The RAF fighters shot down more planes than the Germans could spare.

Then they changed the radio to the Hillegom station. It was a different story. The announcer claimed the RAF lost so many planes they would have to give up flying.

In a debate between Germans and the Brits, I believe the BBC.

Hitler says he doesn't want to fight the British. He is only trying to right the injustice suffered by the German Reich in World War I and gain *lebensraum* (living space) for the German people.

Hitler said that if the British surrender and stop resisting him, he will treat them well. Then they may join him to fight against the Bolshevists, the Russians who are the real enemies. British and Germans should work together to destroy the godless Communists.

The Dean gave me an envelope to bring back to my class so I left the office.

Hitler claims Germany needs more land because the German people are too crowded! But Germany does not seem crowded to the Dutch. It has huge areas of empty land. It's not half as crowded as Holland. And we haven't attacked anybody! If your neighbor wanted your house and killed you to get it, he would punished for his crime in peacetime. But taking over a country is apparently OK. War is the excuse for murder and thieving and destruction. The conqueror is honored, not blamed for his crime,

November 15, 1940

Last night the Luftwaffe bombed Coventry in a massive raid like the one that hit Rotterdam. According to reports, it killed hundreds, wounded more and left the city a wreck. It destroyed an ancient cathedral built centuries ago. They have bombed London so many times, without breaking the English. So now they are spreading out, attacking other cities.

Since Hitler can't mount an attack by sea, he is on a rampage, determined to destroy the rest of their island nation. He did lose more planes in the attack. How long can this go on?

November 16, 1940

Before I fall asleep, I think about our family. Dad makes a living by growing flower bulbs and selling to England and America. Since we can't ship them now, we can't sell them. So he will run out of money. And my tuition is expensive. I feel guilty because he spends money he needs on me so I can go to Hageveld. I know he is broke because I overheard Mother and Dad during vacation trying to figure out how to pay taxes and expenses on the farm in Koegras. Koegras means 'cow grass' in Dutch. That's a funny name for a place—grass is everywhere... If I named it, I would have called it 'The Dunes' because the land is beside the coast and Dunes sounds more distinguished.

"I'm afraid we'll have to sell the farm," Dad said to Mother."

Mother said, "No, Bart. Don't sell the land. If you sell it you'll never get it back."

"You're right, Marie. But we can't afford to keep it. We have to pay the mortgage and the taxes on it and the expenses, but it doesn't bring in any income. We're cut off from our markets in Britain and America. You can't pay taxes with tulips. I thought we were lucky to find a farm we could afford. But now, since the war, it's a liability."

"If you sold the land, the way things are now, you wouldn't get much—not even as much you paid. We have to keep it until the war is over."

"It's in the coastal zone. You can't use the fields by the sea. Not only that, but the Germans have taken down the perfectly good house. They don't pay you anything for the damage they caused and you still have to pay the same taxes. Its *gek** (crazy). We're paying taxes on a house that's not there."

November 20, 1940

When I was home, Dad talked about switching from bulbs to raising a crop he can sell. Like tobacco. We always got tobacco from Indonesia. But since the invasion no more Indonesian tobacco can come in.

Dad sees there's a market for tobacco so he plans to plant it next year. If he can sell tobacco, he'll get money. If he also raises crops, we'll have food to eat. He won't plant as many bulbs, just some tulips to keep in stock for when the war ends.

Dutch tobacco is not as good as Indonesian tobacco. The leaves are lighter colored and milder. They look good but they don't burn well. Belgian tobacco, on the other hand, is dark and tastes terrible, but burns good. He thinks if he mixes Belgian tobacco with Dutch tobacco he might make a good cigar. Dutch men are addicted to cigars. So there's a big demand for good cigars.

Dad thought of a way to get Belgian tobacco. He'll take a trip to Belgium and visit Frans. While he's there, he'll get some tobacco to mix with his own Dutch tobacco. Then he'll blend them to make cigars he can sell.

Dad doesn't know how to make cigars yet, but he got a set of tools from a friend who kept his deceased brother's cigar-making equipment. He'll find someone to show him. Dad can do anything.

November 21, 1940

Mother and Dad are going to Baarle-Nassau, on the border of Belgium where Frans is in school. While there, they plan to go out in the country and buy some Belgian tobacco.

They have to take the train, leaving Annie, mother's helper, and Jo with Alice and Jet and the twins.

To be allowed to travel outside your district, you have to give a reason to get a permit. Their reason will be a visit to Frans. They won't mention tobacco. You can't import tobacco from Belgium.

Dad will have to smuggle the tobacco leaves back to Holland so the German inspectors won't confiscate them. That would make the whole trip a waste of time and money!

November 23, 1940

All Jewish officials were dismissed in October. Hitler claims they are not reliable. That is a lie but it doesn't matter. Hitler is a liar. He does what he wants whatever anybody thinks. He says what suits him at the time. He acts as though saying a thing makes it true.

Now, not only Jewish officials have been dismissed, but even the President of our Supreme Court, L. E. Visser. He is a very intelligent man. Everybody respects him. A group of professors petitioned Seyss-Inquart not to do this. They asked him not to move against the Jews. He ignored them. He does what Hitler tells him. He doesn't particularly care what the Dutch people want.

At the University of Leiden, Professor Cleveringa spoke to the student body, protesting the German actions and praising a popular Jewish professor who had been dismissed. The students, stirred by the injustice, went on strike.

The Germans retaliated. They closed the University of Leiden and threw Professor Cleveringa in jail. They will not put up with rebellion in occupied countries! If they gave in to our requests, no telling what it might lead to!

They do what they please. They'd rather lie than tell the truth. In the beginning they promised if the Jews obeyed their laws, they would leave them in peace. But they don't keep promises. Hitler often promised he would not cross our borders if we did not join the Allies. Look how he kept that pledge!

Many people are hiding. Some are Jews and some are in the Resistance. Others are afraid to be put in prison for disagreeing with the government and some are people who didn't register for the Labor Service. We call them 'divers.' They can't get ration books, of course, so the churches are helping by collecting donated ration coupons. In one town a whole shipment of ration books were stolen from the town hall. Nobody is telling who took them or where they went, but we believe they were stolen to give to the divers.

Holland is surrounded by Germany to the north and east and occupied Belgium and France in the south. The Atlantic coast is walled off. It's impossible to get across the channel without a plane or a fast boat. Some people escape. Usually they make a long journey south through Belgium and France to Switzerland or Spain and Portugal. But it's terribly risky. And you have to be strong to make your way through the mountains.

November 28, 1940

I hadn't heard from Mother and Dad since their trip till yesterday, when this letter from Mother arrived in my suitcase of clean laundry:

"Beste Pim,

We are back from our trip. I'm glad we saw Frans and his teachers and the school. He is a good student and it was wonderful to see him again. But we're thankful to be home in Bennebroek.

Frans has grown. He's as tall as Grandfather Lommerse. He looks healthy. So he's getting enough to eat. He is a good student. The cook at the school is excellent. Belgium now has better food than Holland.

They checked our papers at the station before they let us get on the train and again before we came home. I was afraid they would find something wrong with our permit but they looked at the papers and our identification cards, handed them back and let us on the train. The train was crowded and dirty, but we were anxious to see Frans and didn't mind.

The day we left to go home was windy and rainy. I wore my blue coat with the big sleeves. There's no heat on the trains so I was glad to have it. Dad found a place to get tobacco. He bought as many bags of cut tobacco as we could carry and put them in my sleeves. I was afraid they would ask me to take my coat off and look inside to see what I was carrying, but they didn't notice my overstuffed sleeves. We had good papers. They didn't suspect I was smuggling tobacco.

It helped that Dad spoke German. The guards would rather talk German because they couldn't understand Dutch. They believe everybody should speak their language.

When we got to the station, a crowd was waiting. All the seats were taken. A nice young man named Derek let me take his seat so I didn't have to stand. But I didn't want to take it so he and I and Dad took turns. We shared one seat until Willemstad. There some people got off and we all got our own seat.

The cook at the Brother House gave us a basket of cheese sandwiches because they don't sell food on the train. We shared with Derek, who gave us his seat, and other passengers who didn't bring anything.

I'm glad we saw Frans. I miss him since he's away.

I wish he could come home for Christmas but he can't. We brought him some clothes I got. I bought them two sizes bigger. They're a little loose—but it gives him room to grow.

It's almost St. Nicholaas Eve. The children are behaving so Sinterklaas will bring gifts. This is the best time of the year!"

Mother must have been crying when she said goodbye to Frans. She always cries when she has to leave her children.

Anyway, they saw Frans. Dad got his Belgian tobacco. Now he will learn to make cigars. Dad can do anything.

When the Germans bombed Rotterdam, they set fire to a whole warehouse of Indonesian tobacco and it burned for a week. When the wind blew from the south the smoke smelled so strong you didn't need a cigar.

Chapter 16

❧

St. Nikolaas Eve

December 5, 1940

St. Nikolaas' Song

Zie ginds komt de stoomboot
Uit Spanje weer aan,
Hij brengt ons St. Nikolaas
Ik zie hem al staan.

Hoe stapt trots zijn paardje
Het dek op en neer
Hoe waaien de wimples
Al heen en al weer.

An English Translation

Here comes the steamboat,
From Spain to us here,
It brings us St. Nicholas,
See him stand there!

His horse prances
Back and forth on the deck,
His bright flag dances
In the windy air.

In most European countries, the children get presents on Christmas. But in Holland they get presents on December 5, Saint Nikolaas Eve, or December 6, St Nikolaas Day.

St. Nikolaas, called Sinterklaas in Holland, and his helper, Black Piet, come on a steamship from Spain. He rides a white horse and brings presents and candy. Black Piet also has a big sack to bring naughty kids back to Spain!

No children are missing after St. Nikolaas's visit. It seems like all Dutch kids are good or at least passable or maybe Saint Nick doesn't want naughty children climbing all over his ship when he returns to Spain. Unlike Santa Claus who rides over rooftops and carries presents down the chimney at night; St. Nikolaas also comes when children are awake.

The celebration begins in late November. About ten days before St. Nikolaas Day, children place their shoes by the hearth before they go to bed every night—with hay and a carrot for St. Nick's horse in their shoe. In the morning, they run to see what they find in it. Sometimes they find candy. But when the hay and carrot are still there St. Nick didn't come so there's no treat.

Before St. Nikolaas Day, sometimes a door will open and a gloved hand will throw candy in the room where children are playing. This goes on until December the fifth, St. Nikolaas Eve. On that night Sinterklaas comes to the house with his helper, Black Piet. The saint wears a white robe and a red cape. He has a bishop's miter on his head. He has a long white beard and carries a bishop's crook. He calls each child by name, takes him aside and looks up the child's record in his book. He tells him what he (or she) has done wrong during the year and makes him promise to behave better next year. The children are convinced St. Nick is watching them. Otherwise how would he know everything they did for the year? Then he gives every child a gift. (When I was younger, I wondered why the gifts came in my father's bulb baskets with his company initials on them.)

Besides presents, we each got a chocolate letter—the initial of our first name. My name starts with W, bigger than Jan's J. To make things fair, Dad cuts up one chocolate letter every night and gives us each a piece.

The Dutch name for St. Nikolaas is *Sinterklaas*. 'Santa Claus' is the English pronunciation of the Dutch word. All Dutch children look forward to his day. *Sinterklaas* makes our hearts beat faster and makes us wary especially when we misbehave. He sees and hears everything we do. We think about this more in November, close to St. Nikolaas Eve.

He goes on his white horse to every house in one night. Pieter rides along with him. He carries an empty bag to put naughty kids in.

St. Nikolaas Eve is the highlight of the year. We're lucky. Our Grandmother invites her grandchildren over on December 6, St. Nikolaas Day, and repeats the whole performance, including more presents. She even has the same two men play *Sinterklaas* and *Black Piet*.

When I was an altar boy, the nuns gave the altar boys a box of candy and a gingerbread man, too and the rector had a party for them with gingerbread men and candy. I brought the treats home and mother sampled them. She said, "The rector's candy is better than the nun's." Mother knows candy!

Our St. Nikolaas is really our seamstress's brother. Black Piet is another of her brothers. When I got tall enough to look into the miter Sinterklaas wore on his head and saw his crew cut I stopped believing! But I didn't mention it. Why spoil a good thing?

St. Nikolaas is the best saint on the calendar—he brings presents! But he doesn't come to Hageveld. I miss the St. Nikolaas celebration. I wish I could go home for the night.

December 6, 1940
St. Nikolaas Day

This morning is St. Nikolaas' Day. When I was home, we always went to Grandmother Lommerse's house to celebrate. She would invite all her grandchildren to a party with cookies and candy—both chocolate and gingerbread *moppen* and *speculaas* dolls. The dolls were flat cookies a foot long, baked in a form to look like a boy or girl. We had big glasses of orangeade and could drink as many as we liked.

Aunt Alie, my youngest aunt, lived with Grandmother. She played piano and we sang St. Nikolaas songs until Sinterklaas arrived. He brought wonderful presents. When I was six, I got a priest's outfit with a red chasuble and a white alb. I was so happy when I got it that I put it on. Everybody exclaimed over my new outfit. My grandmother was so proud of me. She knew I wanted to be a priest. Later she invited me over to show her how I would say Mass.

I kept that outfit until it was too small. Then Rector van den Heuvel, where I served as altar boy, gave me one made by a manufacturer of priest's vestments. He bought it for his nephew, who outgrew it. I gave mine to a smaller boy.

I don't remember what anybody else got that year. The red and white priest's outfit was my prize. It made me believe I would become a priest when I grew up.

Grandmother Alie Lommerse was full of love and praise for all her grandchildren. She thought we were all wonderful and didn't need to be lectured. That was taken care of on St. Nikolaas Eve. Now we had a clean slate for the coming year.

I looked up St. Nikolaas in the encyclopedia to see who he was and find out when and where he lived and why he was sainted. This is what I found:

St. Nikolaas was the Bishop of Myra, Turkey, in the 3rd century A.D. He was known and loved for his kindness and generosity. In Turkey in those days a young girl needed a dowry to be wed because eligible men preferred to marry girls who would bring them some money to start their new homes.

One poor family had three daughters but could not afford dowries for their girls. Since they could not find husbands willing to take them, they decided to sell the girls as slaves. St. Nikolaas heard about the girls' problem and threw a bag of gold down the chimney for the oldest girl's dowry so she could be married.

When the time came for the other two sisters to be married, he gave each of them a bag of gold for a dowry, too.

As a saint he was credited with many miracles. He was reported to have saved sailors from shipwreck in a terrible storm. They said he also brought three students who had been killed by a wicked innkeeper back to life.

He is the patron saint of children, sailors and people in need. They don't know his birthday but he died on December 6. So they celebrate St. Nikolaas on that day.

Many churches all over Europe have been built and named to honor him, but only in Holland do they celebrate his name day with presents for children.

December 14, 1940

In December, homes and streets are bright with lighted Christmas trees. In our house we don't have a tree. Our Christmas decoration is a nativity scene. A week or two before Christmas, Jan gets the box down from the attic. Mother unwraps the figures of the Holy Family—Mary and Joseph and the baby Jesus on his little bed of straw, two sheep, one lamb, one ox, one donkey and one camel. A heavenly angel and a star to shine over the stable complete the scene.

We place the scene in the living room a week or two before Christmas and there it stays until the twelfth night of Christmas which is Epiphany. Then the three Wise Men and the camels should appear. They arrived in Bethlehem twelve days after Jesus' birth according to legend. This is the way things are done in proper Dutch Catholic homes.

We all sit around while Mother unwraps the stable, the figurines of the Holy Family, the Wise Men, the sheep, the cow and the donkey. Then she looks in the empty box. She can't find the shepherds. She is puzzled and says, "Oh! There aren't any shepherds. I meant to buy two shepherds."

Dad says, "Then the Wise Men will have to look after the sheep." Our manger scene hasn't any shepherds. It never did as long as I can remember. Mother either forgot to buy them or they were broken. So the Wise Men must double as shepherds.

It is a beautiful scene. But at Epiphany we can only add the camels—the Wise Men are there already—watching the sheep instead of bringing Jesus their gifts of gold, frankincense and myrrh.

After Mother looks for the shepherds she says she'll order them from the store where she got the original figurines. But she always forgets. All the children look at each other and laugh. It is so funny—the same thing happens every year.

Mother says, "Remind me to order the shepherds that go with the set."

It doesn't concern Dad in the least. To him, those old china figures look more or less alike. The Wise Men and the shepherds, dressed in their old fashioned robes are interchangeable.

December 25, 1940

Last night I came home for Christmas. This morning we got up at four AM. I was half asleep when we went to the 'night' mass at five AM. In the church a priest, a deacon, and a sub-deacon celebrated Christmas.

The early mass is called the 'night' mass. After that, we have the 'dawn' mass. There was only one priest to celebrate this. The deacons went into the sacristy. We sang Christmas Carols.

At the 'dawn' mass, nobody paid attention to the priest at the altar except when they quieted down during the consecration. The priest said the words of the ritual over the bread and wine.

After the two masses, we went home for breakfast—raisin bread, tea, boiled eggs, sliced ham and Gouda cheese. It was only 8 o'clock. We ate a hurried breakfast because we had to go back to church at 8:30 to celebrate the mass of the day, a solemn high mass with three priests.

I am in the boys' choir, singing as we proceed to the front of the church dressed in black cassocks and white surplices. The boys' choir and the men's choir sing together but the men are up in the choir loft in back of the church. They don't wear robes because nobody sees them in the balcony. People say children should be seen and not heard. In this case the children are seen and heard, while the men are heard but not seen.

After three masses we are free for the day. There are two days of Christmas; the first day is religious and the second one is social, a day for visiting. "I'm glad that's over!" we said. Jan went to see his friends. Three services in one morning are too many.

When we leave the church we see a few German soldiers who attended the mass. They greet us, but the Dutch people are angry with the Occupation Government so they answer politely but ignore the soldiers' attempts to be friendly.

Dad is polite but distant. He doesn't want to get too close to them. We are doing things against the occupation government's decrees. He can't afford to let them come to our place because they might find out. He wishes them a Happy Christmas and passes by.

As I leave the church, a young soldier stops me. He speaks Dutch with a German accent. "Can I talk to you a minute?"

"Of course," I said.

"It's just that I have a brother back in Bavaria abut the same age as you. You remind me of him. I wanted to wish you a *Vrolijk Kerstmis*." *

"Thank you. I wish the same to you. You must miss your family at Christmas."

"More than you know. I haven't been home for a long time. We lived in Bavaria. My father was a farmer and he was drafted in the army. So he hired a couple to work the farm in his place.

But they turned out to be Nazis and when Dad left, they took over the farm. They make mother work for them. She's afraid of them. When I was home I tried to protect her, but now I've been drafted, too. My little brother Wilhelm and my mother are left at the farm with the hired couple. I worry but there's nothing I can do."

"You speak good Dutch. Where did you learn it?"

"From *moeder*. She is Dutch. She came from Limburg.

"I'm afraid I don't know your name."

My name is Hans. What is yours?"

"I'm William but they call me Pim. Does your mother write? Can't you get a furlough and go home for a visit?"

"I got a postcard once. But the army is short of men. I can't go home unless it's an emergency. You probably think German soldiers want to be here. But I didn't join because I wanted to fight. I was drafted ... I want the war to be over. I wouldn't have said this to you, but you look like my little brother."

"Well, the war is over here. We surrendered and we are living under the occupation. Someday it will end so you can go home. I hope your family is all right."

"Thanks for letting me talk. *Zalig Kerstdagen*."***

"And *Zalig Kerstdagen* to you, too."

I am sorry for Hans—far from his home on Christmas—a German soldier in Holland, where most people don't want him.

But I can't ask him home. He might report things he sees around our place. I sympathize. He said he is not a Nazi. I think he is telling the truth because why lie? Dad had customers in Germany who did not like Hitler at all—farmers, growers and business people not interested in joining the Nazis.

Hitler's party is made up of ex-soldiers and unemployed workers who follow him because they thought he'd help them survive. Things were terrible in Germany after World War I.

There were no jobs and there was runaway inflation. The German Mark was worth so little you needed a wheelbarrow full of paper money to buy a loaf of bread. The German people were desperate. Hitler promised them things—a chicken in every pot and a car in every garage.

I am sorry for Hans, a German soldier living in the barracks. I am a student at Hageveld in Heemstede, studying to become a Priest. We can only see each other in church on vacation—a long time away.

He needs a friend—someone to befriend him in his barracks. It wouldn't be good for him to be close friends with a Dutch boy. We're on opposite sides of this awful war!

*Vrolijk Kerstmis. Merry Christmas

** Moeder. Mother

*** Zalig Kerstdagen. Blessed Christmas Day—the Christmas greeting Catholics usually say.

Chapter 17

❦

The Pilot

December 29, 1940

Yesterday morning Dad gave me an envelope for Mr. Bakker, in Leiden. It's about fifteen kilometers as the crow flies, but farther for a kid riding on a bicycle path.

Leiden is an interesting city. There is a huge windmill standing and waving its arms like an impatient giant right in the middle of the town. I'm fascinated by the mill but people who live there don't seem to notice it. They just ignore it and go about their business.

Dad doesn't tell me what's in his letters. If I'm stopped by a patrol, I'm paying for some bulbs and show them the letter with an invoice and a check.

The real message is between two pieces of cardboard that keep my hat in shape. So far no police or soldiers have ever bothered me. I'm just a kid riding in a swarm of bikes. I carry a book bag and a sandwich—most schoolboys have books and food.

It is safer for a boy or a girl to travel than a man. Germans are suspicious but they watch men, looking for saboteurs, escapees, communists and Jews—but they don't bother kids.

Mijnheer Bakker wasn't in. Mevrouw Bakker gave me a glass of milk to go with my sandwich. We talked and listened to the radio. When he came home, he asked me to stay for dinner. Then he called somebody and wrote a note for Dad. I put it in my hat and kept the cancelled bill in my envelope. I was late. I had to hurry to be off the road before curfew.

I was riding on the bicycle path beside the main road. It was late and there was no traffic. When I was almost home, I decided to take the shortcut through the woods. I don't like to go through the woods at night, but it's quicker than going around the block. The moon sliding through the clouds gave a dim light that barely penetrated the trees. The wind was chilly. Twisted roots sticking up on the path made it impossible to ride. I had to get off my bike and push.

As I came near the end of the woods, close to our field, I heard a hoarse whispery sound like "Help". I froze, frightened. It came again. This time it was unmistakable, "Help".

I looked around in the dark woods. At first I didn't see anything. Then I made out a dark shape. A man was sitting in the bushes, leaning against a tree with his leg stuck out in front. I could tell he was hurt.

"Who are you?" I asked.

"I'm a pilot," he said. "My plane was hit, I was in the tail and it landed in a tree. I hurt my leg when I jumped down and I can't walk."

He was a tall man, too big for me to carry. "I'll have to get Dad," I told him. "I'll be back in a few minutes. Stay here and don't make a sound." That was dumb. He couldn't go anywhere and there wasn't anybody to hear him if he did make a noise. It wasn't likely anyone would come in the woods before morning. German soldiers don't prowl the woods at night. Accidents could happen.

I hurried home, pushing my bike across the frosty field.

When I ran in, Dad was reading the paper. He put his hand out for the answer to his note. But I was too excited to think of that now. I told him "There's a downed British pilot in the woods back of the house. I think he broke his leg."

Dad said "Get a wagon from the warehouse." He told Mother and Jo "Get some blankets and pillows." Then Dad and Jan and I went through the field together. Dad and Jan lifted him in the wagon padded with blankets. It must have hurt terribly. We tried not to hurt him, but the cart was too short for his legs. He could bend his good leg, but the other one just jutted out behind. We propped it on a pillow and rolled up blankets to support it. We had to go slowly.

It took time. If anyone could see us, we must have been a comical sight— Dad pulling, Jan and I pushing, the pilot riding, trying not to make any noise. The old wheels creaked and rattled over the uneven ground. The dark clouds sliding over the moon made it impossible to see the bumps and holes in the frozen field.

We wheeled him into the house, cart and all. He looked like something the cat had brought in and was tired of mauling. He was cold and wet. He looked young, eighteen or twenty; his dirty blond hair stuck out of his hat. His face was thin and his nose and cheeks were strong and bony.

Dad said, "I'm Bart Heemskerk, and this is Marie, my wife and Jan and Pim and Jo. What is your name?"

"I'm Eric. Eric Johnson."

Mother had made coffee and Jo brought him a bowl of soup. He was so hungry he practically inhaled it. So she brought him some *roggebrood* (rye bread) and the soup left in the pot.

It was obvious his leg was broken but we couldn't call the doctor at that time of night. The Germans had a sneaky habit of listening in on phone calls. We couldn't bring him to the hospital. He wore an English uniform. Might as well call the *Moffen* and tell them we had found a British pilot and were keeping him in our living room.

Mother gave him three white pills and a glass of water. She said "For pain."

I don't know how much they helped but they were the only pain medicine we had. She put cream and sugar in the ersatz coffee and asked if he wanted more.

"Thank you so much," he said. "I've had plenty. But I was so hungry and cold in the woods. I hadn't eaten since breakfast."

Dad and Mother put Eric in their bed. Their room is the only first floor bedroom. Mother slept on the couch. Dad brought a cot mattress from the warehouse and put it on the floor in the living room for himself.

Jo and Jan and I went upstairs to our rooms. I couldn't sleep. All I could think of was how to take care of him and hide him so the Germans couldn't find him.

I prayed "Please make Eric safe and make everything all right." But I couldn't concentrate. I was too tired. Everything will work out, I thought. Dad will take care of things. I fell asleep and dreamed of planes breaking up and falling from the sky.

When I woke the sun shone. I remembered last night and thought "There is a reason for everything. It was a miracle Eric was not killed when his plane broke up. There's a reason he survived. And a reason I took a shortcut through the woods and found him. Eric will be safe. If he lived through the crash and the landing, he was meant to be safe.

But after he's better, how can we get him home to England? Dad will figure out a way, I thought.

I dressed quickly, folded back my sheets and blankets and opened the window to let the room air out. Then I went down to check on the invalid. He looked better than last night, not good, but better than when he came in. He was drinking coffee and eating bread and strawberry preserves. He said the jam was delicious. Eric and mother were getting along famously even though neither one could understand each other's language.

Dad had gone to bring Doctor van Aalst. It would be quicker to call but we couldn't chance a listener. When the doctor came he looked at Eric's leg and said it was broken. We already knew that. The doctor looked very serious. He wrapped his leg in a bandage over folded blankets to support it. It was black and blue and twice the size of the left leg.

"Here are some pills for the pain," he said I can't set your leg until the swelling goes down. Then I'll put it in a cast,"

Dr. van Aalst is a good doctor, not exactly jovial, but kind. He was risking his life treating Eric. Helping a wounded British pilot is aiding the enemy. To break the German rules is treason against the Third Reich. If we were caught, everybody in the house might be killed to set an example.

After he swallowed the pills, Eric slept four hours. When he woke he said "My leg feels much better. I was thinking how lucky it was I landed in your tree. And you happened along and found me. And you even speak English." Most people in Holland know some English.

Dad said, "If anything about a plane crash can be called lucky, it was lucky you weren't killed. You'll have to stay here until your leg heals."

And Eric said, "Won't hiding me be dangerous? Maybe I should give myself up and be put in a camp for prisoners of war."

"No. Don't even think it. It is too late for that because we already broke the law by helping you. I have a hiding place where the Germans won't find you."

Dad had made a long narrow closet in the warehouse, hidden by old weathered boards just like the rest of the walls. He added shelves inside the warehouse that match the interior wall and piled crates and old sacks and bulb baskets on top. The furnace in the warehouse keeps the air dry and a little warm. There is no window but in the daytime, light shines down from the ventilation shaft in the roof. At night, moonlight from the sky sheds some light. There is even an old radio in the warehouse we turn on when we're working in there. It wouldn't be unusual to keep the radio on because we forget to turn it off.

"You'll stay in our bedroom for now. When Dr. van Aalst puts the cast on your leg and you feel better, we'll bring you in the hiding place," Dad said.

The whole family crowded in the bedroom like friendly puppies. We wanted to stay around the strange Englishman. Mother brought him soup and crackers. Jo made him flan (custard) for dessert. The boys gave him their comic books. Jo filled hot water bottles to keep him warm. I brought him a book printed in English we happened to have and we all talked to him.

Eric smiled showing regular even teeth. I thought our Dutch teeth were bigger, especially the top ones in front—an irrelevant thought that popped into my mind.

Alice made a suggestion. "When you are by yourself, we could get a little bell for you to ring when you want something."

Dad said, "A bell ringing in the house would be suspicious to anyone who happened to stop in."

"I'll stay home and take care of you. I'll teach you Dutch and you can help me with English."

Dad said "That won't work. People would wonder why you're not in school."

Eric said, "Thank you for finding me and taking care of me. I don't want to be a bother."

Mother came in the bedroom and said, "Eric needs to rest. Everybody clear out now and let him sleep."

December 31, 1940

We had pancakes and bacon and eggs this morning. Jo brought Eric a tray. He said "What a wonderful breakfast!" and wolfed it down as though he was hungry. He didn't seem as sick this morning.

"The pills really help," he told Mother. Jo took his temperature and said it was only a little above normal. I can see by his expression he still has some pain.

The family went to church. I stayed home with Eric and listened to the BBC. I asked, "Do you remember what happened? How come you were in the tail of the bomber since you're a pilot? Why weren't you in the cockpit?

"Our plane was attacked by the Germans and the gunner was hit. The co-pilot took over the controls and I went back to see if I could help. I went into the tail to look at him and there was an explosion. The plane broke apart and fell. The tail landed wedged in a tree hanging over a canal. I don't know what happened to the rest of the plane. I just know it was missing. I don't think the crew survived. Nobody was in the tail except the tail gunner and me. It came down with both of us inside but he died before we landed."

"But you were unhurt? It's a wonder you weren't killed by the explosion or falling from the sky."

"The tree broke our fall. I jumped out. I thought the tail might fall into the canal. I twisted my leg. I knew I had to get away before the Germans came to look at the wreck but I couldn't walk with my knee hurt. I crawled as far as I could and burrowed into some big bushes.

Soon two trucks full of German soldiers came and managed to pull the tail from the tree. They found the gunner in the wreck and must have thought he was the only one in the tail. They didn't expect anybody else, so they didn't look for me. If they searched, they would have found me. It wouldn't have been hard. But they concentrated on getting the wreckage free and carrying it away.

"I could hear them talking. I don't understand the Krauts. But they sounded like they were just doing their work. One was giving orders; it must have been a sergeant. I was afraid they would see me, but they just piled the wreckage into the back of their trucks and drove away.

When I was sure they were gone, I waited, praying for God to send a friendly Dutchman. But nobody came. I kept praying. I got discouraged. Then a miracle happened—you came. And thanks to you and your family, here I am."

"You came down in the right place," I said. "Dad is good at doing things. He'll take care of you."

"I wish I could tell my family so they won't worry—let them know I'm alive," he said.

Anybody with even half a brain would know that was impossible. "We can't let anybody know," I said. "Loose lips sink ships."

We listened to the BBC but they didn't mention Eric's plane crash. How could they? After we heard what the Brits had to say, I changed stations and listened to Dutch news for a while. Eric couldn't understand the language but he wanted me to tell him if they mentioned his plane being shot down. But too many planes fall to describe one individually. The radio only tells us the number of British planes the Luftwaffe shot down. And they exaggerate. We divide what they say by two.

I went to get Eric a glass of water and gave him more pills. After he took them, he fell asleep. I listened to the broadcast, but I didn't learn anything else.

On January 2, the day after tomorrow, I have to go back to Hageveld. I hate to leave Eric. I wish I could stay and help.

The rest of the family will still be here, but I'll have to sit and worry about him. And I won't even be able to tell my classmates what happened. I'm not good at keeping secrets.

January 1, 1941
New Year's Day

In Holland many holidays have two days. There are two days of Christmas, two days of Easter, and two days of Pentecost. We need two days because the first day is a religious celebration and the second day is a feast day to enjoy your family and friends. Unfortunately, there is only one New Year's Day!

Eric spent the day lying in bed in my parents' bedroom. We kept the door closed because we were afraid friends might visit on New Year's Day. We don't want anybody to know he's here.

He can't climb stairs with his leg bandaged. It doesn't seem right to shut him up in the warehouse, either. So Dad and Mother decided to make a call on a relative rather than stay home and have visitors.

At noon we had a big dinner. Afterward Mother and Dad and the twins went to see Grandmother Heemskerk. Jan went to visit his friends. Alice and

Jo and I stayed with Eric and played cards. Around four, Tiberius barked to tell us we had visitors. There was a loud banging on the kitchen door.

"Open up!" commanded a gruff voice. "Open the door!" It was frightening. We knew who it was—the Germans! They must have found out about the airman and came to search the area. Since the ground was dry and hard there were no tracks left by our expedition with the cart. They might suspect, but they couldn't really know somebody was here. We had to hide Eric. I couldn't think of where to hide him or what to do about him being there.

"Just a minute," Jo called loud enough for the unknown presence at the door to hear. Then she said softly "Pim, you and Alice go talk to them while I hide Eric."

"You'd better open the door." I told Alice. "And smile sweetly! They'll be nicer to a girl."

Germans like Dutch girls. And Alice is the type they admire—a young *fraulein* with blond hair and eyes the color of the sea on a sunny day. Two German soldiers stalked into our blue and white tiled kitchen—one of them was short and red haired, beginning to be stout, the other was tall and young. He had dark brown hair and eyes and a long narrow face.

"Do you want my father?" Alice asked, "He went to see grandmother."

They looked so stern and menacing my heart skipped a beat. They weren't Gestapo, just regular army troops with gray green uniforms and tall black boots. The officer said his name was Leutnant Kohlsaat.

He had a thick neck sunk between broad shoulders, a square head, gray eyes and a crew cut. He looked like a military man. Then I recognized the younger one—Hans, the soldier who missed his brother and tried to make friends. But he kept his face straight and pretended not to recognize me. So I did, too.

"We are looking for *Engelse Piloot*. His plane came down in the woods behind *das haus*. We found his parachute. We know he hides. *Woh ist?*" (Where is he?)

Then Jo came into the kitchen wiping her hands on a towel as though she had just come from the bathroom.

"We haven't seen any English pilots," she said. "Yesterday a plane crashed in a tree by the canal. I didn't know there was anybody in it. They had to pull the wreck out of the tree. If a pilot was in it, why didn't they find him?

Then, as though she just thought of something, "Did you look in the canal? If the plane landed by the canal he might have fallen in."

"We looked all around the woods and the field and the canal. But *er ist nicht hier.* (He is not here.) We search now."

Alice said "If someone was here, he didn't hang around. I suppose it would be too risky so close to the crash scene—the first place you would look."

Jo said, "There are some buildings in back where he could hide. Have you checked them?"

"Maybe he broke in through a window. We will search. Open the buildings, please," the Leutnant said. His deep voice made it sound like a command, not a request.

Alice looked up at him with a sweet expression, asking innocently as though puzzled, "How could he be in there? The warehouse is locked and Tiberius barks if anybody comes to our house.

"Open the warehouse. We will look," said Hans.

"You can look," said Alice "but you won't find anybody."

As if he wanted to put in his two cents, Tiberius started to growl. He had made up his mind the soldiers were intruders and he didn't want them around. He growled deep in his throat. Protecting the property was his job. The soldiers looked at our big German Shepard baring his teeth with his ears laid back. They were afraid he might bite them. *"Gut hund,"* Hans said. (Good dog.)

But he kept growling and he looked menacing as a German Shepard can. "Quiet, Tiberius," I said. I would have enjoyed seeing him chase them but they had guns and they would shoot him. I held his collar and asked Jo to hand me the leash hanging by the door.

I said, "Now I'll show these officers the warehouse." We went to the door of the warehouse and I opened it. The men looked it over—every inch of it. They took their time. I pretended to be helpful and named everything— the vegetable bins with our winter store of potatoes, onions, carrots and cabbages, and the shelves where we kept our flower bulbs before we planted them or shipped them in the fall.

They inspected Dad's office. They peered behind the filing cabinets and his big chair and under his varnished desk. They lifted piles of old lumber. They saw everything—bulb crates, planting tools, empty sacks and piles of boxes. They poked at the coal with their bayonets. Did they think a man could be hiding under the coal? They were thorough. I'm sure they would have opened the furnace door but the fire was burning. They moved tables, rapped on walls and poked bayonets up under the eaves. But they found nothing, because nothing was there.

"He might be hiding in one of the other buildings," I said and conducted them painstakingly around the cow barn, the pig pen Dad was building, the woodshed, even Tiberius's dog house and the little shed where my rabbits lived. We went inside the ice cold summer house and the chicken coop. Our entry made the rooster crow and a broody hen fly off her nest.

They climbed ladders up to the haymow, plunging their bayonets in the hay. They speared the cold haystacks in the field. I was trying to be helpful, mentioning places a man might hide. If they thought I was a dumb Dutch boy, maybe they would go away and look somewhere else. But they were still suspicious. They looked over everything in our place. I was thinking of ways to tire them out so they would leave us alone.

Then I had a bright idea. "Have you looked around the convent? There are cellars under it where a man could hide." The nuns wouldn't thank me for sending them to the convent, but Germans are thorough. I knew they would think of it by themselves sooner or later.

The soldiers acted official, not smiling exactly, but at least they remained civil. "We have not looked in your house," the Leutnant, Karl, said. "Maybe you are hiding him in there."

"So close to your barracks?" I said—acting surprised.

Hans said. "You would have seen him, or your dog would. But we have to look just to be sure."

I had no answer to that. The old saying, "A man's home is his castle," came to mind. Didn't the Germans have a saying like that? But I did not argue. Objections would only make them more suspicions. "Come and see," I said, "I haven't seen anyone." I was lying through my teeth. But if they found him, we could all be killed. Helping a British airman is a capital offense. I was lying in a good cause. They were not legitimate police—they were intruders who stamped around our country acting like they owned the place and had to be obeyed. They were criminals.

My heart beat fast. I wished Dad would come home and take care of things. But with nothing else to do, we kept searching. We walked from the fence to the nuns' orchard. I hoped they would leave and go to the convent and bother the nuns. But they turned around and their boots crunched on the frozen field back to our house.

"Where are you officers from?" I asked, thinking that if I could get them talking, they might be friendlier. The *leutnant*, Karl, said, "I come from Hamburg."

Hamburg is in northern Germany. People say northern Germans are more military, more Prussian, while southern Germans, from Bavaria, are more easy-going. I didn't have any way of knowing.

Hans said, "I am from Bavaria. My parents are farmers."

"I study German in school," I said. "I saw some pictures of the castles on the Rhine. Have you ever been to Coblenz? It is on the Rhine River and has an ancient castle."

Karl started talking. He couldn't resist telling me about the glories of Germany. He had been in the castle in Coblenz. I thought he must be homesick. He talked about their *heimat*, their homeland where everything is wonderful. It has to be with the German supermen who live there.

Karl said he had a German Shepard named Max. His dog looked like Tiberius, but Max was bigger. Of course, I thought, everything the Germans had was bigger and better than anything in Holland. It had to be. Their country is bigger and better than ours. I wished they would go back to their *heimat*.

He softened a little when he started talking about Germany, but still intended to search our house. Trying to stop the search would make him certain we were hiding him. He did not trust me. I was an enemy. He had to see for himself. My heart beat so loudly in my ears; I thought Karl must hear it. I hoped Jo and Alice had hidden Eric, but I was afraid the Germans would find him and take him to a prisoner of war camp.

Then they would shoot us to set an example. I prayed harder than I had ever prayed. I tried to make a bargain with God. If He would keep Eric safe, I would do anything—everything he wanted me to from now on.

I hoped Jo and Alice had managed to sneak him into the warehouse after we were done searching. But it felt useless, like praying two and two would be five, not four, that black would be white, that God would tip the earth over and make up be down. I was sure they would find him. It would be my fault. I had not hidden Eric.

We went back in the door between the warehouse and kitchen. I acted like a tour guide. They went through the house, not missing anything. When Hans reached into the cupboard under the sink, a mousetrap snapped shut on his finger. I wanted to smile at his surprise, but I was too scared. They looked in the pantry, in every closet and under beds. They climbed the narrow attic stairs, looked through ancient trunks filled with old clothes. They looked into every place a person could hide, but they did not find the airman.

Finally there was no place left to search. It was getting late. The leutnant ordered us to let them know immediately when we saw him. "There are penalties for hiding an *Engelse Piloot*," Karl threatened. "If you help him, you will be punished. We will be watching you. We will find him." He looked at me as though he thought I might be the flyer in disguise. But I'm too young and too short and I was talking Dutch, not English.

I widened my eyes and gazed back at Karl with the most sincere expression I could muster. He looked back at me, wondering if I was telling the truth.

Then, having searched without finding, they climbed into their big truck and drove away. They weren't satisfied, but it was supper time at the barracks.

I left Tiberius in the entry between warehouse and kitchen. If they came back he would bark. It would stop them for only a few minutes. Hans had a German shepherd himself and knew the dog would bite.

Jo went upstairs and looked out the little attic window.

"They're gone," she called down. Then she went in the parlor and pulled the back of the couch forward. Eric was in the old fireplace, sitting on a blanket in the hole where I once hid to listen to Alice's piano lesson. I almost forgot it was there, but Alice and Jo remembered!

Later, when Dad and Mother and Jan and the twins came home, we told them about the German visitors and the search. Dad praised us for the way we took care of things. Mother looked up at the sky. She was praying, "Mijn God. Dank U!"

Dad said, "They might come back tomorrow but I don't think they'll come back tonight. First they'll think of other places."

"They'll be busy looking in the nuns' potato cellars," I said.

Eric smiled. "I thought our goose was cooked. A guardian angel must have flown over looking out for us."

Soon I'll be back in school. I'll miss the drama. And I won't know what happened. I would like to help him learn Dutch. And the worst thing is, although it's an interesting story I won't be able to talk about it.

Chapter 18

❧

Back to Hageveld

January 2, 1941

This morning we had oatmeal and tea for breakfast. Our big family has a lot of ration cards so we can still add a spoon of sugar. Tea and coffee don't taste anything like the tea and coffee before the war. They say ersatz coffee is made from peas baked until they turn brown and ground up. Who knows what they put in the tea?

The twins were trying to teach Eric Dutch, saying words they thought would be hard for him to pronounce and laughing at his accent. He tried to imitate the way they spoke but he couldn't fool a Dutchman.

"Say Scheveningen," Gerard said. This is a seaside town near The Hague. The Dutch use the word as a test to separate Germans from Dutch people. The Germans pronounce the name 'Shaveningen' but we say 'Skaveningen'. Eric had no trouble but he can't get the guttural 'k' sound. It's easier to teach English to a Dutchman than the other way around. The Dutch learn French, German and English in school. By the time we graduate we speak passable English but students in England don't learn Dutch.

The swelling of Ernest's leg has gone down so Doctor van Alstead put it in a cast. Gre, our seamstress, cut a leg off a pair of overalls and made an opening on that side so he can wear it. She saved the cut-off piece so when the cast is off she can sew it back on again. He has to get rid of his uniform because it's British. What a shame!

I wanted to hear more about Eric's crash. I asked "Were you conscious while you were going down?"

"I was petrified until I blacked out. I thought I was a goner. I can't believe I survived."

The Germans are watching this area. They'll search and search and search some more."

"I hope they don't come here again—not in the house, anyway."

"Since they looked in every crack and didn't find a thing, they probably will look farther out and check the neighbors."

"I wish I could stay home. But I have to go to school."

Jo came in with my suitcase and said, "It's all packed, Pim, and I put in some almond cookies. Don't eat them all the first day."

Jo does so much for me—washes and irons my clothes, packs my suitcase and even adds treats, mostly gingerbread. Gingerbread is good but cookies are better.

Last night Mother made my favorite meal—pork roast with gravy and potatoes and *snijbonen* (cut green beans) and used our best dishes. For dessert she made vanilla *flan* (custard) in a fish-shaped copper mold. The twins always argue about who gets the part of the pudding shaped like the head.

"You got the head last time," Gerard said.

"No, you did," said Ton.

Why do they care who gets the fish head? What difference does it make when it all tastes the same?

January 3, 1941

Jo took me to school on her bike. The freezing wind felt like Siberia. Jo doesn't mind taking me to school. It gets her outdoors. Otherwise she's always doing housework. She's mother's helper and doesn't get much time off. But she shouldn't have to go out on such a cold day.

Dad warned us all over and over," Don't tell **anybody** about our visitor— **nobody,** not even your best friends—especially your friends. If the Germans find out we are hiding the English pilot, we'll all be in danger." He added for my benefit "Don't worry—I'll take care of everything. But remember, do not say a word!"

When we left home, I felt like I was going back to the army. I rode behind Jo. The fine snow stung our cheeks like sharp glass. The tiny flakes were driving past, not piling up in drifts. When the temperature drops, everything will be covered in ice. The predictions are for an exceptionally cold winter.

When we got to Hageveld, I asked Jo if she wanted to come in and have a cup of tea. But she said, "I'd better get home before it gets worse."

She is dressed warmly and going home, the wind will be on her back.

At lunch, the Dean, wearing his black cassock and Roman collar, did not read a story as he usually did. Instead he talked. He warned us to get rid of anti-Nazi material. He's afraid the Nazis will search the school and if they find anything against the occupation government, they would say Hageveld is teaching it to us.

Arie remarked, "They might plant things in the classrooms to make it seem bad for the school. It would be just like them."

I said. "Like the picture of a pig that folds up to make a picture of Hitler's face. Where did you find that?"

"It's just something that's going around. If you don't fold the paper, it's only a drawing."

I picked up my second-hand Greek textbook and decided to replace the cover. When I took off the old cover I saw a message written on the lining, "In case of fire, throw this in." So somebody else didn't like Greek! It was so amusing I snickered. Mr. Nolet gave me one of his disapproving looks. He didn't ask what was so funny so I didn't tell him.

I try to pay attention but my thoughts keep going home. It's frustrating not being able to talk about what happened.

I picture the family relaxing in the house, eating cookies and drinking ersatz. Eric is listening to the BBC; the twins are playing a game and trying to get the best of each other. Their fighting is a nuisance but it's fun for them.

After dinner, Dad reads the paper. We come in to say goodnight before we go to bed and he reaches out and shakes our hand without looking up from the news. Mother gives us a hug and a kiss and says goodnight.

Dad can tell whoppers and act sincere. It's a great ability for dealing with the Germans. They believe every word he says.

If the soldiers come around, Tiberius will growl and bare his long teeth. My geese will fly at them. Those silly geese attack everybody. They haven't learned the boundaries of our farm. They think they own everything—the farm and the street—even the orchard and the Convent—the nun's property.

Dad will act concerned, a good citizen. He'll deny seeing the English pilot—say he'll watch for strangers and let them know if he sees any. They believe he's honest because he speaks German. They trust German speakers but suspect the Dutch. They lie but think we should tell the truth.

Meanwhile Jo and Alice will take care of questionable things that might be lying around like extra dishes or shoes that don't fit anybody in the house. The twins will be listening to the radio. Jan will hide Eric in the warehouse.

Dad's very clever—he's not afraid.

January 7, 1941

This morning, on my way to breakfast I bumped into Potiphar—the man who empties our pots. That's not his real name, just his nickname. He had a yoke on his shoulders with pails dangling from them. He's a cheerful fellow. He smiled and said hello.

"That's a terrible job," I said. "Don't you hate it?"

"It's a poor job" he said, "but my bread is in it."

A picture of bread soaking at the bottom of the pail popped into my mind. It was so funny I laughed out loud.

Mr. Nolet came up behind us. He doesn't think anything is funny. "Heemskerk," he said, "You act like everything is a big joke. Wipe that smile off your face or I'll give you something to smile about!"

I wonder what he was thinking about—assigning more lines for me to copy?

He is a serious young priest, just out of seminary. When he was a baby, someone must have given him sour milk to drink.

He doesn't like my attitude. I'm not crazy about his.

January 8, 1941

Henry didn't come back after vacation. I wonder why. Is he sick? When he left he had a cough. I'd like to know what happened to him but nobody seems to know. When our class came last year, we had a hundred and six boys. Now there are only eighty-five.

Hageveld is like a garden where they planted too many seeds. When the plants came up, the gardeners thinned them out. The school starts classes with too many pupils. They weed the ones they don't need.

Hageveld is a minor seminary. Boys of thirteen of fourteen begin their studies. In six years, the students who remain will graduate. If they decide to go on, they will enroll in a major seminary for another six years. Every year some students are weeded out until the class gets down to size. How many will finish?

It's an honor for a Catholic family to have a son be a priest. The family celebrates when he's ordained. A man from our town was ordained last year at St. Bavo's Cathedral in Haarlem. After the ceremony he and his parents went from Haarlem to Bennebroek in a carriage pulled by two horses. I saw him going past on Bennebroekerlaan to St. Joseph's Church where they had a big celebration to welcome him.

January 9, 1941

Mother wrote to say they got a letter from Mr. Nolet. He said I lack discipline. She asked me what it was all about. I wrote to tell her "Mother, there's no shortage of discipline here. If Mr. Nolet thinks I need some, I'm sure he'll give me plenty."

Discipline comes from the word *disciple* with different meanings. One is a study. Another is to make a disciple of. And another means to regulate or punish. That's the one Mr. Nolet is talking about. He thinks punishment is good for us.

Every day when he comes into our class he writes until he fills all three boards around the room; then erases them and starts over. I write as fast as I can, trying to copy it. While he writes, he gives assignments and more information. He talks so fast—he keeps ahead of us. He talks faster than we can listen.

If I were a teacher, I'd try to interest students in the subjects. I would allow time to let the lesson sink in. He rushes to cram our heads with Greek. I'm not a quick thinker. I shouldn't criticize, but I can't help it—that's how he makes me feel.

January 12, 1941

How is Eric? I am dying to know. Mother writes every week but all she says is everything is fine at home. Of course she can't name names.

They must have got rid of his uniform. I wonder how. They could burn it but metal buttons won't burn. They could throw them in the canal. If he wears old work clothes he would look like a farmer.

"Is his leg healing? Are the Germans coming around looking?"

What if anybody asked me about him? I'd just act dumb.

There's a story about a chicken thief who was caught in the coop with two chickens in his hands. When accused of stealing he said, "It wasn't me who stole them. It was some other guy. I was just passing and I heard a noise. The hen house door was open and the chickens were out. The thief ran away so I was just trying to put them back in the pen. I don't know who the man who got in the coop was. But I never saw him or those chickens before in my life."

Nobody believed him, but it was all he could think of on short notice.

January 16, 1941

The best thing about winter is skating. There are thousands of canals in Holland. When the canals freeze, everybody skates. In Friesland they have the Eleven Towns' Race. The skaters compete to see who can skate down icy canals to the eleven towns fastest.

Our part of the country is not as cold as Friesland and our ice isn't always thick enough to skate on, but this is a cold winter so the ice is as safe as skating on a rink.

Jo brought my skates to school. She knew I'd want them. Last year they were big enough. I tried them on. They're a little snug but I can wear them.

Today we put our skates on and raced on the ice. It's like sailing with wings. I haven't skated for a year, but I didn't forget.

There were all kinds of people on the ice—mothers pulled babies on sleds, little kids wearing skates with double runners, young people twirling and going in circles, and old people skating side by side. It's a scene from a painting: bare black trees and snow on the roofs, skaters wearing bright colored scarves and hats. We had fun gliding and turning and speeding. We fell sometimes but we didn't mind. Dogs ran along, risking frozen feet.

Arie pointed at an orange flag flying from a distant windmill. We skated down to look but it must have been an illusion made by sunlight shining on the moving sails.

We stood in a line to buy *oliebollen* (small round pastries dipped in butter and powdered sugar). We spent our *dubbeltjes* and *kwartjes* (dimes and quarters) on delicious snacks.

Someone stretched an extension cord to a record player on the ice. It was like a party with music and we enjoyed it because we were free from school, our troubles, and the war. It was winter so the sun sets early. We hated to leave but we had to back to Hageveld for supper.

January 19, 1941

Last night rain came down and coated buildings and trees and weeds with ice. The weight of the ice brought big branches down from the trees. I've seen ice coated ground before, but I can't remember so much ice on everything.

Arie said, "Something good came out of the storm. I heard it on the radio in the office."

"How could anything good happen in such a mess of broken branches and fallen trees? There's a lot of damage."

"Some German cars were parked on the street. Some trees fell on them and turned them into junk."

"The mechanics will soon fix them."

They can't. They're flat as tin cans crushed by tanks. And they haven't got the parts.

"God must be sending us a sign to say he's on our side."

"If that's true, why didn't he drop the trees on the German tanks?"

"There's a time for everything," Arie said. "The tanks came in May and that's not ice season."

The wind bends and twists the branches of the trees. The sun glitters on a glass covered world. The long reeds at the canal's edge gleam like Christmas ornaments. We can't go in the woods because branches break off. They sound of a branch breaking is like a gun going off. Icicles hang from the edges of the roof like long bottles and smash when they fall.

We tried to make snowballs from handfuls of ice but the little shards wouldn't stick together. We scooped up handfuls and threw them at each other. They sparkle like diamonds but are not useful for snowballs.

At home, Gerard and Ton must be enjoying the weather. I hope they are feeding my pets and making sure they're safe.

There are two big Chestnut trees by the back door of our house. The overhanging branches might break off and crack the blue roof tiles. It would be impossible to replace the tiles on the ice coated slanted roof.

I have to get up early tomorrow for Morning Prayers and to serve Mass with Father van der Poel. I like to do this once I'm up, but I hate getting out of bed.

Chapter 19

❧

The Winter Term

January 21, 1941

Last year we studied French. The words were hard to pronounce. This year English is our modern language. It's easy for me because I hear Dad using it around the office. When he sold bulbs in America and England, he had to speak English. But he still counts in Dutch. So do I. *Een, twee, drie, vier, vijf, zes, zeven, acht, negen, tien, elf, twelf,* is easier to remember than one, two, three.

Sometimes when Dad thinks in English he absent-mindedly speaks to mother in that language. Mother didn't learn English when she went to school. She laughs and says "Speak Dutch so I can understand you."

Today, in English class, Mr. Zwartkruis wrote a poem on the board by Yeats. I'll write it here.

The Ballad of Peter Gilligan

The old priest, Peter Gilligan,
Was weary night and day
For half his flock were in their beds,
Or under green sods lay.

Once, while he nodded on a chair,
At the moth-hour of eve,
Another poor man sent for him,
And he began to grieve.

'I have no rest, nor joy, nor peace,
For people die and die';
And after cried he, 'God forgive!
My body spoke, not I!'

Yeats

It's about a woman who asks Father Gilligan to come to her dying husband during an epidemic. The priest was tired. He sat down to rest for a minute before he went to see her husband but he fell asleep. When he awoke he hurried to the dying man's house but it was too late. The man had already died.

To his surprise, the man's wife thanked him for coming and seeing her husband. Apparently, while he slept, another priest came. Father Gilligan believed an angel came in his place.

Some boys took turns reading the verses aloud. Mr. Zwartkruis told us our assignment was to learn a poem by heart. We started to discuss our choices.

Arie said, "*Father Gilligan* is an Irish story. It's too superstitious. I'm learning verses from '*The Rhyme of the Ancient Mariner*.' A ship gets caught in icebergs and an albatross flies around the marooned ship. A sailor is so frustrated he kills the albatross. I like it. Especially the line 'Water, water everywhere, nor any drop to drink'."

"That's a good one, too." Mr. Zwartkruis said. But it's a long poem. Learn a few verses. I like 'He prayeth best, who lovest best, All things both great and small; for the dear God who loveth us, he made and loveth all'."

Arie is going to memorize some of the poem and so will I. It's terribly long but it's interesting.

January 22, 1941

In German class today we read the story of William Tell. He was a Swiss archer living in the Canton of Uri. At the time, Austria controlled Switzerland

and a tyrant named Gessler ruled Uri. He put a hat on a pole to represent the Duke of Austria and made a decree that everybody passing the pole must bow to the hat. Tell refused. Gessler arrested him and made him shoot an apple from his son's head. Tell took two arrows from his quiver. He put one in his belt and used the other to shoot the apple.

He was an expert marksman. He split the apple but did not hurt the boy. Afterward, Gessler asked him why he took a second arrow and put it in his belt. Tell replied that if he missed the apple and shot his son, he would have used the second arrow on Gessler. Gessler was furious. He had the guards throw Tell in prison.

Suddenly a terrible storm came up and waves broke the prison wall. Tell escaped and joined a revolt against Austria. The Swiss won the war and kicked out the Austrians. Switzerland became independent. They guarded their freedom and made the motto 'Mountaineers are always free.'

Pieter said "The Austrians of Wilhelm Tell's time were arrogant, like the Germans."

Mr. Verbeem didn't like the turn the discussion was taking. So he explained "It's an old Norse legend Schiller dramatized. Other writers used it too. Rossini wrote an Opera about it."

The teachers don't discuss the occupation of Switzerland. But it *was* in our book. Arie drew a picture of William Tell aiming at the apple on his son's head. We can't say what we think, but nobody told us not to illustrate a story.

January 23, 1941

Today Carl complained there are too many rules. Did he just notice? He wouldn't say anything to the teachers, but just to me. I thought *"Now the shoe is on the other foot. He told Mr. Nolet on me for laughing at the picture and got me in trouble.*

I've forgiven him but I haven't forgotten. I'd like to tell him off. But I restrained myself and took the advice of an old saying, *"Save your breath to cool your porridge."*

Saying 'Shut up' to Carl would be dumb. I'm trying to follow the rules: No smiling, No laughing, Eat what's on your plate, Pay attention in class, Do your work, and above all—No talking!

I'm dying to know what's going on at home. I haven't said a word to anyone about Eric but I can hardly keep from telling Arie.

Keeping secrets is hard for me. "Two can keep a secret—if one of them is dead." We have a whole house full of people. With that many people, how can we keep a secret?

January 24, 1941

Dad hates Hitler and the Nazis. We have to obey the authorities because they have guns, but he can't wait for them to leave and take their ideas with them. Dad's not against Germans, but he hates dictators like Hitler and Mussolini and their tyrannical government.

There are 'V's' all over—on walls and fences and sidewalks. 'V' is for Victory. They began to use it in Belgium and now they're doing it here. Churchill waves his hand holding up two fingers to mean 'Victory' for England. To scribble it on a wall takes only a second. And we use the first four notes of Beethoven's fourth symphony—dot, dot, dot, dash—the symbol for V in the Morse code and tap it on windows as we pass.

Goebbels couldn't get rid of it so he claims the 'V' means victory for Germany.

The Netherlands is one of the oldest democracies. Before the Occupation we were a free country. We could go where we wanted and do what we liked as long as we didn't break any laws. Seyss-Inquart said he wouldn't impose German laws. But he must have forgotten his promise.

Now the Nazis are persecuting the Jews. I can't see why. They are good citizens and well educated. They work in the professions—doctors, lawyers, professors, business people, bankers, architects, scientists and skilled artisans like diamond cutters. They've never done anything to make us doubt them. On the other hand, the Nazis are a collection of hooligans. If anybody is dismissed, it should be the German invaders.

When the Nazis took over in Germany, many Jews fled to Holland. They thought it would be safe in a neutral country.

For hundreds of years the Netherlands took in people who fled their countries. The Huguenots came here to escape French discrimination. The Pilgrims came when it was a crime to read the Bible in England. The Portuguese settled here to escape the Inquisition.

They lived here in peace. So why does Hitler hate Jews? They are cultured and intelligent people. They've contributed great things to the world.

One of the first things the occupation government did was to fire Jewish civil servants. Then in November they even dismissed the President of the Supreme Court, L. E. Visser. The firing raised eyebrows and objections but apparently the opposition was not loud enough to make the occupation government apologize or change their decision.

But when they dismissed Jewish professors at the University of Leiden, Professor Cleveringa assembled the students. He spoke and stirred them up. When he finished, the students were decided to strike. The Germans retaliated by closing the school. The outrage spread to other colleges.

At the Institute of Technology in Delft, students struck in sympathy with Leiden. So the Nazis closed that, too. They made a mistake when they closed the technical school. Germany needs engineers and technicians for their war. Since they closed the Institute, Dutch students aren't learning technology. There aren't many technical graduates for industry.

Hitler was a Catholic, too. He turned against his religion and now he's interested in old Nordic rituals. Catholic priests and Protestant ministers both oppose the Nazis, although the Nazis haven't closed churches. If they did that, the whole population might strike. But if a priest opposes them, the Nazis put him in prison quick as a frog snaps a fly.

Dutch Resistance groups print underground 'newspapers'. It's illegal to print them or give them out or even read them. They are only a sheet of paper written to tell the truth about the war.

Workers deliberately have accidents to damage our machinery. The Germans say the Dutch are slow and dumb. But we managed to build factories and keep them going long before they came.

On dark moonless nights, resistance men blow up railroad bridges to stop the trains carrying war materials to Germany and bringing Jews to prison camps. Dad wouldn't dynamite a bridge. He doesn't like taking chances. But he does other things, like getting papers for 'divers' so they can escape. Mother can't stand having people going hungry. She feeds hungry people who come to the door.

When brains were given out, Dad wasn't standing behind a door. If there's a way to get Eric back to England, he'll find it!

Chapter 20

Mid-Winter Storms

February 2, 1941

This is a free afternoon, but it's too cold and windy to play outside so we're in the Rec room, playing games, reading and talking. I have to copy the Greek vocabulary. That doesn't take any thought. Carl and Klaas were playing cards. Suddenly Klaas said to Carl, "You cheated!"

Carl said, "So did you. I saw you hide a card when you played with Robert."

"That was different," Klaas said.

"What's the difference?" Carl said. "Cheating is cheating."

"I was just checking to see if he was paying attention."

Does that sound like a serious discussion between students or something second graders would argue about?

February 3, 1941

I'm writing in my journal. I'm not worried the Germans will read it because they only read German. Most don't speak English. And why would they bother reading a student's papers?

I remember when German tanks invaded Poland in 1939 from the West and the Russians attacked from the East. The two armies wrecked everything and killed a lot of Polish people. We didn't think that would happen to us. Hitler said he would not cross our border. He'd leave us alone if we didn't join France and England against him.

He lied and we believed him. He was afraid the Western European countries would join together and build up their defenses before he was ready. Meanwhile he was making plans for a surprise attack. When the pieces were in place, he played a different tune. Now he said England and France were going to invade Holland and Belgium and he came to 'protect' us.

We fortified our bridges. But the Luftwaffe flew overhead, dropping paratroopers and bombs. They could not cross our bridges into 'Fortress Holland'; but after they demolished Rotterdam, General Winkelman had to surrender to save Amsterdam and Utrecht and The Hague and the other cities.

We thought the Allies would come to our aid. The French tried but they couldn't reach us. It happened too quickly. France was overcome because they didn't expect the attack to come through the Ardennes. The German Army surprised them and split the French and British Armies. They expected this war would be like World War I. But this is a different war, fought from the air. Rivers and bridges can't save you from bombs.

Hitler has conquered. But he is wrong if he thinks we will join him. You can steal a dog, but you can't make him wag his tail!

February 7, 1941

Eureka! My Greek copying is finished. I stapled the pages to make a neat book, wrote "Greek Vocabulary" on the cover, signed it and put it on the teacher's desk in study hall so it would be there when he arrived.

When he came to the desk, he first reached in his pocket and took out a big cigar, cut off the end and lit up. After a couple of puffs, he let a solid white cloud the size of a tennis ball escape. While the smoke was still close to his mouth he inhaled and drew the cloud back in again.

Then he picked up my copy of the Greek vocabulary and paged through it. When he was satisfied it was complete he called me to his desk. With his bony face, big nostrils and jutting jaw, he's not his mother's best looking. He tipped his head back, raised his eyebrows, and pierced me with a stare through gold-rimmed glasses.

"Heemskerk, what did you learn from this?"

"Not to laugh, Mr. Nolet." I waited a few seconds and then I added "Sir."

He looked to see if I was serious. I kept my face straight and looked into his eyes. If he thought I was defying him, he would assign more copying.

"Be good then and don't," he said.

The whole class watched the interesting scene. But Mr. Nolet leaned back and concentrated on his cigar. I had gone back to my desk when he told me to be good and I felt a weight fall off my shoulders.

Why did a disciplinarian like that become a priest? He should have been a judge to make criminals tremble.

February 9, 1941

I was thinking about Eric. I've never heard of any British airman who landed in Holland getting back to England. Usually they are picked up the minute they land and put in a prisoner of war camp and stay till the war ends. Even if they escape, chances are almost non-existent for them to return home. The channel is too big to swim and too wild to cross without a boat. And the Germans patrol the coast by plane, submarine and ship.

There are three ways to reach England; he could take a boat across the North Sea. But the seacoast is patrolled by the Germans and it would take a good boat and motor. A boat with one person alone would almost certainly not reach the opposite shore.

He could fly across if he could find an unguarded plane with a full tank. That's not likely!

Most people leave going south through Baarle-Nassau, Belgium, France, Spain and Portugal. Baarle-Nassau is a part Dutch, part Belgian province. You can enter it from either country if you have identification. It would be easier for me because guards don't bother young students. Eric is tall and slim, athletic looking. But he can't speak Dutch or French. As soon as he opened his mouth, the guards would tell he was English. He would have to pretend to be mute and brain damaged. An escort could say he was a student going home to Belgium. But he would have to go all through Belgium, across the borders to France; down hundreds of miles to Spain and cross another border and all the borders are guarded.

A man dressed as an engineer or something could take a group through Belgium and France, pretending they were laborers going to work on the Atlantic Wall.

Sweden, to our north, is neutral. If Eric could get to Sweden, he could fly to England but the cold North Sea lies between us.

Sweden is so far away it's like the end of the world to me, or at least you can see it from there.

February 10, 1941

Today I found a *dubbeltje* (dime) on the path. I thought it was a lucky sign.

I told Arie how I felt about finding a lucky coin. He asked, "Do you always find a *dubbeltje* or a *quartje* before something good happens?"

"Of course not."

"Well, why do you believe finding one is a lucky omen?"

"I've been lucky before when I found one. At least I'm a little richer."

"I'd like to test your theory. Give it to me and if it's lucky, something good will happen to me."

I laughed. That might be logical, but I found the *dubbeltje* and it's my luck. "Find your own lucky coin," I told him.

February 16, 1941

Today is Sunday. After Mass, Peter, Arie, Carl and I went out to play a game. Everything was covered with snow melting into slush but it was very cold— not as warm as it looked when we were inside looking out.

"Either your arms are growing or your sleeves are shrinking," Arie said.

"It's cold as Siberia," I said.

"That's where the wind comes from," Peter said.

"Well at least it's snow," Ari said. "I'm sick of all the rain."

"Let's have a snow fight," said Carl. We made piles of snowballs and pelted each other. Other kids joined in. We were like two armies battling each other. The snow got inside our boots and covered our jackets. We looked like living snowmen.

The wind was blowing so hard, my bare wrists froze. I left the fight. I'll ask Mother if she can find an old coat in the attic and turn it inside out to make me a new jacket.

You can't find new cloth in the stores. The factories make plenty but it's all going to Germany to make uniforms for their enormous army.

There are way too many German soldiers stationed everywhere in Europe. Why does Hitler need so many guarding us? We have no guns or bullets. When we surrendered, the Dutch army threw their guns in the canals where they're probably rusting under the water.

February 17, 1941

There is a big crucifix hanging on the wall in the front of study hall. Or at least there was one. The priest took it down and placed it in the lectern to hang a map of Palestine on the wall for an assignment. The class crowded around the map and the tall boys in front hid it. I wanted to see the map so I jumped up on the lectern. That was a big mistake. The lectern was made in two parts and the top was just resting on the bottom, not nailed or fastened together. I guess the carpenter thought the weight of the top part would hold it on the bottom part. They didn't expect me to climb it. When I got on, it toppled to the floor. The crucifix fell out and smashed in a million pieces.

What a crash! Everybody jumped, mesmerized. The teacher came from the back of the room to see what happened. He looked at the overturned lectern and the pieces of the broken cross on the floor. He looked at the students standing around the wreck and saw me on the floor. He asked me what occurred.

"We were leaning on the lectern," I said, "To see the map. It looked solid. But the top was a hollow box resting on the bottom with the crucifix inside. When I jumped up on it the whole thing tipped over and broke the cross in pieces."

Father Straathof raised his eyebrow and shook his head. I waited for him to tell me my punishment. I knew it would be drastic. If laughing at a picture is blasphemy and the penalty is copying a Greek dictionary, what would I have to do for breaking a crucifix? Copy all the maps in the whole atlas?

Father Straathof let his eyebrow down, shrugged his shoulders and shook his head. "Heemskerk," he said. "I might have known you'd be at the bottom of this."

Chapter 21

✦❧✦

A Strike in Amsterdam

February 27, 1941

In Hageveld, the students want to know what is going on. But news is not in our curriculum. They are teaching us to become priests, not reporters. We learn Greek and Latin and Bible History and the usual priest subjects. We are in the middle of the country but it's like the middle of nowhere.

Most of our news comes from nearby cities and towns like Haarlem. But we don't hear much from Amsterdam, the capital. If somebody finds an illegal paper we pass it around. The news sheets are small. Paper is scarce.

The one I saw today, called *De Waarheid* (The Truth) is published by the Communists—but you don't have to be a Communist to read it. The Germans hate these little papers and threaten to jail people for having them, but that doesn't keep them from being passed around.

In the paper, we learned there was trouble in Amsterdam. It started with a fight in an ice-cream parlor in the Jewish section. The Black Shirts or W.A. troublemakers attacked some Jewish men. They didn't expect any resistance. But the young Jews being harassed by the W.A. had formed an Action group to defend themselves. Some young Dutch guys in the parlor joined the fight. They turned the tables on the Black Shirts. The W.A. called the German Police for help.

Jews and Patriots fought the German Police. The police couldn't win. They called in the military, or *moffen*. (*Moffen* means 'muffs'. It's an old

158

nickname for German soldiers because they used to wear tall fur hats that looked like muffs.)

Anyway, the German soldiers outnumbered the Action group. They arrested four hundred and twenty five young men. The arrests did not end the trouble; they only aggravated it. Now Dutch workers, some of them Communists, joined in. The workers were angry because the Germans had disbanded unions. The Communists hated the Nazis because they outlawed Communism. They all got together and called for a one-day strike to protest the treatment of the Jews.

Dutch patriots, Communists, workers and Jews all joined. Streetcars stopped. City offices closed. Everybody—shipyard workers, metal workers, factory workers—walked off their jobs. They crowded the streets waving signs to defy the Nazis.

The strikers demonstrated in Dam Square, the center of Amsterdam. Dutch police were ordered to stop the strike. But there was no way the few policemen could make such a huge crowd of protesters go back to work. The police didn't even try, just ordered the strikers to leave Dam Square.

There weren't enough police to arrest the strikers and there weren't enough jails to hold them. Dutch police weren't excited. The demonstrators weren't doing anything. They didn't have any weapons. They were just demonstrating, waving signs and yelling but not hurting anything.

Rioting is not a Dutch tradition. The police knew that when the sky grew dark and it started to rain and the people got hungry, everyone would go home for supper.

But the Nazis were afraid of losing control. They threatened mass arrests and changed the curfew from 11 PM to 7:30 PM. This made people angrier. So the strikers, not yet ready to leave, kept on demonstrating.

The news spread. Other workers heard about the strike. Haarlem and Zaandam joined in to show sympathy with Amsterdam.

The German authorities overreacted. They ordered the soldiers to shoot into the crowds. Seven people were killed and many more wounded.

When the shooting started the crowds broke up. Then the Germans proclaimed a state of emergency. They arrested Communists and Jews and anybody else they blamed. They imposed fines on cities where strikes occurred and fired their mayors.

Hageveld is in Heemstede, next to Haarlem, but nothing happened here. In rural towns like Bennebroek, there are few organized laborers or Communists.

The strikes surprised the Germans and showed them how we felt about the way they treat the Jews. We don't have guns. We can't fight without weapons. But the German's reaction showed they are afraid of losing control. If the strike would spread, Germany could not put the insurrection all over the continent of Europe down because invading Russia has spread their armies too thin.

March 2, 1941

The strike ended but Seyss-Inquart and his top deputy, Hans Rauter are tightening control. Rauter is a friend of Heinrich Himmler, the second most powerful man in Germany, after Hitler. Rauter has more access to Hitler than Seyss does.

Amsterdam, Haarlem and Zaandam are quiet. Many strikers were arrested. Some were executed. Others put in jails, like the 'Umbrella' in Haarlem. Its nickname comes because it has a round roof resembling a big umbrella. Since the Germans have taken it over, it's notorious for cruelty.

Jews who were arrested were sent to Westerbork, a detainment camp in the arid eastern part of the country. From Westerbork, Nazis put them on trains to send to camps in Poland.

There are no trials. There are no lawyers to defend the men they arrested. Many were shot. It's impossible to find lawyers. Dutch lawyers may no longer practice in our courts. It's no use, anyway. The Nazis say if you are arrested it proves you are guilty because if you weren't guilty they wouldn't arrest you. That's their logic!

Thoughts about the war fill my mind. I can't concentrate on Geometry. Math does not come easy to me.

Today, walking on the path around the school, Arie said, "You're so quiet lately. Is something bothering you?"

I'm tempted to tell him what is on my mind but I can't. So I said "I'm just waiting for vacation."

"That's a long way off," he said. "Wasn't the stew tough today?

"It tasted like old leather shoes with the shoestrings left in."

"Do they feed the teachers the same food we eat?"

"They wouldn't take it. They'd go on a hunger strike."

Arie smiled. "Can you imagine priests striking?"

"No. They're too peaceful."

"What makes people belligerent, anyway? What makes a man like Hitler get an army, march them into another country, shoot people who fight him and take over?"

"I don't know. What gets into them? Why do they want to rule the world? Are they crazy?"

"Maybe their mother didn't teach them how to behave."

"Or there's something in the air in central Europe."

"Germany is landlocked and has no way to the Atlantic or the Pacific or the Mediterranean. Their only seaport is on the North Sea and it's frozen in winter. Maybe the Germans want to get out but the other countries are too close so they take over the other countries.

"Hitler's on a rampage. Taking over Europe—Denmark and Norway and Belgium and Holland and France."

"He's going to build a wall around Europe so nobody can get in or out. It will be a prison."

"Or an asylum."

March 9, 1941

Today was cool and windy. But the ground isn't frozen and it's not raining. Carl and Arie and I walked around Hageveld, avoiding muddy puddles.

Arie asked Carl, "How do you like German?"

"It's not hard. It's a lot like Dutch. But their history is different, all about wars and fighting. First they had the Kaiser and now Hitler came along, telling whoppers. I'm writing good ones in my book."

"Somebody should. Like 'We do not want to lie and cheat.'"

"If he doesn't want to lie and cheat, why doesn't he quit? Nobody is forcing him to do it!"

"And 'Great liars are great magicians.' He admires liars and brags about them."

"And 'My will decides'," said Arie.

"You can either be a Christian or a German. But not both" Carl said.

"But worshipping Hitler is law in Germany. Hitler Youth have to swear obedience. Even unto death—so help me God."

Arie asked, "If he doesn't believe in God, why does he swear in God's name?"

"He uses God's name to say he's telling the truth."

"Remember Faust—he sold his soul to the devil? The devil granted him whatever he wanted for twenty five years. After that, he had to give his soul to the devil. But when the devil came to claim it, Faust reformed. So the devil didn't get his soul after all."

March 10, 1941

In Germany, after World War I, there was a great depression. The government printed huge quantities of paper money and the German mark became worth so little that a loaf of bread cost a barrowful of paper marks. Everybody's life savings were gone. Salaries were worthless. The people were desperate.

The French marched into the Ruhr, where the industry of Germany was concentrated, because the Germans could not pay the reparations dictated by the Versailles Treaty after WWI. This threw people in factories and mines out of work.

Hitler served in World War I as a corporal. After the war he was an angry ex-soldier with no money or prospects. He joined the Nazis, the Worker's Party, and took over the leadership. At a political rally in the Buergerbraukellar in Munich, he tried to take over the government in what was called "The Beer Hall Putsch."

The meeting was in progress and state commissioner Gustav von Kahr was speaking to three thousand people when Hitler pushed his way into the beer hall with armed storm troopers. He jumped up on the table and fired into the air. "The revolution has begun," he announced. He forced the leaders of the party, Hans von Seisser, the head of the police and General Otto von Lossow, the head of the Bavarian army into a room and told them to join his revolution at the point of his pistol. While they remained under guard, he told the people they agreed to join him.

He sent for General Ludendorff, a famous German General who hated the new Republic. Ludendorff agreed to join Hitler. He talked to von Kahr and von Seisser and von Lossow and the three men were released to appear with Hitler on stage. They all made speeches in support of the new government.

The Berlin government sent orders to suppress the rebellion. Kahr, Lossow and Seisser left Hitler and brought in the police and troops to put it down. They ordered the Nazi party dissolved. But Ludendorff marched the storm troopers into Munich and took it over and proclaimed a new revolutionary government.

On November 9, 1923, Hitler, Ludendorff and Goering with the storm troopers reached the center of Munich. Armed police stopped them, firing broke out and three Nazis and sixteen storm troopers were killed. The rest fell on the ground to avoid being shot. Hitler jumped into a waiting car and left for the safety of the country.

Hitler ran away, Goering was wounded and the Nazi party seemed to be ended. For their revolutionary efforts, the leaders were tried and convicted. On April 1, 1924, Hitler was sentenced to prison for five years. But for some reason, he was very well treated in the fortress of Landsberg where he served his sentence.

While there, Hitler wrote his book, "Mein Kampf" which means 'my journey.' It was filled with his ideas of German superiority and hatred for other people, especially Jews. He said the Germans were supermen and all the other people were only worth being slaves. He made the Jews scapegoats, blaming them for Germany losing World War I. He practiced speaking to become an orator. He realized being a good orator was the path to power.

When he got out of prison he ran for office as Chancellor. He promised that if he was elected, he would bring prosperity to Germany. There would be 'a chicken in every pot' and every German family would be able to afford a 'people's car.' But in 1933, when the last democratic elections were held in Germany, he still did not get a majority of votes. He persuaded the head of the government to appoint him anyway.

He used intimidation as a weapon. People, who did not agree with him, mysteriously disappeared. Some were put in concentration camps and some were killed. People who saw what was happening and knew they were in danger, left the country.

His reign of terror was felt on *Kristallnicht*, in November, 1938. His bullies smashed windows and assaulted Jews. They wrote Nazi slogans all over and rioted. Most Germans were too sensible to listen to him. Many

Jews fled to America. Some went to countries like Holland, where there was freedom of religion. It seemed like a good idea. But Hitler occupied Holland so Jews are not safe here. Hitler hates Jews.

March 11, 1941

In German, we translated the story of the Pied Piper. Rats invaded Hamlin Town. They were all over everywhere. They bit the babies, ate the food, and overran every building. People were at their wits' end.

Then a piper came to town dressed in a many colored suit. He promised he would get rid of rats if the councilors would give him a bag of gold. The desperate councilors gladly agreed.

The piper played his tune and charmed the rats with lively melody. They followed the piper and he led them into the sea to drown. But when he came back to get his bag of gold, the councilors cheated him. They felt safe because he could not bring the rats to life.

Then the piper played a different tune. He charmed their children and they followed him out of town, The people never saw their children again.

Hitler is like the pied piper. He uses stirring music to mesmerize the Germans. He lures them with immense parades and colorful banners. His huge columns of soldiers, his tanks and planes make them feel powerful. He tells them they are the greatest people in the world. They are stirred up by his speeches. They believed his promises and follow him like the children who followed the Pied Piper.

Chapter 22

Easter Sunday

April 9, 1941

April is tulip time. Tulips of red and yellow and white are blooming over the fields in the bulb district. Before the war we made floats covered with hyacinths and held parades from Lisse to Hillegom and Bennebroek. But this year there are no celebrations. The only parades we see are soldiers marching or army trucks passing or planes flying overhead.

It's Easter. Today we attended services at St. Joseph's Church. The sanctuary was filled with lilies to celebrate Christ's Resurrection. The voices of boys in the choir singing hymns entranced listeners.

Pastor Schmidt preached. He is known for his long sermons. He kept on and kept on, long after the time for him to sit down. When he finally finished, the curate read a letter from the Archbishop, Cardinal de Jong. It said we should feed the hungry and help the Jews and other fugitives. Seyss-Inquart and his Deputy, Rauter would be furious if they heard it. Pastor Schmidt didn't want to read it. But the bishop said it should be read to the congregation. So Pastor Schmidt made the curate read it.

After the service we hurried home for breakfast. Eric can't come to church. When we got home he was looking at maps in an atlas.

"Are you learning the way to Spain?" I asked.

"I'm trying," he said. "But those Dutch maps aren't easy."

I reminded him "Those are the ones the old navigators used."

"I'm not a navigator," he said. "And I can't read the Dutch names."

We hadn't eaten before mass so we had breakfast—*uitsmijters*—two slices of bread, covered slices of ham and topped with fried eggs. They are delicious. We had imitation tea to drink. It doesn't taste like real tea but we are getting used to it. I drink black tea but the twins drink it with milk. After we finished, the boys left to visit friends.

Dad said "Archbishop de Jong is breaking their rules. If he's not careful, they'll find a cell in the Orange Hotel to put him in."

"He's so brave. He says what he thinks," Jo said. "If the Nazis hear about that letter, I wouldn't be surprised if they arrested him. In fact I'd be surprised if they don't.

"They don't want demonstrations in Utrecht," said Jan. "They had enough in Amsterdam."

Utrecht is one of the oldest communities in the Netherlands. It is the seat of the Dutch Catholic Church. They tore down an old Roman fort to build the Cathedral and the Square. The bell tower has 365 steps, one for every day of the year. It was built in 1023, over 800 years ago. Cardinal de Jong has his office there.

Dad said, "Everybody agreed the Cardinal wrote a good letter."

"Pastor didn't read it," Mother said. She won't criticize a priest but hates it that he is pro-German.

The sun streamed through the tall dining room windows. I'm glad to be home. Everybody is healthy, Eric's leg is better, and my pets are all here. Eric is like family—he learned some Dutch words which he speaks with an English accent. He's here in Holland, wishing he was in England.

He can't go out so he gets his sun from the window. When the geese cackle and the dog barks, he knows someone is coming down the path. He hides until he thinks it's safe.

He's tall and blond, looks like a Dutch farmer. Mother found old work clothes for him. Shoes were a problem because he has long bony feet. But Dad found some old leather for a cobbler to make him a pair of boots.

He wants to leave. Dad knows men who are guides to get people out. Eric wants to get back to his own country on the other side of the channel.

After breakfast I visited the Teeuwens, our next door neighbors. They haven't any children and sort of adopted me because they took care of me when mother had the twins.

They were sitting in the kitchen, with coffee and cookies. I hadn't seen them since Christmas. I pulled up the tall wooden chair I always sit in. *Juffrouw** Teeuwen is short and round and comfortable looking. She wears her pale hair pinned back in a bun. She hugged me. "You're growing, Pim—getting too big for your chair."

"It still fits me and I like to think of it as mine—unless you give it away." I smiled, remembering that I once asked a visitor to move because he was sitting in my place."

Juffrouw Teeuwen asked how school was treating me. But Mr. Teeuwen changed the subject. He wanted to talk about his trip to Amsterdam. "The day the strike started I went to Amsterdam on business. But when I got there everything was closed. The trains stopped running. I was stuck with no way to come home.

"It all started in an ice cream parlor where young people were hanging out. The Black Shirts in Amsterdam ere harassing the Jews. They've done it before. But this time the *Knokploegen* got involved. They were sick of the Black Shirts' shenanigans and decided to put a stop to it. So they fought back. (*Knokploegen* is a name borrowed from history. They were the tough guys, the Dutch patriots in the Eighty Years War that freed The Netherlands from Spain.)

The Green Police, the Dutch Gestapo, arrested a group of Jewish and Dutch young men in the ice-cream parlor where they hung out. That's when the skirmish began."

"The Green Police claimed the men threw acid at the Black Shirts. They arrested the Dutchmen and the Jews and the owners of the ice cream parlor. The owners were blamed because they let Jews gather in their place. Afterward, the Green Police plastered posters all over Amsterdam saying they had put the young men in a prison camp. They thought it would discourage anybody who might have ideas."

"I bet that made the Amsterdammers mad," I said, emptying my cup. I would have liked another cookie, but I had two already. In Holland you get two cookies with two cups of coffee. The coffee we get now is ersatz but the cookies are delicious. But only cookie crumbs were left.

Mr. T leaned forward. "The workers were mad at the Nazis because they outlawed unions and made them work longer for less pay. The action of the Green Police was the last straw. All the workers and Commies hate Nazis. So, that Saturday in February, they called a strike. They asked everybody to stop working for one day to demonstrate their opposition to the Black Shirts."

"We read about the strike from an underground newspaper somebody brought to Hageveld. Did you actually see what happened?"

"I took the train to Amsterdam and got there when the strike was starting. Streetcars quit running. The harbor was deserted. The traffic stood still—except for the Police. The crowds in Dam Square held up signs. They were angry at the Nazis and they wanted them to know this is Holland, after all, not Germany. The workers felt safe demonstrating. They thought there was safety in numbers. With so many people demonstrating, the police couldn't arrest them all."

"The Germans were shocked. They couldn't believe their eyes. In Germany, strikes are against the law. There haven't had any since 1933. They thought the Dutch were subdued and wouldn't dare oppose them."

"What did the police do?" I asked.

"There was nothing they could do. They stood around like they do at a parade. The workers weren't doing anything but waving signs. The police believed they would demonstrate for a while and go home when they got tired of the strike. The protesters had called for a one-day strike. They planned to go back to work the next day."

"How did Seyss take that?" I asked.

Mr. T was getting stirred up. He wiped sweat off his high forehead with his handkerchief.

"Seyss was in Vienna. Rauter was in charge. He was outraged. He ordered the mayor to break the strike. The mayor couldn't stop the crowds gathering. He had some posters printed saying 'If everybody cooperates, we shall end today's confusion' and put them up where the people could see them. That didn't satisfy Rauter. He doesn't understand the Dutch. We're used to quiet government, not an iron hand. We obey the laws but we don't like to be bullied. Rauter didn't know what to do. He went into a rage, forbade demonstrations, and declared military rule, posted severe penalties. His actions added fuel to the fire. The strike spread. People in other cities—like Haarlem and Zaandam struck to show their support of the Amsterdammers."

"If the Germans had ignored them, they would have ended that afternoon. But SS troops rolled down the streets by truckloads. The people hung around to see what would happen. Rauter told the troops to fire into the crowds. Seven people were killed and forty wounded in Amsterdam. There were some injuries in Zaandam, too. I don't know how many.

"When the shooting started, the crowds melted like snow in summer. Nobody wanted to be shot. Now the Nazis are clamping down, afraid of another strike. They can't afford to have anything happen to damage war production."

Chapter 23

~❦~

Eric's Escape

April 10, 1941

Eric walks without limping. He's learned some Dutch words although he'll never get rid of the English accent. He's ready to go home.

Dad said "Tomorrow a guide is going to take some men out and Eric is going with them. You'll bring him to Leiden to meet the group. Then they'll go south by bicycle through Belgium, France and Spain. They won't have to pass the train inspectors."

"How can he cross the borders?"

"Eric has good papers. He'll pretend he can't speak. The guide will explain he has a brain injury and do the talking for him."

We were sorry he was leaving. Mother was worried. She said "We'll be waiting to hear from you."

Eric said, "Don't worry. If God saved me when my plane was shot down and after I landed in the tree, it must mean he still has some use for me. So I think he'll take care of me now. When I get to England I'll send you a message on Radio Orange. I'll say I saw fields with yellow tulips when I flew over Holland."

"Fine," said Dad. "But don't give any details about your escape or it might end the route for others who follow."

"Getting a message on the radio will be great," Gerard said. "If you get home we'll know you made it, but how will we know if you don't?"

Then he realized it would be impossible to let us know if he didn't get out. Mother smiled and we all laughed. Dad got identification papers from the town office. The forms looked official with the right stamps and his picture.

Dad managed to scrounge a bike, too. Since the Germans are stealing bikes and there aren't any new ones, getting it was like a miracle. The bike he got is rusty and the paint's worn off. But the frame is strong and the gears work. Of course the tires aren't guaranteed. When he leaves he can drop it anywhere. Somebody will take it.

Dad got it from our bicycle repairman, Joop. who put it together from old parts. Joop is a good mechanic and he can fix anything. But he has very peculiar hands. There is an extra finger on the outside of both hands. Whenever I see him, I pretend not to notice. He has extra little toes, too. I've never seen anybody else who has six fingers and toes. He has very wide feet but you don't really notice the extra toes because his shoes cover them.

Eric will take the 'new' bike tomorrow and I will use Frans' bike. I use it because I don't have my own. Both bikes are black—I wonder why? If they were different colors, it would be easier to tell them apart.

From Leiden, they'll go south. It shouldn't be hard to do in Holland. There are so many bikes here they look like swarms of mosquitoes. The Germans can't stop them all. Biking is the way we get around. The occupation forces took our cars and trucks. Even if you had a car, you couldn't drive it because you can't get benzine without coupons and only people like doctors and firemen get coupons.

Dad gave Eric some money. My job is to show him the way to Bakker's house—where I was coming from when I found him in the woods. Then I'll drop him off and come home.

When people are going to work and school, the crowds are biggest. Dad told me to be very careful when we get there and if the window shades are still down, we should just pass on by. Dad would like to bring him to Leiden, but it's safer for me. German soldiers don't bother schoolboys.

We will all miss Eric. Mother treats him like another son. I have to laugh at the way they talk together. She speaks in Dutch; he speaks English. But they seem to understand each other with a little help from the rest of us.

Tonight Mother made us all get down on our knees and recite the whole Rosary, praying Eric will have a safe trip. She believes prayers can end the war. And she is doing her share.

Our Trip

Well, Eric and I started out on the road to Leiden. Dad arranged for him to join a guide taking a group out of Holland by the usual way, going south to neutral Portugal. Eric was as eager to head home as a racehorse is to reach his stable when the race is over.

It was sunny when we started. We took raincoats and wore tennis shoes but carried our shoes in saddle bags to keep them dry. We were prepared for the rain we knew would be sure to come. It always rains in April.

Mother and Jo packed two lunches, a small one for both of us to eat on the way to Leiden and another for Eric to eat on the way down. I planned to come home after Eric met the guide. There were ham sandwiches on bread from baker Oudt, last fall's apples from the attic, a little shriveled but still sweet, and a pint of milk in a thermos. There was enough to eat before we got to Bakker's, in case they didn't serve coffee, and a lunch for Eric to take on the trip. The second lunch was bigger because it had to last.

Everybody said goodbye and hugged Eric. He's been here so long he seems like one of the boys, another brother. Mother was emotional and her eyes shone with tears. She was afraid he'd be caught. She thought our Bennebroek home was safer and didn't want him to leave.

Dad took out his billfold and gave Eric guilders. He also put small packages of tobacco and cigarette papers in a bag for him. Eric doesn't smoke, but Dad said "Use it for barter. People like tobacco more than anything."

Dad warned us "When you come near Bakker's house, check to see if their blinds are open. If the blinds are closed, don't go there." Everybody closes their shutters at night on account of the blackout and opens them in the morning if all is well. If there is any trouble, like a police visit, the people don't open them. So we use them to signal; if the blinds on a house are closed in the morning it's a good place to stay away from.

The Germans come at night when people are sleeping because it takes time to wake up and realize what is happening. The surprise gives the intruder the upper hand. There's no time to tell the neighbors about it, so we signal by leaving the shutters closed.

We rode on our *fiets*, (bikes). Eric's was taller than mine. Dad bought it from our bicycle repairman. It was put together from old parts and looked decrepit. But it was better that way. Old ones are not as conspicuous. I used the one Frans left behind when he went away to school. He didn't need it. It was not a bad bike, although sometimes the chain fell off. I should have it repaired, but it wasn't necessary. When the chain fell off, I would just stop and put it back on. It only takes a minute.

We started out early in a swarm of bicycles riding like the wind as the people hurried on their way to work. We all had to go the same speed—fast— or be hit by the ones that followed. As workers reached their destinations, they dropped out. After an hour, Eric and I were the only ones still riding on the path.

At the outskirts of Leiden, we came to a little grove. I decided to stop because there was bound to be a commotion at the house. It was coffee time so we reached into our lunch bags. There was no coffee, of course, but we drank cold milk and ate a couple of butter cookies. Jo put them in for a treat. She knows we love sweets.

When we got back on the bikes, I told Eric "We're almost there. I'll go ahead to see if it's safe. You go slower and stay behind. If everything is all right, I'll wave and you can come on. If not, I'll just ride on to the bridge over the canal at the end of the street. We'll stop there and feed crusts to the ducks. If anything is seriously wrong we'll need to go back home and tell the folks."

I didn't expect anything to go wrong, but I didn't want to take chances.

Bakker's house is on a long narrow street, in a neighborhood of brick houses in a row with small flower gardens in front with pink, white and blue hyacinths that are in bloom now and early red tulips with blossoms too big for their short stems. A bird sang from the top branch of a tall tree. Strong east winds pushed big white clouds west and rippled the grass. There never was a nicer day for Eric to start his journey.

When I was a half block away, a muddy truck came down the street and parked smack in front of the house. A man in a green uniform got out while another man stayed with the truck, watching the street. This was a disaster! The Green Police are neither regular German Army nor regular police, just the worst sort of Nazi troublemakers. I recognized their uniforms.

I was so shocked I could hardly breathe! How could this happen? Somebody must have told them! Maybe they suspected Mr. Bakker was in the resistance. They must have been watching him. And now they came to capture the escapees.

I kept riding down the street without slowing. My mind whirled like a windmill's sails in a strong wind. I didn't turn my head or glance behind. Eric followed. We rode straight on until the house, truck and soldier slid from sight.

At the little humped footbridge over the canal I waited for Eric. We got off our bikes and watched the scene of ducks and swans swimming and bobbing their heads fishing in peaceful water. Everything had changed. Our plans were shattered. Eric would not start home today.

I said "I don't know what's going on, but you saw the man in the green uniform. He's a German, and we don't want him to notice us."

"Like the Gestapo?"

"Not the SS. The Green Police, a different kind. But they aren't there to read meters."

"Now what shall we do?"

"I don't know. But we can not go near that house. We'll have to go back to Bennebroek and see what Dad says."

Eric was terribly disappointed. Giving up now—when he waited so long and was finally beginning was too much.

He considered a moment, "Maybe the soldier coming was just a coincidence."

"That's no coincidence," I said. "That was an incident! Luckily we saw the man in his green uniform."

"Let's stick around. See if they go away. Then we'll go back and see what happened."

"No, that was a warning sent from God."

"Let's wait a little while and see. Maybe they'll go away. Maybe something will turn up."

"Something will turn up all right—another German truck and more police."

"I can't go back now." Eric said. "I have to start. I'll go by myself. I'm all set. I have food and money and a bike to ride on. The Belgians will help me get to France. They don't like the Nazis anymore than you do."

"Neither do the French, but how can we reach the Resistance?"

"It's been done."

"But you'd never make it. You don't have enough money; you don't know the way and you can't speak the language. Even if I went with you,

I wouldn't give a *dubbeltje* (dime) for our chances. We could probably get to Belgium and through to the French border, but how could we cross into France without help? We'd be arrested because we don't have a travel pass. And since you're not in uniform, they'd shoot you for a spy."

"I'll travel at night and hide in the mountains. The French partisans would help."

"How? The German army looks for them all over and they can't find them."

"I don't know. But I have to start. I don't want to go back."

"It's a long way south. I don't even know how far it is from Belgium to Spain. From here to Belgium must be a good many kilometers. And that's the shortest distance. France is huge and Spain is humongous. And you have to cross the Pyrenees. You'd get lost in the high mountains."

"Call your Dad. Maybe he can set up another plan."

"That's another detail. We can't call home. If the Germans knew the meeting place, they probably know the escape plan. They listen on telephones. They'll be looking for calls from Leiden. Calling the house right now would put the family in danger. After you crashed behind our house, they suspected us of hiding you. They've been keeping an eye out for the British pilot. Germans are intelligent and very thorough. They'll never give up until."

"I'll go alone," Eric said. "I can't sit here. England needs pilots. And with a little luck, I'll get back home."

It would not be safe. He needed a guide who spoke French. It would not even be safe with someone who was green as new grass. But an idea came to mind. I remembered that Steve van den Berg telling me some students escaped going north, leaving through the port of Delfzyl.

Steve's home is in Leiden. He finished Hageveld last year and enrolled in the university here. He's living at home now because when the students demonstrated against firing Jewish professors, Seyss Inquart closed the Universities.

Steve had said there was a way of going out through Delfzyl. It was a shorter trip than going south to Spain and Portugal.

I thought a minute and told Eric "There is another way—through Delfzyl. A factory there makes chemicals the Swedes need to make steel. Dutch freighters sail from Delfzyl to Sweden to bring it to the steel mills. A friend at school told me some students got on a freighter in Delfzyl and sailed to Stockholm. Sweden is neutral. If you could get to Sweden on a Dutch freighter, you could go to your embassy there and they would put you on a plane to fly to England.

This sounds like the way to go, I thought. Steve lives in Leiden. I'll call him and ask how we can get to Delfzyl."

Eric agreed. He wanted to go home so badly, he was up for anything. If I told him to swim, I think he would put on trunks.

We rode to the center of Leiden and found a pay phone. You have to use tokens in pay phones. Dutch coins are too tiny to operate them. Luckily I had a few tokens in my pocket. I looked up Steve's number for the operator. I was lucky again. Steve answered the phone.

"Steve, this is Pim." I said. "I'm in Leiden and I'd like to see you. Could we possibly get together?"

"Sure. I'm not busy. I'd like seeing you. Where are you?

"We're by the windmill. How far are you?"

"Only a couple of blocks—there's a coffee shop across from the windmill. I'll meet you there in ten or fifteen minutes."

"Great! See you then."

Leiden's windmill was so big and so close we couldn't miss it. And the coffee shop was right across the street. It was a typical café—dark paneling and windows facing us. We saw customers sitting around sturdy wooden tables. A parrot with bright red and green feathers perched over the door. The parrot was a talker. When we came in he squawked in a loud voice "*Sluit de deur.*" (Shut the door!) The guys in the café looked up at the bird and laughed.

Eric sat down at a table by the window. I went to the counter to get two cups of ersatz. I hated to spend money for the awful stuff but we couldn't take a table without buying something. We'd feel too conspicuous standing outside.

Eric was looking out the window at the enormous mill with huge sails turning in the wind. "What a sight!" he said. "Right in the middle of town. And nobody is paying the least attention. They don't even look at it!"

"It's no big deal," I said. "The windmill's been there for centuries; everybody in Leiden is used to it."

We waited while our coffee cooled, looking around. The young men at another table were telling jokes. The bad tempered parrot was picking at his gaudy feathers. The coffee tasted terrible but it was hot. In a few minutes Steve came in and joined us.

I introduced Eric, speaking softly. The other customers glanced at us and went on talking and laughing loudly at some private joke.

"This is Eric." I told Steve. "He wants to leave. This morning we came to meet a guide. But the Green Police were there first,"

"No! What happened? Did they see you? What did you do?"

"We didn't stop. Just rode on by."

Eric said in English. "We were hoping you would help so we called you."

I looked at the young guys at the other table to see if anybody noticed. They didn't appear to be listening. So I leaned forward and rested my chin on my hand, fingers over my lips and frowned at Eric. I wanted him to speak Dutch or keep quiet. It didn't look like any officials were in the place. But you have to look out. You can talk Dutch or Italian or French or Flemish. Nobody finds German unusual. But you can't speak English!

Steve said "You were lucky and you did the right thing. I would have made myself scarce, too. Anybody would. Since they closed the University, they ordered students to register and serve in Germany. The churches told us not to so most of us are refusing. I'm watching out for the police so they won't catch me."

"Last year you told me some students from Leiden University left from Delfzyl on a Dutch freighter. I wonder if Eric couldn't get out like that."

"It's worth a try. If he can get on a ship to Sweden he'll be home free."

"But we don't know how to get to Delfzyl. There aren't any signs and we can't wander around Holland like lost souls asking for directions. I know it's a port up north in Groningen. But you've been there. And your Aunt Katrina lives there. So you must know. Can you tell us? I've never been outside of North Holland."

Steven is slim and dark haired, with long legs. He's quite ordinary looking until he smiles. Then his face lights up. He gives an impression of confidence, like a man who knows his way around. He's older than I am and wasn't in my class at seminary, but sometimes when we walked around the school, we bumped into each other and talked.

"Heemskerk, you amaze me," he said. "Such bright ideas! Is Eric the only one who wants to go?"

"There was a guide but we can't get in touch with him. We don't know where the others are. So all I know is Eric. If he gets to Delfzyl on a freighter to Sweden, he can go to the British embassy there. They'll fly him to England. But we need a guide to get to the port."

"Getting to Delfzyl isn't hard. I'll guide you. But we'll need money to eat on the way. How many guilders do we have?"

We added our money. Eric had the thirty guilders Dad gave him, Steven had fifteen. I had five and change. Fifty guilders. Was that enough for three?

"It's not much," Steve said. "But it will have to do. When we get to Delfzyl, Aunt Katrina will feed us and give us a bed. And he can stow away on a Dutch freighter. We can get to Delfzyl. But sneaking on a freighter under the eyes of the Germans will be the hard part—the trick of the year."

Eric said, "We're wasting time. Let's go while the sun is shining!"

Mother always told me to use the WC before we left home. Since one was available in the coffee shop, I followed her advice. When I came back to the table there was no more discussion. Steve and Eric, between them had settled things.

But I had misgivings. What would Dad think about me going without asking him? On the other hand it was logical to leave. What else could we do?

Eric was happy as a pig in a puddle. When plan A doesn't work, you have to go to plan B. We would go north instead of South. A slight change. Going back to Bennebroek would get us nowhere. Eric was ready. Steve would lead us. Eric would start his journey tonight.

We left the café. When we opened the door, the parrot squawked "*Sluit de deur.*" Everybody in the café laughed at the raucous parrot who thinks he is in charge of closing the door. It was the only phrase we heard him speak.

The three of us strode back to the pay phone in the square, heads high, feeling better. When we met Steve, we were tense, uncertain. With Steve we had confidence.

He called his brother, Kees. "I'm taking a bike trip with friends from Hageveld. I might see Aunt Claire. I'll be back in a week. Tell Moo and Pa. I'm on vacation and I'll tell you all about it then.

"Let's get moving," Eric said, "Daylight's wasting." We got on our bikes and headed for the road north.

When we left Leiden, the sky was vivid blue. But the weather is moody in Holland. The sun shines to get us out. But it didn't keep being sunny. The wind shifted; dark clouds blew overhead. And rain fell in buckets.

At first we were in a swarm of bikes. I had to let my parents know where we were going. But phone calls might be monitored. I didn't want the Germans to know about our trip. Then I thought of Uncle Piet. He sees Dad a lot. He wouldn't mind stopping for coffee at the house. I called him and said, "When you see Dad, tell him I'm taking a bike trip with friends and I'll be home Saturday or Sunday so I can go back to Hageveld on time."

Uncle Piet said he would pass my message to Dad and told me to have a good time. Afterward, I felt better. I didn't know what Dad would think. Were we doing the right thing? I couldn't tell him where we were going. All I could say was we were safe. Dad would figure it out. At least he would know we were all right.

In the rain, traffic melted away. We kept on, hoping the thick dark clouds would move out to sea and let the sun show. Our raincoats and hats did the best they could to keep us dry, but our feet and hands and faces were wet as the crows huddled on the fences. It rained on and off all afternoon.

Hardly any cars passed. Dutch people can't get much benzene, so there aren't many vehicles on the road. We saw a big draft horse pulling a wagon and an occasional civilian vehicle.

Later an army convoy overtook us and a truck at a time swept by. Each one gave us a bath as it splashed through the puddles. The caravan went on forever. The muddy water annoyed us so we pulled off the path and waited under a bridge for the parade to end. They were German trucks but they were on their way north and didn't ask us where we were going. We were only kids on bikes. If they stopped for every bike they'd never get where they were going.

While we waited under the bridge, Steve said, "Sooner or later we'll come to a checkpoint. What will we say when they ask where we're going?"

"Something logical—something they won't question," I said.

"What would they believe? We all have to say the same thing," said Eric.

"In North Holland, we'll say we are going to Dad's farm at Koegras," I said, "but after we pass that and keep going north, I haven't the faintest."

Steve had the solution. "We'll say we're going to work on the Atlantic Wall."

Hitler is building an enormous wall around Europe from the North Sea along the Atlantic Coast all the way South to the Mediterranean to protect Europe from a British invasion. The Atlantic Wall is unbelievably humongous. Nobody knows how many men are working on it or their locations.

It's so long even the Germans can't keep track of it. If we tell them we're going to work on the wall, they'll have to believe us because so many thousands of laborers are going to be working on the wall in so many places.

"Where should we say we are headed?"

"Emden," said Steve. "We'll say we're going to Emden because we're going in that direction and it's where the wall starts."

If we went south they'd be suspicious we're trying to leave because escapees go south through Belgium and France. But going north wasn't a known escape route. We wore work clothes like wall builders or ditch diggers or laborers.

"Makes sense to me. It's the perfect reason to travel."

"Remember the good news, bad news jokes?" I asked.

"Sure. What's the bad news?" Eric asked.

"You can't speak Dutch,"

"Details, details." Eric said. "I'll fake it. What's the good news?"

"The Germans can't speak it either."

"Just say *ja* or *nee,* (yes or no) if anybody questions you," Steve told him. "If they keep on asking, look confused and say, *"Ik weet 't niet."* (I don't know).

"I'll tell them you fell during the war and hit your head. And you can only say a few words."

It's a true story as far as the fall during the war goes. He made up the part about why Eric can't talk. Steve is another Aesop, full of fables.

The soggy paths and drippy tree branches made riding uncomfortable. Every kilometer took us farther from home. As we rode through the rain, I started to worry. I wondered how we could smuggle Eric on a Dutch freighter. Wouldn't boats be guarded by German soldiers? How could he get past them? How could we get him on the ship?

I figured that was the sticker. If we could get him on the ship, it would take him to Stockholm and from there the British embassy would fly him to England.

When the clouds cleared and the rain stopped I felt things were getting better. We rode in order. Steven first, then Eric and I brought up the rear.

Eric said, "I'm thinking of an old song. 'It's a Long Way to Tipperary'."

"You can sing if you have enough breath," said Steve. "But not in English."

As the sun went down, we looked for a place to sleep. We had to get off the path. We were tired and cold and hungry. We were the only riders on the dark road. We wanted a warm place to sleep. But we didn't see any inns. And we didn't dare go up to a strange house. We might walk into a place filled with Germans or where sympathizers were staying.

This was dairy country. On either side of the road were fields where cows huddled together. Creeks and rivers flowed through them. There were more cows than people. Some were black and white. They were Holsteins. There were some red and white cows, too but their colors didn't show in the dark.

We noticed a thatched building standing by itself in a chilly field, with haystacks standing around. It was not a house where people lived or a cow barn. It looked like an empty stone shed.

"Let's see if we can get in that little coop," Steve said. "We can't ride much longer."

We lifted our bikes over the fence around the field and pushed them across the bumpy pasture. I reached the little building first and tried the latch, praying it was unlocked. God had big ears and he heard me because the door opened easily, hinges creaking. We went in and carried in our bikes. Bikes are scarce and we didn't want them stolen. Without them, we'd be lost.

The thatched-roof shed held old dented pails, milk-cans and rusty tools. A pole ladder leaned against the wall, the way to the loft. When we closed the door it was almost pitch dark. But we didn't care. We were glad to be under a roof. We climbed the shaky ladder. Up in the loft it was lighter because there was a big opening, a window the farmer used to bring hay to store. A pale moon shone, intermittently covered by wisps of clouds. There was nothing except old hay left from winter.

"What's for supper?" Steve said.

"Not much."

Steve prayed, "For what we are about to receive we thank you, Lord." I wish I could say the food miraculously expanded like the loaves and fishes in the Bible, but it didn't. There were still a few small apples, dry bread crusts, broken cookies and a little milk. Enough to satisfy us but nothing over.

The moon was all the light we had but our eyes grew used to the dimness and it was enough. We tried to pile some hay in place to make beds but the hay was stiff and matted. It was no use. We were exhausted. We lay down in the hay with our clothes on. I hate spiders. I hoped there were no spiders in the hay.

Eric said, "That song is still going round in my head." And he started singing:

"It's a long way to Tipperary; it's a long way to go,
"It's a long way to Tipperary, to the sweetest girl I know."

The music was sad. It sounded Irish. I wondered where Tipperary was, but I was too tired to care. I fell asleep.

The next morning I heard cows mooing, sounding like they were complaining. I wondered where the sound came from and why there was hay in my bed. Then I awoke. It was beginning to get light. We looked at each other. I thought we should leave before the farmer came to do the milking. Steve and Eric and I climbed down the ladder and left the shed. There was a tank full of rain water outside and we used that to rinse our hands. There were some bushes and trees in the pasture and we took advantage of them, too.

Eric said, "A regular convenience, as good as you could want."

A brown-eyed cow was cropping grass in the field. The cow had everything she needed—water to drink and grass to eat. But we were hungry and thirsty.

Steve looked at the gentle animal and asked, "Does anyone know how to milk a cow?"

None of us ever milked a cow, but I'd seen Ton do it. It didn't seem hard. So I got an old dinged pail and placed it on the grass where she was munching. Then I squeezed and pulled on two big soft udders. The little cow moved away. She didn't like my effort. Steve pulled handfuls of fresh grass and held it out to her. That got her attention. She reached out with her tongue and swallowed a mouthful. He and Eric fed her more grass and while she ate, I tried to get into position to milk her. Milking looks simple but it's a skill. It took a few tries before I managed to get anything in the pail. When I collected about a quarter of a liter, we poured some in our empty jars and drank it warm. Cows give a lot of milk, so we didn't think what we stole would be missed. The cow didn't seem to mind but if she did, she couldn't tell.

An orange kitten mewed to ask for a share. I squeezed a stream in the kitten's direction. It was cute to see how she caught it in her mouth. When we finished our milk I rinsed the pail and put it in the shed. Then I gave the cow a pat on her shoulder to thank her. She mooed to show her appreciation.

We left before anyone came to milk the cows.

"How far do you think we traveled yesterday?" Eric asked.

Steve said, "I don't know where this is but we're still in North Holland. We haven't crossed the Afsluitdijk."

This is the huge concrete dike built to connect the province of North Holland with the province of Friesland. It could not be too far from where we were.

A brilliant sun rose in the clear blue sky. Our path ran beside a smooth flowing canal reflecting the world like a wavy mirror. We came to a village and smelled the wonderful aroma of fresh baked bread. "Look," Eric said, "A bakery."

The baker was a big man with red cheeks and a big apron over his stomach. He had a round bald spot in the hair on top of his head like a monks' tonsure. He smiled at us and asked, "Where are you boys from?"

"Heemstede," I said.

Steve said, "Leiden."

Eric didn't know what to say. He thought for a minute and then he said the first thing to come to his head—"Amsterdam." Luckily there were no Germans standing there to wonder why it took so long for him to answer. I'll tell him to say Lisse next time, because that's where the license on his bike came from.

"We're on vacation," Steve said.

I asked the baker "How much is a loaf of bread?"

He pointed to the price on the glass case. Brown bread is a guilder." That wasn't too much.

We got three loaves of warm bread. "Wait," he said and gave us each a pat of butter on a cardboard chip. "You look hungry. Like some ersatz too?"

"Thanks," we said, so grateful for the breakfast. He seemed happy with our small transaction, and since he gave us butter, I gave him a little bag of home-grown tobacco and some cigarette papers.

He looked and said. "It doesn't look like Dutch tobacco. What kind is it?"

"It's a mixture. Dutch tobacco is mild but it doesn't burn well so he added some Belgian leaves to make it burn better."

"Thank you," he said. Tobacco is expensive."

We sat together at a little table in the back of the store and ate our bread with butter that melted as soon as it touched the knife. It was *heerlijk*. When we left the bakery we saw another store across the street. Since the baker sold us bread without coupons, I asked the smiling woman behind the counter if she would trade a bag of tobacco for some Gouda cheese. She agreed to trade a wedge of young cheese for tobacco. We added a few guilders.

Buying without coupons is strictly *verboten*. They call it black marketing and apply a hefty penalty for this to both the buyer and the seller. But fair exchange is no theft. And since buyers and sellers would both be penalized for breaking the rules, neither could tell.

The Nazis invaded our country, stole everything we had and sent it to Germany. They instituted rationing of our food and now they punish us for selling our own food without paper coupons. They make laws and when we can, we break them.

The Second Day

It was a perfect day. We traveled in a flock of bikers, passed a checkpoint without any fuss and stayed on the road going north.

After a good night's sleep and a bright morning, we made good time. We felt optimistic that today would finish our trip and reach Delfzyl. Nobody was paying any attention to us. We thought we would get Eric on a freighter and head home.

Pedaling made us hungry. We stopped beside a bridge over a canal to finish our bread and cheese and rest. My legs chafed. I wasn't used to riding so long. I'm sure Eric and Steve felt the same. But they didn't complain so I didn't—we just kept on riding and looking at the scenery.

In the middle of the day we saw a small café. Steve and Eric bought ersatz coffee and I had imitation tea with milk. A friendly couple ran the café and gave us each a cookie. They must have been sorry for us. We were such a mess. We took the time and used their bathroom, to tidy up. I washed but I didn't have a comb. I could only run my fingers through my hair.

After we started out again, big clouds blew across the sun and the wind was chilly. But we were comfortable in our coats and sweaters.

Jagged lightning flashed in the distance as we came to the little town of Roesbeek. We kept some distance between us. Steve went first and Eric next. I followed close enough to keep them in sight in the swarm of bikes. In the center of the town we saw six or seven German trucks parked and about twenty troops standing around. There was a huge crowd in the middle of the road. They stood around tense, silent, waiting.

On the left side of the road was an old stone town hall. On the right side there was a good sized restaurant of rose colored brick. Throngs filled the road between the buildings. When we got close we saw six men tied to posts in front of the town hall. Behind them, sandbags were heaped against the wall. We took in the scene at a glance. The men were hostages who were going to be shot to punish the town for sabotage. The townspeople were witnesses.

Nazi soldiers wearing tailored green uniforms and tall black boots were standing on the sidewalk in front of the hostages holding rifles at their sides. Grim-faced townspeople looked helplessly at the drama staged by the Germans.

The SS Commander in charge spoke in German. Most everybody in Holland can understand German now. In a loud voice, he announced, "Last week saboteurs blew up the railroad bridge east of town. We took six hostages from the town and warned you that unless the criminals came forward, the hostages would be shot. The perpetrators did not surrender. Therefore, on the order of the Reichs Kommandant, according to the law, the hostages will be executed. This is a warning. We won't be trifled with. Today only the hostages will be shot. If it occurs again, we will kill every man from eighteen to fifty and burn the town. If anyone wants to confess, speak now or we will shoot the hostages.

Steve and Eric and I looked at each other. We could not believe the brazen effrontery of the *moffen*. They were going to shoot six innocent men—they admitted it themselves. And they wanted witnesses?

The soldiers faced the hostages who were standing bravely holding up their heads. Then an amazing thing happened. A wiry old man stepped up to the SS captain. He could not have been a saboteur. He didn't look like he had enough strength to fasten explosives under a bridge and blow it up. What did he want with the commander?

He spoke clearly and with authority. "These men are not guilty. They had no part in any sabotage. Let them go."

The crowd began to raise their voices. "Let the hostages go! Don't shoot them. They didn't do anything. They aren't guilty. Let them go!"

The people echoed him, protesting loudly. You couldn't hear every word, but you couldn't miss what they meant. The people were angry, ready to mutiny. The soldiers looked uneasy. They had guns, but the protesters greatly outnumbered them. They realized the soldiers could not shoot them all.

The old man held up his hands to quiet the crowd. He continued, looking directly at the German commander. "If you shoot these men, you will be committing a grave injustice. The people of Holland will not forgive you. These men are not saboteurs. Men do not destroy bridges in their own back yards. The men who blew up the bridge left a long time ago. If you try to stop sabotage by killing innocent men, you are not thinking clearly. This will make the people angry and increase sabotage because you didn't catch the guilty men. The saboteurs are still out there."

"If you must kill somebody, kill me."

The Captain was the picture of arrogance. He tightened the corners of his lips in an expression of righteous satisfaction. If he felt threatened by the crowd, it did not show. He showed his power, indifferent to the crowd and their hatred. "You are only one man. I have orders to shoot six. Which man will you die for?"

"Listen to me. Do not commit this injustice. Hollanders will not forget this."

The Captain said, "I will let one of the hostages go in exchange for you. Choose who you will die for."

The old man persisted. "I am an *advocaat*. There is no need for *advocaaten* any more because Germans disregard our laws which Seyss Inquart promised to protect. I will not be missed. But these men are needed. Adrian van Dyck, here, is the last doctor in town. He takes care of everybody who is sick. He even cared for one of your soldiers. Since the invasion, there is a shortage of doctors."

The Captain said, "If that is your decision, I will let the doctor go."

"Do not do this terrible thing. Take everything we have, but spare our lives. Have Germans changed from a civilized people and become so cruel they kill innocent men? Hitler wants Holland to join his Reich. Killing every man, woman and child will not win us. Only kindness can change our minds."

The Captain did not want to listen any more. His patience was gone. He would not wait. He said to the squad, "Free the doctor and tie the old man to the post."

The soldiers cut the rope and let the doctor go. They took more rope and bound the *advocaat* to the post. Their heads were high. Their faces emotionless. The doctor looked dazed. When he was released he could not stand so friends supported him. The soldiers moved back and stood in a line facing the hostages, with their weapons at the ready. I thought of Herod slaying the Innocents and Pilate washing his hands.

The soldiers seemed to shrug. They were only following orders, their stance implied. At the Captain's command, they raised their rifles. He barked '*Feuer!*' and the loud crack of guns split the air. The crowd watched the hostages still tied to the posts slump in death.

Then a deep bass voice began to sing, "*Ik heb u lief, My Nederland.*" The Dutch anthem, 'I love you, my Netherlands.' Other voices joined in singing.

> "*Waar de blanke top der duinen,*
> *Schittered in de zonnegloed,*
> *En de Noord Zee vriend'lijk bruisend*
> *Neerland's smalle kust begroet*
> *Juich ik op het vlakke strand*
> *Ik heb u lief mijn Nederland.*"*

The Commandant walked to his long black car, ignoring the crowd. The red, white and black swastikas on the car's fenders whipped in the breeze.

The Germans knew they had done a terrible thing. As the soldiers walked away, there was no swagger in their steps. They climbed in their trucks and left. People surrounded the fallen men, untied them from the posts and carried them away. It was over. But the bullets that missed the sandbags against the wall, left fresh gouges in the stone.

"How could this happen in Holland?" I asked.

"How long can this go on?" Steven wondered.

"Until the war is over," Eric said.

After the war the Germans will want to forget this outrage. But we will remember. The gouges in the stone of the town hall mark the deaths of six innocent men.

An English translation—of *"Ik Heb U Lief, Mijn Nederland."*

> *Where the white tops of the dunes,*
> *Glitter in the shining sun*
> *And the North Sea's friendly breeze*
> *Greets Holland's coast,*
> *Shout I on the narrow strand,*
> *I love you, my Netherlands.*

The Joyless Night

As we left Roesbeek, the storm that had been threatening hit with force. Bolts of lightning split the sky. Thunder boomed. It seemed God was angry at the senseless killing. We were tired from riding, cold as herring in the North Sea, empty as a pail with a hole in the bottom. I could scarcely keep riding. I wanted food and warmth and a place to rest. I was lost, lonely and sick for home.

But the storm stopped and we reached a town. It appeared we were the only ones awake. The shutters were closed on the windows of the houses and stores were not open, not even a kroeg or a roadside café. We were riding down a business street where all the buildings were dark. In the sky, only the moon and distant stars shed a pale light. It was almost curfew, when day and night meet.

Then we saw a tiny blade of light between a door and its frame. We had to get inside soon. Steve knocked on the locked door. Steve rapped again harder. We could hear movement inside and someone came to the window. We pressed our faces against the glass. It was only a drugstore but we thought if they let us go in, we might get something to eat—licorice or cough drops or peppermints. I was so hungry I would eat toothpaste.

A young woman moved the edge of the blind and looked out at us. She pointed at the sign GESLOTEN, (closed) printed in big black letters. I nodded to show I understood. We had to speak to her. Steve flashed a big-toothed smile and she smiled back. Then, thank goodness, she cracked open the door. "Sorry. It is past closing. I must go."

"Please," said Steven. "We came a long way today. We need a room to sleep. Can you help us? Do you know any place where we can stay tonight?"

"There's an empty building behind the store," she said. "It's only a storage shed but you can stay there if you want. Where did you come from?"

"From Roesbeek," said Steven, "where the Germans shot six hostages."

"So, they did it. Those bastards. We wrote petitions and letters to the Commandant and Rauter and Seyss-Inquart. Everybody begged them to listen but the Germans mean to show us they are the bosses," she said. "The Resistance blew up a railroad bridge last week. The Germans are furious—they wanted to find the men who did it. So they took men in the town hostage. But nobody would or could come forward. If someone had confessed they would have tortured him to find out who is in the Resistance."

"They tied the hostages to posts and shot them in front of the town hall with the whole town watching."

"How terrible! They think terrorizing us will put a stop to our opposition. It won't work. Their actions only make things worse. You'd better go before anybody sees you. Go straight down the street to the intersection, turn right at the corner. Go down a little way and turn right again at the alley. I'll meet you in back of this building."

We were too tired to walk the rest of the way. But we knew she could not allow us to go in the store after closing. So we went around and found the dark building behind the store. The young woman opened the gate to the alley and we entered through a heavy old wood-plank door. In the shed, a bulb hung from the ceiling which made a feeble attempt to light the room but wasn't very successful.

"I'll get you something to eat," she said and left us. We looked around and saw nothing. The shed was as bare as if a cyclone had passed through. There were no chairs, no beds and not even any blankets. But behind a door in the corner, there was a little W.C. with a toilet and sink. We took turns using it. Then the girl came back carrying a crumpled bag of ham sandwiches, a thermos of ersatz coffee and a white stoneware pitcher with a half cup of milk for our coffee.

"The coffee was left from lunch," she said. "It's not fresh but I heated it so it's nice and hot.

"It's wonderful," Eric said.

"We're hungry enough to eat horses." Steve said.

"We haven't had anything since noon," I added.

We gobbled the sandwiches and drank every drop of coffee. It tasted delicious. We were starving. Steve remembered his manners and introduced us. "This is Eric and this is Pim and I'm Steve."

"I'm Nicole. I'm glad to meet you. I'm sorry the room is so bare."

"Nicole, you are a guardian angel," Steve said. We all fell in love with her. She was about eighteen or nineteen. She smiled and showed her cheeks had dimples. Her eyes were brown and her hair the color of ripe wheat.

Eric wanted to express his gratitude. He spoke English when he said "Thank you for helping us."

"*T is niks.* But you are English," she said in surprise. It dawned on her that he must be a diver, which is what we call fugitives. But she did not follow up by asking Eric where he came from or how he got here. She didn't want to know. She might be in the underground but I didn't ask that either.

I said, "Nicole, we want to give you something. We don't have a lot of money but we do have tobacco." I handed her the last two packages.

"*T is niks,*" she said again. "You don't have to pay me. But thank you for the tobacco—it's better than money now. I can trade with it.

We told her about the hostages and the *advocaat.* She knew the doctor and one of the men who were shot. Then she left, apologizing because she didn't have a better place to offer us. She picked up the bag and the coffee pot—the things she had brought in with her. She said she would bring breakfast in the morning.

We felt better. We were grateful to be in a shelter, under a roof.

I said, "Last night we slept in a hayshed; tonight we are in a storage shed. Where will we sleep tomorrow—in a shack?"

"In Delfzyl, we'll have beds," Steve said.

"I might be on the boat going to Sweden," Eric said "or just getting on."

The threadbare carpet that covered the floor of the shed might have been a nice Persian rug once, but its pattern was faded and its surface flat as canvas. It was all we had to lie on. We bundled up our jackets to make pillows for our heads and covered ourselves with our rain coats. Since drinking hot coffee and eating sandwiches we were warming up a little. Eric told Steve, "So far we have been lucky," he said. We even passed German checkpoints but they didn't stop us."

Steve said, "But we aren't there yet. And if anybody told me last week that I would be riding a bicycle in the rain and sleeping in empty buildings, living on bread and water, I' d have thought they were *gek* (crazy)."

"Don't forget the milk," I said, half asleep.

"We were luckier than the hostages," Eric said. "But why were they shot? For nothing? And we survived."

"I don't know," Steve said. "The war makes people crazy."

I thought of my parents. Were they worried? and Eric's parents. He was missing for months. They knew his plane had crashed and hoped he was in a POW camp. But for all they knew, he might be dead. I prayed Eric would get home safely, but before I could finish I fell asleep.

In the morning I woke in the dark room and remembered where we were. Steve opened the door that led to the store. A tiny garden bordered the flagstone walk between the shed and the back of the store. Short-stemmed Red Emperor tulips were in bloom. A robin sang his morning song, pecking in the dirt. Nicole brought us a pot of tea and a tray of cheese and buns. We ate it all and felt so grateful. I wanted to give her a few last guilders, but she would not take our money.

She said "*T is niks*" and I could only thank her.

We picked up everything, even the few scattered crumbs and left no sign anybody had slept there. Then we washed up as well as we could in the W.C. and said goodbye to Nicole.

As we rode away, the wind was pushing whipped cream clouds across the sky. I could see a patch of blue. In Holland we say that if enough blue shows between the clouds to make a pair of britches, the sky will clear. I hoped so. We had our share of rain.

Delfzyl

Next we got on our bikes, went down the alley and had some uncomfortable hours. If you haven't been riding on a bicycle for three days you might not realize how the seat chafes. But Steve and Eric didn't complain so I kept my *zaniking* (complaining) to myself.

At nine we saw a bakery with a sign that proclaimed "Banket" in gold letters. It was not a banket bakery any more. They had no sweet cookies or butter-frosted cakes or apple tarts in the window as they must have before the war. Now there was only bread. We each got a mug of ersatz coffee and a warm bun. They tasted good but we spent our last guilders. I was glad Nicole had refused our money as we had nothing left to pay.

The bicycle path we rode on was crossed by bumpy roots and muddy holes we had to go around. The scenery here was different from North Holland. The windmills were little, bright colored whip mills, not like our big stone mills in North Holland. They are too small for living quarters. The miller's family must live in the houses close by.

Gray and white gulls were dipping and turning and gliding overhead and yelling with shrill voices, so aggressive that if we were eating food, they would have snatched it from our hands. Maybe they thought we would throw them scraps of food. The road we were following was close to the North Sea. We could not see the water but we could smell the salty sea. There was some bicycle traffic and a few trucks hurried by. They didn't pay any attention to us. We were too ordinary.

Shortly after eating, we saw an army truck parked on the side of the road. We didn't think about it. We had nothing to hide. We were almost to Delfzyl. But when we came up to the truck, two soldiers jumped out. "Show your documents," a strong young trooper said.

Steve handed them his well-worn card with his picture on it. They took it and asked him, "You are from Leiden? That is in the tulip district. What are you doing so far from home?"

"I'm going to work," he said. "They closed the University so I have to find a job. I thought I'd look at working on the wall."

"That is good. Here we have plenty of work. And you," he said to Eric, "Are you from Leiden, too?"

"Nee," said Eric, as instructed.

"Where are you from?" he asked as he took the paper from Eric's hand. Then he read "Bennebroek. Are you looking for work, too?"

"Ya," he said.

Then the soldier took my identification card. "You are from Bennebroek. But you're only fourteen. You aren't old enough for working on the wall. Where do you go to school?"

"I go to Hageveld," I said. "I'm on Easter vacation. I don't go back to school until next week."

The man seemed satisfied by our answers. But he had another question for Eric. "Where did you get those boots?" he asked. Eric was wearing his English boots because he had exceptionally long feet and the boots the cobbler made weren't as comfortable. Dad had tried to age them by smearing them in mud and we had gone through enough rain to soak them out of shape. They still looked English to the trooper, though.

Eric didn't answer. I don't know if he understood the question.

Then Steve said, "He was hurt in the war. He can only say *ya* or *nee*. The doctor says he must learn to speak again. But if you talk slow he can understand what you say."

"Is that so?" the trooper said. "Things like that happen in the war. I got hit in the head once myself, but it didn't affect me." Just then a big dark cloud came over us and the wind increased and blew the trees around. I heard a crack like a branch breaking off a forest giant.

"Go," I thought urgently. "Don't stand around talking to us." He must have had the same idea or caught it when it flew from my mind.

"Good luck," he said loudly enough to be heard over the sound of the wind. "They can use all the help they can get. It takes a lot of men to build a wall around the Atlantic. Just keep on this road and you'll come to the right place. Tell them Kurt Schneider sent you." The soldiers got back in the truck. The storm was coming toward us fast.

We rode on toward Delfzijl against strong wind and cold rain, miserably wet and uncomfortable. It was like trying to swim against the tide. Even our shoes were full of water as we pedaled on. After a while the rain stopped and the wind stilled. It was a friendly storm. It made the troops leave. And we survived.

Chapter 24

Delfzyl

It was noon when we reached Delfzyl. We were tired—worn out from riding. We were dirty from riding through showers that soaked our clothes but failed to clean them. We were so hungry. We couldn't remember eating warm food or a good meal.

Steve said, "I hope I remember the way to Aunt Katrina's."

"Well, you have the address," I told him. My mother told us "If you don't know, ask. You have a good Dutch mouth." I almost said that although it wasn't polite. But Steve had no problem finding Aunt Katrina's place.

The house was set on a little street of tidy homes and neat lawns. Pink tulips stood guard in front. The brick walls were painted white and the roof was glazed blue tile. It was smaller but in color it resembled our house in Bennebroek. It had a Dutch half door and when we knocked; his aunt opened the top half to see who was there.

I didn't see myself in a mirror so I don't know how I looked. It couldn't have been much better than Eric and Steve. They resembled scarecrows that had been standing too long in the field. In spite of our appearance, Aunt Katrina recognized her nephew and opened the bottom of the divided door to let us come in her kitchen.

"Come in," she said. "But first put your bikes in the shed so they'll be safe."

When she saw the dirt we tracked on her white tile floor she must have cringed, but she hugged Steve and kissed him on both cheeks. "Steve," she said. *"Hoe gat't met U?* (How are you?)

Steve said. "Aunt Katrina, I'd like you to meet my friends. This is Eric Johnson and Pim Heemskerk. Pim is from Hageveld. And Eric dropped from the sky. We came all the way from Leiden."

She said 'Hallo' to us and we shook hands all around. Dutch people always shake hands when they meet. It is a necessary ritual. If the sky fell on Holland and everybody came out to see what was going on, they would all shake hands before they tried to put it back up.

"Has something happened in Leiden?"

"Not recently. Nothing you don't know about. We came on account of Eric. He's a flyer. His plane was shot down and landed in a tree behind Pim's house."

Aunt Katrina smiled and said, "And you weren't killed? You are all right? How did that happen?"

Eric didn't understand the question or didn't know how to answer so he replied with a Dutch phrase he'd learned. "*Hallo. Hoe gaat 't met U?*"

Aunt Katrina's face resembled an old painting of a Madonna. Her eyes were blue. Her eyelashes and hair were so pale they were almost white. She wore her hair in a big bun on the nape of her neck. Her voice was brisk and bossy. She sounded like a teacher or a nurse.

"Your accent is English," she said to Eric. But you speak a little Dutch. How long have you been in this country?"

"I came the day before New Year's," Eric said. "I learned a few words."

Aunt Katrina looked at me doubtfully, comparing me to Steve's height. "Were you in Steve's class?" she asked.

"No, I'm only in my second year," I said. "He graduated last year."

"How do you like the seminary?"

"*Fijn,*" I said. Then I added "Most of the time."

Then she said "You boys must be hungry. We'll have lunch. Then you can tell me everything."

An iron pot heating on the stove filled the room with a delicious aroma. Although the pan was covered, it smelled of ham and onions. It had to be pea soup.

"You can wash before we eat. Steve, you use the bathroom upstairs?" Eric used the little washroom while I waited. On our trip we to used bushes instead of porcelain facilities. After being without plumbing, the bathroom was a luxury.

The little room was spotless with snowy white towels. After we finished washing, the clean towels were dirty. It was a mess but the dirt would come out in the wash.

Aunt Katrina set the table with a white tablecloth on top of a thick Oriental rug that protects the wood top. She filled our bowls to the brim. *Heerlijk** (delicious)

There were slices of fresh bread, butter, and Edam cheese and strawberry preserves on the table. And she poured tea—not the imitation kind we make from brown tablets in hot water—but real pre-war tea with the scent and taste of tea leaves from a china teapot.

"Honest to goodness tea! We can't get it any more," I said.

"We have a friend Kees, a sailor. He brought it back from Sweden."

The pea soup tasted better than anything I've ever had. We ate everything but the silverware and the dishes. I would have licked the bowl but I didn't want to be rude. We finished the loaf, the cheese and the preserves. It was the first hot meal I had since I left Bennebroek.

Aunt Katrina had a Dutch kitchen with walls that were light yellow on top and had blue and white Makkum tiles on the bottom. A Zaanse wall clock hung between the door and the window with pear shaped brass weights. Every quarter hour it played a tune and the bell chimed to count the hours. On the windowsill was a vase holding flowers. They looked like Darwins.

"Such beautiful tulips," I said, "Pink Trophy. Dad won a prize for them once."

"Oh," she said. "You're that Heemskerk! Is your father Bart? I met him at a flower show in Lisse a few years back. I didn't know you were his son. There are so many Heemskerks in North Holland."

"Way back during the tulip mania, their ancestors probably came from the town of Heemskerk. All the Heemskerks aren't necessarily related, they are named for the town."

Aunt Katrina came from Leiden. But she fell in love with a good looking man from *Friesland* many years ago and came to live here. It's cold in North Holland but colder in Friesland. I wondered if she missed living in our area, where it isn't exactly warm, but not as frigid.

"What is going on at home?" she asked.

"Not much," Steve said. "The Germans are still cracking down on young men. They closed the University and want us to all sign up and go to work building their camps or work in Germany."

"Tell me about your trip from Leiden," she said "and how you happened to come here."

"It's a long story," said Steve. "Pim is from Bennebroek. He was hurrying to get home before curfew. He cut through the woods behind their farm and stumbled on Eric.

Eric is a pilot. His plane was hit and broke in half. The tail landed in a tree with him in it. When he jumped down he broke his leg. He hid in the bushes from the Germans until the Heemskerks took him home and stayed until his leg healed. Now he wants to leave.

Pim and Eric went to Leiden to meet the man who was supposed to guide him out. But when they came near the house to meet the guide, they saw two Germans hanging around. Pim called me and we met in the coffee shop by the windmill.

We talked it over. The best way for him to get out seemed to be taking a Dutch freighter from Delfzyl. Eric and Pim wanted to go that route but Pim didn't know the way to Delfzyl so I came along to show them."

Aunt Katrina's eyes widened and she said to Eric "That's amazing, almost unbelievable. You might have been killed when your plane crashed. You might have been caught when you landed and put into a prisoner of war camp. But the Germans didn't catch you. You must have a charmed life."

"Ja, ja," said Eric in Dutch. Then he switched to English. "I was lucky. I think of the other men who were in the plane when it was shot down. I wonder why I landed safely and the others were killed?"

We couldn't think of any answer to Eric's question. Nobody even tried. Steve said, "We need to get him on one of the Dutch freighters that sail to Stockholm."

Aunt Katrina raised her eyebrows and wrinkled her forehead in thought. Then she said, "Some students stowed away on a freighter in January. Since then the Germans doubled the guards. Escaping from Delfzyl is harder now."

"Well, there's an old saying, 'Where there's a will, there's a way.' We'll see if it's true," Steve said.

"Uncle Pieter is at his office in the port. He'll be home a little after six. Maybe he can think of a way to get him on a boat."

"When do the freighters go?" Eric asked in English. Steve translated for Aunt Katrina.

"There's one in the harbor now that leaves tomorrow. But getting on it will be very difficult—like getting a camel through the Eye of the Needle."

Then she got up and shook her head. "Would you *jongens** (young men) like a hot bath? I've got some clothes in the attic from Menno. You can wear them while I wash yours.

We took baths in her upstairs bathroom, Eric first and then Steve and last me. We dressed in the soft old clothes she laid on a bed. The slacks were too long but I rolled up the pants. Steve has stork legs so his were high water pants—useful for wading. But Eric's fit like they were made for him.

Her radio was tuned to the Dutch station in Hilversum, to listen to the music. When the news came on, the announcer said Germany invaded Greece and Yugoslavia. Their great and glorious army was winning. Another victory we didn't like to hear about. The Greeks had been fighting Mussolini's troops a long time but the Greeks held the Italians off. Since Hitler went to Greece to help the Italians the Greeks haven't got a beggar's chance. The German Army will roll over the land like an ocean, no matter how steep or rugged.

Aunt Katrina turned the radio off. She said "I heard about Greece yesterday. It's terrible for those people. But what can anybody do?"

She asked Steve what was going on with her relatives in Leiden, where she came from. They talked about their family and while we enjoyed our baths, she washed our dirty clothes and hung them on the line. We sat around waiting for the wind to dry them.

Aunt Katrina started preparing dinner. We helped—I peeled potatoes, Steve cut up red cabbage and cored apples while Eric set table. Aunt Katrina had a beef roast in the iron pot oven with a lid. She put in a big hunk of butter to brown it and enrich the gravy. The soup we had for lunch satisfied my appetite but the smell of food cooking made me hungry again.

Soon after six, Uncle Piet came home. When he saw us he threw up his hands in mock surprise and said, "We've been invaded again! Who are these guys?"

"You know Steve, your nephew," she said. "These are his friends, Eric Johnson and Pim Heemskerk. They came all the way from Leiden on their bikes."

Uncle Pieter is a typical northerner, tall, blond and big-boned with red cheeks from the cold wind, and eyes gray-blue as the North Sea. Steve told him Eric's story of the tail of the plane hung up in a tree.

Uncle Pieter speaks Fries, his native language. It is a Nordic language related to Icelandic, not like Dutch which is derived from German. Signs in the Province are in both Dutch and Fries. Fries children have to learn Dutch in school, but Dutch children do not learn Fries. So we spoke in three languages. Eric spoke English to me; Steve and his uncle spoke Fries; Aunt Katrina spoke Dutch to me because I don't understand Fries. I tried to follow the conversations. Steve had to translate the Fries and I translated the Dutch into English for Eric's benefit.

Steve asked Uncle Pieter, "How can we smuggle Eric on board?"

"There must be some way," Uncle Pieter said. "I haven't figured it out yet. If he could speak Dutch, he might sign on as a deck hand, but if he only speaks English, that's a dead giveaway. You don't speak Swedish, do you?"

"No. I'm English and no linguist. I don't speak German either," Eric said.

"Maybe you could work with the men loading the ship. They don't talk a lot while they work—mostly they just yell and swear when things are messed up as they usually get."

We ate a big supper—roast beef and red cabbage and baked apples with whipped cream. While we ate, we thought of ways Eric could get on a ship. After supper, Uncle Pieter said "I'm going to the pub and talk to Kees. His ship sails tomorrow. Maybe he can figure it out."

After he left, Eric was hopeful. "I could be a loader. I can carry stuff from the dock to the boat and swear a bit."

Steve said to me, "We could create a diversion to distract the guards, give them something to see. We could set off fireworks or start a fire. The guards would be afraid the chemicals would explode. While they were putting out the fire, Eric could sneak past them and get on the boat."

"If we had fireworks. But we don't. A fire could get their attention," I said doubtfully. "But they'd suspect sabotage. They might search and find Eric. We can't do anything to aggravate them. They would take hostages. If anything happens it has to look like an accident."

Uncle Piet was gone over an hour. Aunt Katrina said, "Don't worry. Kees and Piet will put their heads together and think of something."

Almost as soon as she spoke, Uncle Piet returned, wearing a pleased expression and carrying a package. In it was a uniform his friend Kees got from the laundry to bring back to the ship. He told Eric to try it on.

When you are in uniform, people don't look at your face. 'Clothes make the man.' They look at the uniform instead. The uniform was a little roomy, but when Eric put it on, he looked like a Dutch sailor!

And better still; Kees had gone back to his ship to get an identification card from a sailor who was about the same height and was blond like Eric. In uniform, and in weak light at the gatehouse, the guards should not notice the difference between Eric and the sailor's picture on the card. He could pass. He wouldn't have to say anything but the name on the card. If they spoke to him, Eric would cough and pretend he had a bad cold. Kees would talk to the guard.

Kees told Uncle Pieter to bring Eric to the pub in the uniform a few minutes before it closed. Kees would bring the identification card. When they left the tavern, they walked together. The guards examined the ID cards at the gate to see if they all had them. In the poor light, the sailors' faces were hard to notice. After all, they were in uniform and had their identification. The guards would not expect ringers.

Sailors are boisterous. The German guards did not appreciate their unruly behavior. In the dim light in the guard's station, walking with the others in uniform, Eric should pass inspection. The guards would be glad to let them through so they could go back to their game.

Eric had to pronounce the name printed on the card. The guard had a list of the sailors. The card was real. The guard with no reason to suspect anything would check his name off the list. Eric was about the same height and coloring as the man on the picture. Once on the ship, Kees would bring him to his quarters and he could hide there until they were safe at sea. Then Kees would inform the Dutch captain there was a stowaway on board. The captain would help him. When they got to Sweden, Eric would leave the ship with other sailors going ashore. Then he would go to the British Embassy. They would fly him back home.

In uniform, Eric became Tinus Janssen. The first name was pronounced Teenus. It's easy to say. The second name was even easier. The Dutch pronounce Janssen as *Yonson* instead of Johnson as the English do. It is practically the same name. It means 'the son of John.'

To board the freighter, Kees said the sailors would act rowdy and create confusion while they waited in line. Dutch sailors and German guards don't fraternize. Dutch sailors resent being bossed by Germans. The German soldiers think the sailors are crude, not military when they wait at the check point. The noise the sailors make should draw the guards' attention and keep them from noticing Eric. So he should be able to get on board with the rest. Especially with the uniform he wore.

It was time to say goodbye to Eric. In spite of myself, tears came to my eyes. Uncle Piet gave him a *borreltje** to steady his nerves. Then we all hugged Eric and said goodbye in different languages. Steve said *Dag*. Aunt Kristina said *Vaarwel* and I said *Bon voyage*, because Grandmother Heemskerk spoke French on important occasions. She thinks it shows class.

Eric said, "When I get to England, I will ask the announcer on Radio Oranje to say "Yellow tulips are blooming in the fields of Holland.' Then you will know I made it home safely. And when the war is over, I will come back and see you." Then he left in sailor's uniform, walking down the street with Uncle Piet. I wondered how Kees would get the uniform back. Eric didn't take his other clothes with him. Kees would have to find another uniform.

Then it was up to him to play his part. We waited tensely for Uncle Piet to come back and tell us if he got on the boat safely. It was only a short time but it seemed like hours before he came and said, "The sailors left the pub together with Eric and Kees in the middle of the crew. He could speak his name like a Dutchman. If we don't hear any more tonight, he passed the test and will sail with the tide in the morning."

That night Steve and I discussed our departure. "Aunt Katrina thinks we should stay another day and rest up," he said.

I objected. "The sooner we leave the better. Everybody will be safer when we're gone. If we leave early in the morning, nobody will see us. The neighbors won't notice that three came but only two are still here and wonder about the other one."

I was right and Steve agreed that Aunt Katrina and Uncle Piet would be better off without us. Nobody would suspect such a quiet, inconspicuous pair of working against the German authorities.

However, if anyone in the neighborhood asked who their visitors were, they would say we were students who had to go back to school. Steve wasn't a student but they didn't know. He still had his Hageveld identification card. He was free to take his time. But I had to start class Monday.

Tomorrow morning Steve and I would go home. Easter vacation would be over. I'd go back to school and Steve needed to find a job so they wouldn't draft him for the Labor Service.

Leaving Delfzyl

Steve and I slept upstairs that night. It was the first time since we left home that we slept in beds on real mattresses, with sheets and blankets and pillows. The bathroom had a tub and shower, too. We were clean from our baths but hot water was such a luxury we took showers anyway. Steve's aunt gave us flannel night shirts. The room was chilly because Aunt Katrina opened the window to let the bedroom air out. Dutch housewives kept the windows open in the daytime unless it was actually raining or snowing in. We closed the shutters for the blackout of course. Our beds soon warmed up and we got comfortable. I prayed Eric would have a safe trip and fell asleep.

When Steve opened the shutters at first light, we looked toward the sea. We couldn't see the harbor itself because buildings were in the way, but in the distance we saw the dark waves breaking against the rocky shore.

We believed Eric was safely aboard the freighter and would sail when the tide came in. When he got to Sweden the British would fly him home. And his family would be so happy to see him come home after his long absence.

After getting so far without being caught, the weight slipped from our shoulders. The trip home would be easier. Going home is shorter than going out. We wouldn't have to worry about Eric at checkpoints. And now we knew the way.

We would have more food. Aunt Katrina made us *uitsmijter* ham for breakfast—(two slices of bread with a slice of ham and a fried egg on each piece).

"Are you sure you want to start today?" she asked. "It's windy and it looks like rain. Stay a day and rest up."

But we knew it would be better for them if we went. Steve said his parents would worry and I said I had to go back to school Monday.

"Thank you so much," we both said. "But we have to go."

"What do you want me to do with the bike?" Uncle Piet asked.

"Give it to someone who needs it." I told him.

"But take off the license plate," Steve said.

Uncle Piet said "A bike with good tires is worth a few guilders. I'll sell it and give you the money."

I was happy with his suggestion. He gave me forty guilders. I gave half to Steve for our expenses on the trip home. Every dubbeltje we started with was gone.

"That's very generous," we said. He hugged us both. Aunt Katrina had been up early and made sandwiches for our travels. She hugged us with tears in her eyes.

"Say hello to the family in Leiden for me," she told Steve.

Steve said he would write when he got home and they would know we made it safely. They had been so good to us. We couldn't thank them enough for their kindness and help. We rode away. When we looked back, they were standing there waving at us.

As we left Delfzyl, we heard the long sound of a foghorn. We thought it was Eric's ship blowing its horn and sailing away.

Now the wind was on our backs. Pedaling was easier. It looked like our troubles were over. We'd reached our goal! The fog cleared. Gray gulls were gliding on the wind, trees bending, flowers blooming, the sun shining.

After an hour we stopped to rest and drink coffee. Steve said, "I can't wait to see Nicole. She's such a wonderful girl. Don't you think she's beautiful, Pim?"

"Are you *gek* (crazy)?" I asked. "If we stop and see Nicole, it could put her in danger. She knows Eric was English. She knew we went to Delfzyl. When she sees two of us returning she can't help knowing Eric got on a ship."

"But Nicole helped us. She's our friend."

"If the Germans find out somebody escaped, they'll investigate. They'll question everybody. They won't quit until they find out what happened. They'll punish everybody including your Uncle Pieter and Aunt Katrina. Think what they would do to Nicole if they knew she helped a British flyer.

"Nicole would never tell."

"Not on purpose. But there is a saying, 'Two can keep a secret if one of them is dead.' She doesn't know anything but if we talk to her, she'll guess what happened to Eric. We should to go straight home and hope nobody's looking for us."

"I have to say goodbye to her," Steve insisted. "Just a few minutes."

"It's not a good idea."

Steve looked like a cat that lost her last kitten. I was ruining his dream. "I must see Nicole."

"Write. Send her a letter,"

"How can I? I don't even know her last name."

"It's easy. There's only one Nicole at that store. Address it to Nicole in care of the store."

Steve nodded but he couldn't be convinced.

To change the subject I asked," Where will we sleep tonight?"

"We started out early enough so we should be able to make it to the hayloft," Steve said.

"In the shed we used before? It was not bad if you don't mind hay dust and spiders."

He laughed and I thought it was settled. We rode along the path unaware of what fate planned. Suddenly my rear tire went flat. So, pushing our bikes we walked a long time. When we came to the next town, I asked a Dutch policeman where we could find a repairman. He waved his arm and told us, "Paul Oosterman can fix it. Go down the next street to the school. Turn left to the canal; follow that until you come to a church, make a left after that and then a quick right. After about three blocks you'll see his sign on the garage."

Seeing he'd lost us, he said, "Left at the canal and right at the church, you can't miss it. If you can't find it, ask for Paul Oosterman. Everybody knows him."

We followed his directions and found the garage. Then we waited and waited. Of course he wasn't home! Finally he came, patched the tire, and charged three guilders. It was reasonable but the unexpected charge depleted my cash, We still had a long way to go.

He said "You had a loose chain, too. I tightened it a little. It should be all right to ride if you're careful, but when you get home it needs to be fixed properly."

"It's been that way a long time. When the chain comes off, I put it back on. But thank you for fixing it," I said.

We rode past the drugstore where Nicole worked. Steve slowed down, looking at the window, hoping she would appear. The temptation was too much. He couldn't resist stopping. "I'm sorry, Pim. I can't leave without seeing Nicole."

It was not safe. But we went in the store. Nicole was waiting on a customer. When she finished she smiled at Steve. "What a nice surprise." She was looking at Steve. "Are you going home now?"

"Vacation is over," Steve said. "School starts Monday." There were no more customers. I knew the two of them wanted to talk so I walked to the front of the store, looking through the window to the street. They spoke softly. Nicole wrote her address on a sales slip.

Steve took it from her. "I'll remember it. When I get home I'll send you a letter. Please say you'll write. I'll write even if you don't. But please do. As soon as I can I'll come and see you."

A lady came and stood at the counter. We'd have to go. Nicole reached under the cash register and handed Steve a package wrapped in wax paper. "Here are some rolls from the bakery," she said. "They're good. Take them for lunch."

We shook hands and said goodbye. Steve didn't kiss her but I could tell he wanted to. When we left, he smiled, but it was a sad smile. He was not a happy guy.

Steve gave me one of the rolls from Nicole. I hated to take it. It was probably her lunch.

When we left town reluctantly, we stopped by a bridge over a canal, to eat and watch the barges going by. We leaned our bicycles against the bridge supports while we rested. They were only a few meters away. Suddenly, out of nowhere, three boys on two bikes came up the path behind us. One boy grabbed my bike, jumped on and off he went without a 'please' or 'thank you' or even a 'sorry.'

"Give me back my bike," I yelled. But he rode on fast as he could. The boy and my bike were soon lost in the distance.

Steve said, "There's no point chasing him. Even if we caught up with them, we couldn't fight three. So climb on in back. We'll ride together."

He pedaled and I sat behind him. We could have reported the theft, but we didn't. The police would ask questions. And it wasn't likely they'd find it. There are so many bicycles everywhere and they're all black.

I was sorry for Steve. It would be harder to pedal with the extra weight. But he had the longest legs and he was strongest. His bike was too big for me. So we rode on with me hanging on behind him.

About five kilometers down the path, we found my bike lying in the dirt with scratched paint and the back fender bent. But I put the chain back on and straightened the fender, and I could still pedal it. The thief didn't know how to fix the chain or he didn't want to bother. It was an accident he richly deserved. My faith in justice was restored!

"That's twice," I said. "First the tire blew and then a thief came and stole my bike".

"I hate to mention it, but there's a saying, never two without three."

"That's just superstition. What else can happen?"

We hurried to make up lost time. We stopped only a few minutes to rest and eat. And when we rested, we held on to our bikes. But nobody tried to take them. After dark we reached the little shed. And it was still unlocked!

"The owner doesn't believe in locks. He must think the cows are guarding it," I said.

"He probably doesn't care if somebody uses it," Steve said. "There's nothing inside anybody would want."

We climbed the ladder to our sleeping place in the loft. Now the shed seemed to me to belong to us. Like a hotel room or a rental since we used it before. Now I know how squatters feel when they move into an empty building.

We ate a supper of cheese sandwiches and last year's mealy apples. The moon was sailing through thin clouds and the stars were tiny pinpricks of light so far away they hardly shone. There were no sounds at all. I felt safe and fell asleep. Then I woke to the roar of many planes flying west. We knew they were bombers, flying to Britain.

"Why is Hitler so vicious?" I asked Steve. "Why does he want to kill everybody? We never did anything to him. And he has plenty of territory. Why can't he be satisfied with what he has and leave us alone?"

"Why do the nations rage?" Steve said. "I haven't any idea how a conqueror thinks or why he wants to own the world. Only God knows."

"And the devil." I said.

The planes passed over and it was quiet again. I slept. In the morning the little brown-eyed cow was grazing near the shed. So I milked her and this time I felt like an expert. I tried to show Steve how to milk. But he said, "I'll leave that to you." After we drank the warm milk I patted the little cow's side to thank her, but how can you thank a cow? She didn't even know what a favor she did for us. We left a little milk in the rusty milk can cover for the orange kitten. Then we walked our bikes through the morning dew, lifted them over the fence and rode south. The wheels sang as they turned, "Bennebroek, Bennebroek, Bennebroek."

By noon we were hungry. The food we brought from Delfzyl was gone and we had nothing but bread crusts and milk for breakfast. "Let's stop at the first café we come to," Steve said.

We found a small cafe beside the canal with two tables set outside in a park-like setting. We watched swans gliding by, the white feathered parents and their smaller, darker babies. Their reflections in the blue water, framed by drooping willow trees made a lovely scene. There were two old men with long fishing poles on the opposite side of the canal. They hadn't caught anything. I wondered how long they had been fishing.

Our dinners were crisp fried fish and potatoes. The cook gave us a newspaper to wrap the leftovers. Afterward we rode down the path, our hunger satisfied.

But the old saying "Never two without about three things happening" was right. A mean black dog sprang out of a flower field and chased us, barking. He attacked me, bit at my ankle and tore my pants. I couldn't get rid of him and he couldn't get me off my bike.

"Throw him the fish!" Steve yelled.

I didn't want to, but he kept jumping up so I threw him the package. He stopped chasing and tore at the package.

"You should have told me you were hungry and I would have given it to you," I said. I'd rather have him chewing on my fish than my ankles.

Return to Bennebroek

Steve and I rode side by side on the wide path. The clouds filled the sky but there was a patch of sky so we knew it would clear up. Eric was on his way home. That lifted the heavy weight from our minds. We came to a checkpoint. Two of the Green Police asked for our identification and where we were going. Steve said we were going back to Hageveld after vacation.

Steve's old card showed he was a student. They looked at his picture and then at him. He was old to be in a minor seminary. But they asked no more questions and turned to a rider coming behind.

We were riding on top of the dike beside a canal. The trees waved branches in the wind and birds were riding overhead. We were glad it wasn't pouring. The canals were full after all the rain. A barge moved slowly by, the captain and his wife on the deck with a gray Keeshond. A Keeshond is a dog with a curly tail and dark circles around its eyes that look like spectacles. It makes a good barge dog because it's small and clean and friendly.

For a while we seemed to be moving at the same speed as the boat was floating, but then it went faster and left us behind.

Steve said, "How do you feel now that you have struck a small blow against the Nazis?"

"Wonderful. We should be in the escape business. We could call it Heemskerk and van den Berg, Travel Guides."

"Or Travel Now, Pay Later. Why did you put your name first?"

"Alphabetical order."

"But then I would be first. Berg comes before Heemskerk since we don't go by the v's. There are too many vans and vanders and vers in the Netherlands."

"I thought it sounded right, but if you like, you can put your name first.

"But what would we do for money while we waited for the end of the war?"

"I don't know. It wouldn't work anyway. We couldn't advertise.

"Shucks, I need some kind of business or I'll have to register with the labor board."

"You should have gone on the ship with Eric,"

"I would have. But I couldn't let you go home alone. And Kees had only one uniform."

I don't know a thing about Friesland and Groningen. In Friesland they have their own language. I couldn't understand them if they didn't know Dutch. Without Aunt Katrina and Uncle Piet, Eric couldn't get on the ship. We were helped by so many coincidences. So many things just 'happened' when we needed them.

"Do you believe in destiny?" I asked.

"Yes. I call it Providence."

When we finally came to Heemstede, close to Bennebroek, I asked Steve to come home and stay with me overnight. But Steve wanted to go to Leiden. He was as eager to get home as a horse when it smells its own barn.

"We'll get together again," he said. "Soon. After next week."

I laughed. 'After next week' is a standing joke in our family. Dad says it whenever he doesn't want to do something. It usually means 'never.'

"I'll be in school until August," I reminded him. I thought "We'll get together on my vacation." I took the road to Bennebroek and Steve went on to Leiden.

I started worrying about what Dad would say. I would have liked Steve with me to soften his anger when I came back. I had gone a long way without permission.

When I came in the yard Max barked, the geese honked and acted glad to see me. Mother cried. Jo and Alice and the twins gave me hugs. Dad was not upset. My uncle had called and told him I was safe but he didn't know where I was.

Everybody wanted to hear about our trip. They listened to my saga. Dad knew from Mr. Bakker that we hadn't met in Leiden. Mr. Bakker was thankful we didn't come to his door. Soldiers had come looking for divers but found none. Mr. Bakker was afraid we would walk in while they were there and would all be caught. He couldn't warn us. It was lucky we saw the German truck with the soldiers at his door.

"Going north to Delfzyl was a smart move," he told me. "I was in the dark until Uncle Pieter told me you called. The call helped but it didn't tell me where you were. When the soldier came to Mr. Bakker's home he searched. When he left Mr. Bakker called off the escape. He couldn't tell you because he didn't know where you were. If you had been there, it would have been a disaster. Somehow there was a leak and they were checking. But when nobody came they went home."

The soldier we saw didn't know it, but he saved our lives.

Mother said, "Eric's mother will be so happy. She must have worried all this time. And now she'll have him back!"

"And after the war, I hope he'll come back to Holland," Jo said. She hid him in the fireplace hole. She took care of him while he lived with us.

Alice said, "I was so used to seeing him around and listening to his English and I miss him."

Gerard and Ton wondered when Radio Orange would broadcast the message about yellow tulips.

Dad said, "First he has to get to Sweden and then he'll go to the British Embassy. They'll fly him home. It will take a while."

It is only six days since I left Bennebroek, but it seemed longer. I expected Dad would be upset at me for going to Delfzyl without asking, but he wasn't. He thought we had done the only thing we could."

Mother warmed up stew for me and Jo made pancakes with melted butter and sugar. I ate four, but who was counting? The twins ate their share, too.

"Did you worry?" I asked Dad?

"I knew you were with Eric. I wondered about Delfzyl because you said you would be back in time for school. You couldn't get back that quick if you went south."

After I ate last night I wanted to write about my trip in my journal. But I was too tired. I kissed Mother goodnight, shook Dad's hand and went to bed.

Now it's Sunday. Tomorrow I have to go back to Hageveld. What gets my goat is I can't tell anybody. It would be so much fun to brag about my trip.

Chapter 25

An Upsetting Game

April 20, 1941

Jo took me to school on her bike. It made me feel like a little kid again. Last week Steve and Eric and I were riding our bikes through the country. We had been cold and wet and frightened and hungry, but I felt like a man.

After class was over we played volleyball. It was windy but the exercise kept us warm. We were enjoying the game. The volleyball sailed over my head. I jumped for it, but I tripped and fell and landed on my knee. I couldn't get up.

"What's the matter?" Carl said.

"He's hurt his leg," Pieter said.

Even with Ari and Pieter helping, it hurt so much tears came to my eyes. When I tried to stand my leg buckled under me. But Ari and Pieter were both strong. Half being carried and half painfully limping along, they got me to the nurse's office.

Sister Martha, our nurse, bandaged my knee. Somebody told the Dean and he came to see how I was.

"It's only a sprain, Pim. You'll be all right in a day or two. In the meantime, if you can't kneel, sit in the back seat in chapel where you'll be less conspicuous.

"Why does everything happen to you?"

I often wonder.

April 21, 1941

Last night my knee swelled up so much I couldn't sleep. I took off the bandage. That didn't help. This morning Sister Martha called Doctor van Kamp.

"It's not broken, just badly bent" the doctor said and smiled at his joke. Now I have to use crutches. "Be patient and it will heal." I don't have a lot of patience so that didn't help but he gave me pills that do.

I'm frustrated. How could jumping for a ball make me have an accident? When I fell off my bike and scraped my knee, I got back on and rode home.

April 22, 1941

I'm learning to use the crutches and with help, I go to class, to chapel, and to the dining room. I'm glad when I can just sit at my desk.

Today is Frans' seventeenth birthday. I wrote him a birthday letter to tell him we miss him. He is in a boarding school in Baarle-Nassau, on the Belgian border. This is a little piece of the Netherlands that is both Belgian and Dutch. The two countries own it jointly. I don't understand how but they both govern the same land. It's an odd situation but they don't fight about it. It's just an odd Dutch solution to a problem!

Frans is two years older than I am. He's a nice brother, always in good humor. He gets along well in school and has plenty of friends. He's tall and handsome like Jan. I wish I was like him.

The school Frans attends is a novitiate of the Brothers of the Christian Schools, a Catholic Order founded by Jean Baptiste de la Salle. He's studying to be a teacher.

Jo was sixteen on April 6. We couldn't celebrate her birthday because it was Lent so she couldn't have a cake or a party till after Easter.

We weren't home on April 6. We were on the road to Delfzyl when Hitler invaded Greece and Yugoslavia. But we didn't find out about it until we got to Delfzyl.

Today we talked about it in Greek class. The German diplomat, von Ribbentrop, explained the invasion saying they sent their army to 'protect' Greece and Yugoslavia. This is the same excuse they gave for invading

Belgium and Holland. Who are they deceiving? The only country that Greece was fighting was Italy.

Hitler's army didn't help Greece. They came to help Italy because the Italians were losing. Hitler couldn't stand to see the Italian Army's defeat. The Greek army was doing quite well fighting them off until the Germans jumped in.

In October, Mussolini sent his army to invade Greece. The Greek army fought hard and kept the Italians out. General Metaxas led the Greek army. Metaxas was a military genius who had led the Greeks in four wars. But in the middle of this one, General Metaxas died. The Greeks fought on without him. Italy still could not win. So Hitler sent the German army.

Hitler doesn't like Mussolini. But Italy is his ally so he can't stand to see them get licked. It would look bad for the Axis.

April 23, 1941

Mr. Nolet teaches Greek. He admires the Greeks and often tells us about them. They were the first to establish a *democracy*. The word is a combination of the word '*demos*', the people, with '*kratos*', and authority or rule. It means 'the power of the people.'

The Greek army is still fighting with the British Expeditionary Force helping. In the old days, the mountains made their country hard to invade. A small force could hold off invaders at a narrow pass. But now planes fly over mountains and bomb the armies.

Hitler wins every time but he's running out of countries in Europe to defeat. When Alexander the Great was thirty, he wept because there was nothing left to conquer. Hitler can go on. He can see the oilfields in the Caucasus. He needs a lot because his tanks run on oil. That's one thing Germany doesn't have.

Hitler will kill two birds with one stone by 'protecting' another country and stealing their oilfields.

April 24, 1941

Arie drew a cartoon of me falling with legs and arms going in all directions like a windmill. I can't see much humor in it. I can hardly go up or down stairs. I can't take a shower because my leg needs to stay dry. I'm as patient as I can be but it's not healing quickly enough.

April 25, 1941

The Dean told Dad what happened. Mother sent a letter and Jo put extra cookies in my suitcase. They didn't last because kids stopped to visit and sampled them.

Jo brought me a book about a big stone tower in Delft where gunpowder was kept to defend the city. In 1674 officials came to inspect the stored gunpowder. Somehow they must have caused a spark and the huge tower exploded. It wiped out everything for miles around. Buildings and people flew up into the sky and rained down all around in pieces. It sucked the water out of the canals, erased the tower and everything around the tower vanished.

The blitzkrieg was like an explosion. It turned the Netherlands upside down. Many Dutchmen were killed. The ancient buildings of Rotterdam are gone. After the war they'll rebuild and renew the center of our port city, but it will never be the same.

The explosion in Delft was an accident; nobody meant it to happen. But Hitler bombed Rotterdam to punish us and show his power!

April 26, 1941

When Hitler's armies marched into Greece and Yugoslavia, Yugoslavia surrendered but Greece fought. The British Expeditionary Force came to their aid but could not save Greece from Italy and Germany.

The famous pass of Thermopylae has fallen. In 480 BC the Spartans defended it against the Persians, in 279 BC the Greeks defended it against the Gauls, and in 191 BC the Syrians defended it against the Romans. The invaders didn't win. This was the fourth battle of Thermopylae. The Greeks fought desperately to hold it. Two big countries attacked a brave little nation. If the Greek Army had better equipment, they might have won.

When a country beats their swords into plowshares, it's no surprise if they can't defend themselves. The country with the biggest army and the best weapons wins. The losers do the ploughing.

April 28, 1941

It's Sunday. I can't go out and exercise so I'm writing my journal.

When I think of people in mountainous countries, I remember Frans saying "People living on steep hills have to grow one leg longer than the other."

Dad agreed, "Cows and goats in mountain pastures have longer legs on one side, too."

How funny the goats would look when they came down the mountains and stood on level ground!

Geometry is hard for me to remember but I have no trouble remembering jokes. The brain is divided into sections. In my brain, the math part is smaller than the humor part.

April 29, 1941

A Swastika flies over the Acropolis. A heroic Greek soldier was ordered to remove the Greek flag. He climbed on top of the Parthenon that crowns the mountain and took the banner down. Then he wrapped himself in the flag and jumped from the top of the Citadel three hundred feet to his death.

I don't think I could jump off a mountain. I couldn't even climb the Acropolis because I'm afraid of heights. This was a spectacular leap and a wonderful example of patriotism, but what good did it do? And how did it hurt the Nazis?

I think a live patriot is better than a dead martyr. Somebody said once "He who fights and runs away, lives to fight another day."

The British Force left for Crete, a Mediterranean island in whatever would float. I looked in an Atlas. They might not be able to hold on to that, though.

The Germans are flying like the Supermen Hitler claims they are. We are praying God to end the war. What do they expect him to do? Send lightning to destroy the German Army? Make an earthquake or a volcano erupt or send a flood? so tanks couldn't run. A foot army wouldn't be so strong. In the Bible God helped Daniel and Gideon and David destroy their enemies.

So many dictators have risen –Alexander the Great, Ivan the Terrible, Genghis Khan, Hannibal and Napoleon. Sooner or later they are all defeated by their enemies. They can't ride on top very long. This war started in 1939 with the Polish invasion. Poland was invaded. How long before the end?

April 29, 1941

Dr. van Kamp came and examined my knee and told me I'd have to stay off my feet a while.

I asked "How long will it be?"

"A few weeks. You have a sore tendon. If you don't give it time to heal, you'll end up with a trick knee."

"Great! My knee is playing tricks already—it keeps me from playing, but not from studying."

April 30, 1941

The British left Greece. They were rescued from Belgium last year and now they're leaving Greece—it's Dunkirk all over again. This war seems it will never end.

The British are doing what they can to defeat Hitler and his war machine. They need help. Canada and Australia are sending troops but they're a half world away.

Can Churchill get American aid? In World War I, the Yanks helped defeat Kaiser Wilhelm. Now Hitler is invading Europe all over again. Germany is ready to get up an army at the drop of a hat, march into all the little countries and take over. How can they? Isn't it against the law?

Chapter 26

Home from Hageveld

May 1, 1941

My knee was not healing fast enough because I have to climb the stairs at school. So Dad came to bring me home. I couldn't even say goodbye. My friends were all in class. It's like a vacation only I still have assignments.

I'll miss my friends. But the food is better at home!

May 2, 1941

I'm sitting at the dining room table listening to music on the radio. We can only get Dutch stations on this old radio. The announcers tell us what the Germans want us to believe. British broadcasts are forbidden. The Dutch radio stations are full of German propaganda. To keep us from listening to the BBC and Radio Orange, we had to turn in our radios for a junk set they gave us. It only receives local broadcasts. Dad kept our good Phillips radio and turned in an old one from the warehouse. It's even Steven—their junk for ours.

Dad hid the good radio in the air vent on the warehouse roof. Evenings at 9 o'clock Queen Wilhelmina speaks from London on Radio Orange. The only way to hear her is by climbing up to the top of the warehouse using bulb shelves for a ladder. Then the listener opens a sliding door to the vent in the ceiling and turns the radio on, keeping the sound low. The one who is listening tells the rest of us what she is saying. She always ends her speeches with "We are one day closer to Liberation."

Getting the broadcasts is awkward, because we can't all go up in the loft and we can't carry the radio down. We don't want the Germans to know we listen to the BBC.

On Dutch stations they make speeches, give news broadcasts and play music from great composers, like Bach, Beethoven and Brahms. Hitler likes music, too, especially Wagner's music. He acts like an emperor and I think that's the way he feels when he hears it.

May 3, 1941

I was doing my English assignment and drinking ersatz when Dad and Rinus came in from the field. "How's the knee?" Dad asked.

"Pretty good," I said, although it hasn't changed much.

"Do you feel up to *de tulpen de koppen*?" That's cutting blooms off to let the bulbs grow bigger. It's easy when the weather is nice.

"Sure," I said. "I'll be glad to help,"

But mother thought it wouldn't be good for my knee. She called Doctor van Kamp and he said I shouldn't walk in the tulip field because I'd be sure to twist my knee.

Dad and Rinus drank their coffee. When they finished, Dad said, "The world is full of willing people. Some are willing to work. The rest are willing to let them."

"You know where you fit in," Rinus told me.

"I'm willing but the doctor said I can't."

"When your leg is healed, I'll see you make up for it," Dad said keeping a straight face but I saw a twinkle in his eye.

May 4, 1941

When Norway surrendered last year, King Haakon went to England and Major Quisling was put in charge. It was a disaster because the Norwegians hated him. They use his name as a synonym for **traitor**. We call traitors quislings, too now. The very name quisling suggests a turncoat.

It's almost a year since Holland was attacked. Last May we were enjoying the fine spring weather. In the back of our minds we were afraid of Germany, but Hitler promised he would not cross our border if we didn't help the Allies. Our government wanted to risk offending Hitler so they wouldn't even negotiate, discuss our predicament with the Allies. If the little countries had joined France and England, would we have been able to defeat him?

In 1939 Hitler's army invaded Poland. France and England declared war against Germany. We mobilized our army to be ready if Germany attacked. We thought we could defend the bridges over our big rivers to keep them out of our coastal areas. But if they did manage to get across the rivers, we would flood the low land to keep out the tanks until the Allies could come to help. But we didn't even try flooding.

Hitler only promised he'd leave us alone to gain time. He was planning to invade Holland when he said he would leave us alone to make us feel safe. The best time to attack is when the victim is sleeping.

Dad said "Hitler's a liar. You can't believe anything he says. If Hitler said the sun was shining, I'd take my rain coat and umbrella."

May 5, 1941

Seyss-Inquart and Hitler are on top of the world. Germany successfully overran Yugoslavia and Greece. Europe is a big prison. Great Britain is the only country standing. The sun shines on the Third Reich.

We have shortages of sugar and butter. Cigars and tea and coffee are memories. But we can't complain too much as long as we can eat.

When I see RAF planes flying over, I think of Eric.

May 6, 1941

The land around the house is depleted, no good for flower bulbs. Dad grows potatoes and vegetables and strawberries there. If you grow the same thing all the time, you need to change crops to restore the soil. He has a better field in Hillegom where he grows tulips. He was going to look at his land there and I rode behind him.

But we had a surprise—there was a little English Spitfire in Mr. de Vos's field, right next to Dad's.

He asked "Where did the plane come from?"

"It's a mystery to me," Mr. de Vos said. "It's was there when I got up this morning."

"Have any German soldiers been around looking at it?"

"I haven't seen anybody."

"It must have run out of benzene and glided down for a landing.

"But where's the pilot?"

"He must have bailed out before the plane came down. There aren't any footprints on the ground around it."

Dad said, "Sitting in the open like that, you'd think it would be surrounded."

Mr. de Vos said. "I haven't seen anyone."

There were no footprints in our field either.

I wanted to look inside, but Dad said we'd better leave it alone. He thought the Germans would come to pick it up.

It looks like it's in good condition. The Germans will want to study it and see how it compares with their small fighters.

If they took the pilot, why didn't they take it? Or leave guards?

May 7, 1941

This morning we went to High Mass at 9. Dad sat in the choir loft. Mother, Alice and Jo have seats on the left side of the center aisle. The twins and I sat on the right. In St. Joseph's, men and women and boys and girls do not sit together. The men are on the right and the women on the left. That's the way it's always been.

The pastor, Jansen-Schmidt said Mass. There would be a long boring sermon. I wouldn't mind the boring part if it wasn't so long. And I wouldn't mind the length if it wasn't so boring. The pastor didn't tell any jokes or stories today. His stories are usually interesting. That's what I like best.

Since I can't kneel, I had to sit. People must have wondered why, but I could hardly turn around and explain.

As usual half a dozen German soldiers stood in the back. They sang louder than anybody. They want us to know they're Catholics, too. We don't like them here. They don't belong. But they sure can sing!

When we came home and had coffee, Dad went to Hillegom to see if the Spitfire was still there. I rode on the back of Dad's bike. The plane was gone. We hadn't seen it come and we didn't see it go. While we were in church they took it away.

Jo said, "Maybe we should see if the pilot is around."

Gerard said, "No, if the plane is gone, somebody must have taken it. Maybe the pilot filled the tank and flew away."

"He couldn't take off from such a little field," Ton said. "The runway is too short. He'd hit the trees."

It's a mystery to me. Where would anybody get fuel? There isn't any except for what the Germans have.

May 8, 1941

Dad is on the Town Council. He knows about everybody in Bennebroek. The Chief of Police is Willem Kranenburg. H's a friendly man. Dad likes him although Mother is careful around him because the Germans control the police. Willem he has to obey their rules or be replaced.

Bennebroek is such a small town it only has two and a half policemen— the chief and one full-time and one part-time. There's little crime here because everybody knows everybody. Nobody could commit a crime without being caught.

Today the Chief stopped by to see Dad. We were drinking coffee when he came. Mother gave him a small cup of ersatz and brought out her best cookies. He ate one and looked as though he liked it.

After he finished his cup of ersatz, he told Dad, "There was something odd on Radio Oranje last night."

Dad raised his eyebrows. "I thought we weren't supposed to listen to that."

Kranenburg shrugged. "Most Dutch people aren't, but it's different for me. The Germans want to hear what the British say on Radio Oranje. But most of them don't understand Dutch. So they want me to report anything interesting."

Dad said, "The British wouldn't broadcast anything they didn't want Germans to hear."

The Chief said, "I know. I'm not telling secrets. But I heard an odd remark. It sounded like a message in code meant for somebody in the bulb district. The announcer reported something a pilot said. 'Flying over tulip fields in Holland I saw so many yellow tulips, the fields were painted yellow.'

It doesn't make sense. Why would the pilot mention only yellow tulips? And why twice? Why mention tulips at all and then only yellow ones? There are just as many red and white tulips. Didn't he see them?"

Dad said, "Maybe the pilot saw the yellow tulips because they show up better from the air. Or he likes the color yellow. I like orange myself."

Jo thought of an explanation. "Maybe he's color blind and can't tell yellow from red."

The Chief did not accept this. "It sounded like a code to me. 'Yellow tulips' must mean something. It must be a message for somebody, probably here in the bulb district. But for the life of me, I can't think what it was all about."

Dad brushed it off. "Well, there are fields of tulips all over from Leiden to Haarlem. I wouldn't worry about it."

Kranenburg had another cup of ersatz and another cookie. He complimented Mother saying "I can't remember ever tasting better cookies."

"They are good," Mother admitted. "Jo got them from *bakker Oudt*."

The Chief might have said these were the best cookies to please Mother. He might not have had them before because Oudt's is the Catholic bakery. The Police Chief is a Protestant. The Protestants buy from Sijtsma's bakery. Mother has tried both bakeries. She thinks Oudt's cookies are best—he uses more butter.

I was happy to hear about the yellow tulips but tried not to show it. I wished the Chief would make himself scarce, so we could talk.

Finally he left. We knew it was a message from Eric. We missed the broadcast, but Kranenburg told us because he thought Dad might figure it out. He was right. Dad knows the meaning but he couldn't tell the Chief.

This was the news we waited for! Now we know Eric got to Sweden and back to England. We don't know how, but he reached home. When the war's over we hope we'll see him again and hear about the cruise on the Dutch freighter to Stockholm and how he flew home.

May 10, 1941

A year ago today the Blitzkrieg came to Holland. Now it's spring again. The birds are singing and tulips and hyacinths decorate the land. The apple trees in the Nun's apple orchard are covered with drifts of pink and white.

When our Army surrendered, the Germans let the soldiers go home. They said they were being kind, forgiving us for fighting them. But they made the officers report regularly so they could keep an eye on them. Usually the men just signed the register and went home. But the last time they had to report, they had a big surprise. The Germans told them to buy round-trip train tickets. The officers thought they would sign in and leave as usual. But this time the Germans arrested them and sent them to a P.O.W. camp in Poland. People are stirred up, furious at the officer's internment.

The Germans also instituted rationing. Our country is rich in food. Milk, butter and cheese are some of our biggest exports. Everybody in the country had to register and get I.D. cards to buy food. On the cards the people had to tell their religion. It was just one thing on the form, a formality. But the Germans know our religion and they are rounding up every Jew they can find and sending them to Westerbork, a refugee camp in Drente. From there they are putting Jews on boxcars and shipping them to concentration camps in Poland.

We have a new symbol of resistance—the V. You see them painted everywhere, on fences, walls and buildings. It is Churchill's sign for Victory. You hear it knocked on walls, too—da, da, da, daa. That's a V in the Morse code--three dots and a dash.

V for victory began in Belgium. At first, patriots painted the letters R.A.F. on walls to encourage people. Painting three letters took too much time, so they switched to the V.

It caught on. In January, Colonel Britton, an editor on BBC asked everyone to write a V on every wall. The symbol spread to Holland. The BBC encouraged patriots to write the letter V wherever they could. They started broadcasts with the first notes of Beethoven's Fifth Symphony—da, da, da, daa. People would knock it on a door as they passed. The letter is being written and knocked on doors and windows all over Holland.

Goebbels knew he could not stop them so he is using the V himself. He dropped pamphlets saying V means victory for Germany. So the Dutch paint the V in orange letters for the House of Orange, thus for Queen Wilhelmina.

Wonders never end. Rudolf Hess is one of the Nazis' leaders. They say he is next to Hitler as leader. He flew across the North Sea in a small plane and landed in Scotland. He wanted to make peace. Was he Hitler's ambassador? It's a mystery but we don't think it's likely. Hitler hates the Brits.

The rumor is that Hitler sent him because he wants Britain to leave Europe alone. Maybe Hitler is tired of the bombing and wants a truce. If the RAF doesn't bother Europe, he might promise not to invade their island.

Some say Hess is different than the rest of the Nazis. They support Hitler for the power they can get. Hess worships Hitler and does whatever he can for the cause. But if he thinks he can end the war with Britain, it won't succeed.

May 14, 1941

On BBC we hear they passed the Lend Lease law in America. The Americans will make arms and supplies and give them to the British. The English are running out of money and can't buy them. When the war is over, the U.S. will get them back. It sounds great for the Brits.

President Roosevelt favors the English and he's against Germany. He's a descendant of the Dutch. We think he would like to declare war against the Nazis, but America has an isolationist Congress. They don't want to send troops. But they passed a Lend Lease law to help the British against Hitler. They will send supplies to Britain to help them fight.

Alice asked, "What does that mean?"

Dad said "They are making equipment for Great Britain to lend Churchill. After the war is over, they will return the planes and tanks and guns.

The twins said, "The stuff won't be much good after the war. They might just as well give it to Britain."

Dad said, "Planes are shot down faster than British factories can replace them. If the Brits can't get planes for the RAF, they can't survive because that's their only hope. Britain will be defeated if they can't get planes. Roosevelt is willing to help Great Britain, but the Americans don't want to send their men to die on the continent. They think Europeans should take care of their own wars.

Churchill said "Give us the tools, and we will finish the job." England can win if they get enough planes. Germany has the biggest army in the world. Britain's best hope is the RAF.

May 15, 1941

The Dutch radio is talking about the British bombing Hamburg and the Luftwaffe bombing London. So it's a standoff. Which air force can beat the other? Churchill says the Germans are losing more planes than the RAF. But Goering will not stop bombing England as long as he has a plane left to fly. Bombing is devastating both countries but neither one will give in.

In North Africa, Rommel's troops are fighting the British and the British counter- attack. Why are they fighting in Africa? Does Hitler think he can conquer that continent, too?

Chapter 27

Hitler Attacks Russia

June 22, 1941

Today Hitler attacked Russia!

Molotov announced the invasion saying: "At 4 A. M. today, without declaring war, German troops attacked our country.

"This war was forced upon us, not by the German people, but by the bloodthirsty Fascist rulers who have enslaved Frenchmen, Czechs, Poles, Serbians, Norwegians, Belgium, Denmark, Holland, Greece and other nations."

He didn't mention the treaty Russia signed with Hitler in 1939 when Germany and Russia attacked Poland from the east and the west, so he didn't waste words describing the treachery of Hitler toward his former Ally, either. But he made this grim prediction: "Napoleon suffered defeat and met his doom when he attacked Russia. It will be the same for Hitler."

Hitler's excuse is he needs *'lebensraum'* for the German people. He swallowed Europe, one small country at a time. Now he's maybe going into a country many times larger than Germany—with an impressive army.

June 24, 1941

Everybody in Holland is talking about the Russian Front. The German soldiers were as surprised as we are. It will be dangerous. They'd rather stay safe in Holland.

The German army has a long march before they reach Moscow. Even if the soldiers ride in tanks and trucks, there aren't enough vehicles for all of them.

The border is over 2000 miles long. So long a front needs millions of soldiers. Where will they get so many? By drafting men from the occupied countries?

An army travels on its stomach. It takes tons of food to maintain millions of men. The German Army doesn't bring enough food with them for a long campaign. They harvest food from the countries they invade. Will they get enough food in Russia to feed their troops? And where can they find enough fuel for their tanks?

It's a long way to Moscow. They will run out of supplies.

June 25, 1941

The Russian plains are immense but the German army is taking giant steps across them, meeting little resistance. The radio announcers say their Generals expect to reach the capitol and force Stalin to surrender in a few days. Their army is speeding like an express train on a clear track.

Dad hung a map of Europe, Russia and northern Africa on the back of the door to the dining room. He puts pins in the map to mark where the army has reached. Keeping track of their army would probably be frowned on by the Germans. So when the door is open it is hidden behind the door.

Today was a nice day. Uncle Piet and Uncle Nick came over for coffee. Dad showed where the invasion is going on his map.

Uncle Nick said, "At that rate, it won't be long before they reach Moscow. If Russia can't defend their capital from the blitzkrieg, the war will be over."

"It's not going to be so easy," Dad said. "Stalin is letting the Germans go deep into the country. Then his army will surprise them by making a big circle around their army and cutting them off."

Uncle Nick said, "Hitler seems indestructible."

Jo said, "Don't forget. Pride goes before a fall."

If his fall is a match for his pride, it will be a big fall!

Uncle Piet said "Hitler is *gek* (crazy)—too big for his britches."

The uncles agreed that war could end by Christmas— January or February at the latest.

"They better get out before winter sets in," Jan said. "That's what defeated Napoleon."

"Is it really going to end?" Mother asked.

"It's going to take time," said Dad. "All we can do is watch while the two big countries fight. I'd say 'May the best man win' but neither one qualifies."

Churchill had a comment, too. He said "If the Devil were to attack Hitler, I'd at least make a favorable mention of Hell in parliament."

Dad said "This is the beginning of the end. Hitler has reached his peak. From now on, he's going down."

Nobody has ever defeated Russia. Not even Napoleon with his glorious French army. Hitler believes he is greater than Napoleon or any conqueror who ever marched into another country to kill their people and ransack their land.

Everybody is wondering what will happen here. The invasion of Russia will take German troops from the West. They'll have to get more soldiers from somewhere else. Most able-bodied German men are already in the army. If there are fewer German troops here, it will take pressure off. Hitler will have to take men from the occupied countries.

We are waiting, doing what we can. Mother feeds people who have nothing to eat. Dad and his friends help 'divers' hide. Dutch patriots blow up bridges.

If England invades, Hitler will be fighting on three fronts—Europe and Africa and Russia.

Someday Holland will be liberated! We'll celebrate with parades and dancing in the streets and watch the German Army slink out like a whipped dog, head hanging low and tail between its legs.

Chapter 28

❧

The Citroen in the Straw

July 12, 1941

Yesterday Klaas Schipper drove over in his Citroen. He parked behind the warehouse where his car couldn't be seen from the street. Klaas lives in West Friesland, about 40 miles from us. He is a member of the Bulb Growers Association. Dad is the chairman so he thought his visit was something to do with that.

Klaas is a very friendly man. Dad likes him a lot but since he lives so far away and fuel is hard to come by, he was surprised to see him. Mother served coffee and while we were drinking it, the reason for his visit came out. He wanted a favor.

"Will you hide my car?" he asked Dad.

The Germans are looking for transportation. They can't buy it because civilian goods aren't being made now. They steal whatever they want—cars, trucks, bicycles, motor bikes. Since they are the only ones who can get benzene, Klaas's car is not much use to him—or any other Dutch man. But he wasn't going to let a German thief get his car—not if he could prevent it.

Dad didn't want to refuse his friend, but it would be asking for trouble if he hid the car on our farm and the Germans discovered it. You couldn't park it in the barn or the warehouse—the soldiers are always snooping around. If they found the Citroen, they would confiscate it and punish the property owner. Dad thought about where he could hide it. Then a brilliant idea came to him. There is a big roofed-over area where he stores bales of straw to keep them from rain and snow—bedding for the cow. So he told Klaas he could take out some bales of straw in the middle of the pile and put his car under the straw. He said "I can't promise the Germans won't find it, though."

Klaas agreed and we all went to work pulling out the rectangular bales in the middle of the pile to make room for the car. Klaas drove his Citroen into the space we created. Then the twins and I piled more bales of straw on top of the car. When we were finished, it didn't look too different. The pile was neat and little a higher but who was measuring?

Klaas thanked Dad profusely for his help. Then he got on the bike he'd taken from his car, and pedaled off down the street. He had to reach his home before curfew and it was a long ride.

Dad warned us, "This is a secret. Don't think about it. Don't talk about it. Don't even think of talking about it."

Ton said, "Of course not."

Gerard added, "If the Germans found the Citroen, they'd take it away."

So now we are the only ones on Schoollaan to have a car. We don't own it. We can't drive it. We can't even show it to anybody. But it's a good feeling to have a car—even if it's hidden under the straw.

Dad doesn't have a car. He says we don't need one. The land in Holland is flat and there are bicycle paths beside all the roads. Riding a bike is our transportation. Everyone over ten years old rides a bike. It's good exercise. Before the war, even the queen sometime rode one.

Chapter 29

❧

Starting a New School

September 1942

I go to St. Henricus Prep School now. It is different than Hageveld. Classes begin at 8:45 and end at 3:45, followed by a study period until 5:30. Mathematics is the first class, followed by the same studies we had at Hageveld—Languages, History, Religion, Science, and Music, which is choir. The teachers come to our classrooms as always, but there's not the same emphasis on *Silentium*—Silence. We have to bring our lunch because it's not a boarding school. We have a half hour of physical education a week—mostly exercise. The class is held at the girl's school because that's where the gym is. But we get plenty of exercise walking a half mile to the bus stop in Heemstede mornings and afternoons. Sometimes we play soccer after school. That's my favorite sport. I'm not too good at it. I haven't played much. But it's fun to play.

I like my teachers, Brother Albert teaches English. He gives interesting assignments. Our history teacher is Brother Willibrord, a nice man but a little impatient if you can't answer his questions. Brother Alexis teaches Math. He's a fast talker. You have to listen and get what he says the first time, he doesn't chew his cabbage twice.

There's a drawback to changing schools—I had to give up my plan to become a priest and choose a new occupation. I don't plan to be a bulb grower like Dad. I don't like the work, especially digging bulbs in summer. Now I don't know what I should do.

As long as the country is occupied by the Germans, there won't be many opportunities for young people. My advisor suggested I might go into medicine. I don't know if I could be a doctor but I'm thinking about it.

In our family, almost everyone knows what they want to be. Frans is studying to be a teacher. Alice will be a pharmacist. Jo will marry her boyfriend. The twins, Ton and Gerard, will go into Dad's business—raising tulips and flower bulbs. Henrietta is still too young to decide. Jan is clever—good at making things and figuring things out. He likes plants and growing things. I like music best—playing the piano. I'd like to take lessons and be an organist. But Dad says that's nice but not a vocation because you can't make any money in music. He sings in the choir and plays the violin like a professional but earns his living by selling flower bulbs and developing new tulips. Since he can't sell as many now, he is growing tobacco and making cigars. Selling tobacco is illegal according to the German government. But Dutch men need cigars. He 'gives' them to friends. They give him things in return, like money.

The way he learned to make cigars was a lucky happening. Mother feeds people. She gives a meal to anyone who asks for one. She has a table outside the kitchen door in nice weather. When she gives people meals, she sits down and asks them questions like where they came from and where they lived before the war. She wants to know if they need anything and tells them to come back if they need another meal. Once a man from Rotterdam stopped and asked for food. She asked him what he had done before the war and he told her he was a cigar maker. So she said, "You should talk to my husband."

She arranged for Dad to meet him and it ended up that he stayed with us and showed Dad how to make cigars. All he wanted in return was a bed and his meals. That was good for them both. Dad learned to make cigars and Mother gave him a warm bed and three meals a day, plus ersatz at coffee times. These are in the morning and in the afternoon. On Sunday after church we have two cookies with our coffees. He liked staying with us although it was not exactly luxury. But he said it was more comfortable than sleeping under the bridge, where he'd been sleeping.

What would it be like if you could earn a living doing what you enjoy most? That wouldn't seem like work. If everything you need would magically appear you wouldn't have to worry about money. I would like to play the pipe organ or conduct an orchestra. Wouldn't that be wonderful? Dad says this is the real world so I will have to work at something when I'm through ULO. That's what we call high school.

I won't graduate until 1945 and I'll have to serve a year in the military after that so there's plenty of time to decide.

Chapter 30

Jan Goes to Germany

When Jan was eighteen he was supposed to register for the labor force (or live in hiding and risk being caught in a sweep and taken to Germany). Then he might have to live in a labor camp under prison conditions, working in a munitions factory, helping the German war effort.

But Dad had a friend, Kees Mantel, who owned a farm in Germany where he raised flower bulbs before the war. He didn't raise flower bulbs now, but he raised plants there. Kees had an official permit to go back and forth across the border with his two sons in his truck, growing plants and food in Holland and Germany.

So Dad got Jan papers to go to Germany and work on Kees' farm. It suited the Germans as they needed to keep their farms producing food for the war. Jan wanted to stay home on our place and hide whenever the Germans came looking for workers. But Dad didn't want to risk him getting caught so he decided Jan should go and work for Kees.

Jan had papers that gave him permission to enter Germany and stay at Mantel's farm. He did not have their permission to re-enter Holland, of course. In the Germans' view, he didn't need a pass to come back to Holland—he had to stay in Germany and work on the farm.

When the family or the sons traveled back to Purmerend, Holland, they smuggled him in under the farm produce in the back of the truck. When they started out from Germany, he would ride in front for a while, but before they reached the border, they hid him in the back with whatever the truck was carrying.

But one day the Germans had a surprise checkpoint miles before the border. The young men saw a tank sitting on the road. It was too late to hide. Two German soldiers approached the truck.

Jan said there was a soldier pointing a gun in his face, asking for his permit to cross into Holland. The soldier said "Show us your papers." And Jan said he didn't have them.

The soldier asked "Why don't you have papers?"

Jan thought fast. "I lost them."

"How did that happen?"

John answered "Remember the big air raid in Wuppertal three days ago? The house I lived in was hit and burned down. My papers were in the house. That's why I don't have them."

Since the Mantel boys both had their permits and John was riding in the front looking just like what he was, a farm laborer, the Germans believed him. They let him go, warning him to get new papers before re-crossing the border.

That was a close one. If they hadn't believed him, all three of them would have been imprisoned and tried for smuggling a person across the border, a serious offense.

On their trips back and forth between Germany and Holland, they took bulbs and plants to Germany and wheat and potatoes back to Holland. There was plenty of wheat in Germany but the Dutch couldn't always get it The occupation rules would not let them bring it in.

Sister Momboer
January, 1943

Sister Momboer is a German nurse who came to work for us when Mother had a baby. She took care of her and the baby as long as Mom needed a nurse. There haven't been any babies in our family for a long time. But she'd cared for all of us in turn and she became a friend.

Yesterday afternoon she came over for a visit. Mother asked her to stay for supper. It was nothing special—just fried fish and beets and potatoes and a flan (pudding) for dessert. Everything went like a Dutch clock. The house was comfortable. We ate in the kitchen because it's cozy. We were enjoying the meal when the radio, which was on so we could listen to music, interrupted the broadcast with a speech by Adolf Hitler. He always yells and screams like a maniac and Dad doesn't like him. When she heard him, Sister jumped to her feet, raised her right arm in the Nazi Salute and shouted 'Heil Hitler!'

Dad is always polite, but he feels so strongly about Hitler, he forgot about his manners. He raised his voice and corrected Sister "We do not salute Hitler in this house. We are loyal to our Queen."

Dad hates and detests *der Feuhrer* for invading our country. Sister was shocked by his unfriendly statement and left immediately. If she didn't, I think Dad would have asked her to go.

It was cold and rainy outside. The poor lady had to get on her bicycle and go home without even finishing her dinner. It was probably the best meal she had all week. I felt so sorry for her—she looked so crestfallen. She didn't apologize. She just went. I don't expect her to come back.

Mother likes Sister Momboer. I'm sure she said something to Dad later when they were alone. *"Bart, she couldn't help it. That's just the way she feels. She is German after all and he's her hero."*

And Dad would have said *"Not in this house!"*

Sister has light brown hair which she wears in a braid twisted up around her head. She has a forceful profile with a strong nose and chin. She is short and a little stout but she looks like a German maiden—one of the **ubermench**, the master race.

Chapter 31

The Atlantic Wall

March, 1943

The whole Atlantic Coast from Norway to Denmark to Spain is so many thousands of miles long Hitler doesn't have enough soldiers to defend it from an invasion. So he's going to build a wall around it. When it's finished, it will be bigger than the Great Wall of China. The Chinese wall was built over many centuries. Hitler ordered his wall to be done immediately. It is incomprehensible. He plans to erect this humongous barrier with wars being fought in the east and the south and Britain bombing Germany and everything else going on. Where is he going to get workers? And how will he find the material? There isn't enough concrete and steel in Europe.

Of course he will take workers from Holland, France, Belgium, Denmark and every occupied country to build his Atlantic Wall. If you are a man with no job and live in an occupied country, there is a good chance you might have to work on it. He will need soldiers to watch the workers, too. He'll have to force them to build it.

Pouring concrete, reinforcing it with steel girders, and digging foundations are heavy work. And the Germans aren't known for feeding their workers well, so they'll be hungry. The weather is guaranteed to be rough with storms blowing on the coast from the Atlantic. The wind blows from West to East, when it's not blowing from Siberia.

Hitler must be crazy. He has a battle going on in Africa, another one in Russia and he is trying to help the Italians fight, too. Great Britain and

America are breathing down his neck so he decides to build an enormous wall. How long can he keep fighting? Why don't his generals end this insanity?

The Atlantic wall was more than 1700 miles long on the north and West, from Norway to Spain—plus 400 miles along the Mediterranean Coast. It had 15,000 concrete bunkers, was 3 ½ meters thick and was the largest building project ever. It used 1 ¼ million tons of steel. There were 300,000 men building it. Hitler had lost so many men that he could not realistically spare so many to build his wall.

Note: A Dutch Architect, Jaap Penraat, smuggled 400 men to safety under the pretense they were laborers going to build the wall.

Chapter 32

⁓◈⁓

The Lost Bombers

April 12, 1943

The twins, Ton and Gerard, and I were weeding the fields behind our house. The sky was filled with puffy white clouds against the blue. Suddenly we saw huge Blenheim bombers coming from the west, from England. They were unbelievable. To avoid being seen on radar, they were flying lower than I ever saw before. They were going to bomb Schiphol Airport in Amsterdam— quite near us by air. I wondered why they came without their fighter plane escorts, the Spitfires.

Suddenly, out of nowhere, an angry swarm of German fighter planes, Messerschmidts attacked the huge bombers.

Yesterday, the Messerschmidts had landed at the airport. When the British bombers approached Amsterdam, the little planes were waiting. It was no contest. The big, slow bombers could not maneuver fast enough to escape. The fighters picked off the bombers like shooting ducks in a nest. All of the bombers were shot down. One broke up in the air over our heads. Pieces of broken planes rained down, falling like missiles. I've never been so scared.

The roar of planes, booming guns and banging explosions were as terrifying as a million fireworks. The shooting and destruction of the bombers happened right over us. We threw ourselves down in a ditch and prayed God to keep us safe. Bullets from the Messerschmidts rained down. The little fighter planes looked like toys compared with the huge bombers.

239

Their machine guns seemed to be aimed right at us in crazy maneuvers as they shot down the big planes. We tried to protect our heads with our arms, but we kept stealing looks. We could not help watching the terrible battle.

It was like a fireworks show, only magnified many times and with the earsplitting noise happening everywhere at once. All the British planes were hit. One exploded in mid-air. The crew tried to escape by jumping out of the planes. But the fighter planes went after them and used them for targets, shredding their parachutes and sending them plummeting to earth. None of the planes could fly back to England.

Hyacinths were blooming in the field nearby. We could see pieces of metal mingled with the bright colored flowers. The debris landed on everything but we were not hit.

Uncle Frans and Aunt Ann live half a mile away in a residential area. The brick structure shows on the bottom of the home's wall, and there's wood siding covering the brick on top of the wall. It's a pretty house. Their three children are younger. I don't see them often. I didn't know the secret revealed when the roof and side of the house split open—a Jewish couple living in their attic.

When the air fight happened, an engine with part of a wing attached hit Uncle Frans' house, sheared off a wall, and exposed the hidden room under the roof. Fortunately, since it was daylight, the couple was downstairs or they would have been killed. They just used the attic for sleeping and stayed downstairs the rest of the time. They only hid when searches were going on.

Although their hiding space was revealed, the Germans were too busy picking up the remains of the bombers to notice. Or perhaps they saw it and thought it was just an ordinary attic with a bed in it because of the crowded living conditions in Holland.

The rest of the huge wing, from the engine to the tip, fell three feet from our house. The cockpit with the crew fell into a small canal nearby. The crew were killed and the men who parachuted from their planes were all killed.

The raid was terrible. It cost the British many pilots and crewmen and seven big bombers. It might not have happened if they had attacked the night before, protected by Spitfires. In the darkness the Germans would not have had it all their own way. Spitfires could have taken out many Messerschmidts. A Spitfire is small, like a child's model plane. One landed in a nearby field once. We marveled at how small a contraption it was. But in the air, it can do amazing things.

While we watched the air fight overhead, it seemed to go on forever, but it was only a short time. Then German soldiers came into town on their trucks. They picked up pieces of the broken planes. They picked the bodies off the ground and threw them in the back of their trucks without any respect as if they were only debris.

Where we had been working before the attack happened, a piece of a plane was lying in the field. "Missed us by a hair," Ton said. We three boys ran into the house, trembling from the terrible shock of what we saw. Mother and Jo and Annie were in the kitchen. They had made a big pot of ersatz coffee. We got cups and sat around the table drinking it with milk. There is no sugar and ersatz without sugar tastes terrible. It was not anything like coffee, but it was hot.

"Those poor young men," mother wept for what had happened, "and their poor parents."

"It was right over our house," Jo said. "We could have been killed, too!"

"There must have been a guardian angel watching over us," said Annie.

"If our guardian angel was shielding us, why didn't he protect the men in the bombers?" I asked.

"The bombers shouldn't have come in daytime," Gerard said.

"Where are Dad and Alice and Jet? I asked. I needed to see everybody to know they were safe. Jet sat by the table,

"Dad's at a meeting, but he'll be back soon," said Mother. "Alice went to work."

When Dad came home, he said "Uncle Frans' house was hit and we need to help fix the roof."

The house was smashed. A plane's wing fell on the roof and tore off the side of the house. His neighbors stood around trying to figure out what to do. They wanted to help and brought whatever scraps of wood they could find to rebuild the missing wall. There is no new lumber now so we used junk. We were lucky to find some old beams taken from a decrepit potting shed.

"Looks like a monk's job," Dad said, "But it's the best we can do." Dad is a great believer in good workmanship. Now we can't do things right, though.

The hidden room under the roof still has to be repaired. When it is finished, the Jewish couple can move in again. They have gone someplace else until we are sure it is safe. The neighbors could have seen the hiding place but apparently nobody reported it or the Germans would be looking for them. The Nazis are absolutely insane about finding Jews and sending them to Concentration Camps. We don't think any NSB members noticed. There aren't many Dutch traitors here in the bulb district. Not like in Amsterdam. Almost all Bennebroekers are loyal to our Queen.

As long as I live I'll never forget the horror of the battle in the sky. How could the German pilots attack the British pilots who were bailing out? How could they be so cruel? They are airmen, too. Shooting down planes is one thing, but shooting defenseless men hanging from parachutes is like shooting soldiers who have raised their hands to surrender.

Tonight we prayed fervently, thanking God for keeping us safe and we prayed for the flyers and their families.

The British didn't know the fighters were already at the Amsterdam Airport. They were warned the Messerschmidts were coming and meant to bomb the runways to keep the Germans from using Schiphol airport as a base. Somebody told them the planes were coming tomorrow.

The Germans must have captured British spies and used them and their radio equipment to send misinformation. They are good at that.

Chapter 33

Our Wonderful Show

May, 1943

Louis van der Wal and I are giving a play. It's a take-off on an opera. His father will let us use his house. It has a big living room and dining room connected with French doors between. We can use the living room for the stage and the dining room for the audience. To close the curtain we will shut the French doors. We can seat 30 people at a time.

We will rig up a spotlight from a headlight of an old car, powered by a battery. There are still some old clothes in our attic we can use for costumes.

And we have a talented pianist, some good singers and a crew of assorted actors. So we will have songs and skits in our funny opera. The pianist, Marie, says nobody can be killed in the opera because it is against her religion. So the man who is attacked can only be hurt, not killed. But he can yell like he is being killed!

The local milkman heard us practicing and he had tears in his eyes. He was wounded during the war and had a metal plate in his chest. He pounded himself on the chest and made a loud bang. He said, "And they're the greatest!" This was so funny we had to keep from laughing for fear of hurting his feelings.

Our closing scene is a big portrait of Queen Wilhelmina, with the spotlight shining on it. I wrote a poem that ends "They will never subdue us, those who have wounded our hearts." The climax will be the Netherlands national anthem. It might be heard ouside the house but this is a very strict Christian neighborhood and we think nobody will report it. We'll display the Netherlands flag and the Royal flag. We only invited our friends, patriotic Hollanders. So many want to come we will give two performances!

Chapter 34

❧

Ein Prosit

August 12, 1943

"I heard the Germans are transferring Bennebroek Troops to the Russian Front," Dad said at breakfast today.

I wonder if they'll be easier on us when there aren't as many of them here," Mother said.

"At least they won't have as many spying on us," Dad said.

"Does that mean all the troops will leave and we'll get our school back?" Gerard asked.

"No, their replacements will use the barracks."

Things are not going well for the German Army in Russia. They started like a blitzkrieg with great leaps and strides. But that changed when Stalin's armies met Hitler's. The Russians let them pass deep into the territory for a while and then surrounded them, trapping them in a place where they can't cross a river.

The Nazis can't get enough supplies of food and fuel for their troops and it will get worse when winter comes. The Germans will freeze. They don't have the right clothes and equipment for the terrible Russian winters.

The soldiers in Bennebrook would rather stay in Holland. Hollanders are peaceful and disarmed—our soldiers dumped their guns in the canals when they surrendered. The Germans don't want to go to Russia and fight fierce enemies equipped with tanks and guns.

Some of the new soldiers coming here aren't even German. They don't speak German or any language I've heard before. They dress differently, too. They wear cheap uniforms. Where do they come from?

There are still plenty of Green Police around—looking for Dutch workers. Their trucks are running all over Heemstede, Bennebroek and Hillegom, picking up workers in raids we call *razzias*.

Men who escaped from the labor camps say they were kept in unheated barracks surrounded by barbed wire fences complete with armed guards and dogs to watch them. They worked long days, eating miserable food, sleeping on wood planks and were treated like slaves. If prisoners are too sick to work or die from the cold and hunger, the guards don't care. The Germans send other men to take their place.

Lou is eighteen and out of school. I'm almost seventeen but still in school. We stay on the farm and watch out for *razzias*. We don't want to be caught in a sweep. So before we go to town, we always ask Rinus if German trucks are around.

At breakfast, Mother said, "You need a haircut, Pim." So Lou and I got on our bikes and went to Bennebroek. The barber's name is Goof Zandvoort. Goof is a good name in Dutch where double o's are pronounced with a long 'o' sound so we say *Gofe* to rhyme with loaf. In English, *Goof* would rhyme with roof and they would laugh at the funny name.

Riding to town, the sun shone, birds sang, and everything was lovely. But just when we came to the barbershop, a big dusty German truck drove up and parked on the side of the street behind us. My heart stopped, too. I didn't know whether to go into the barbershop or drive off. Bicycles can't outrun trucks. And running would make them notice us—if they hadn't already. I looked at Lou and he looked at me and we came to the same conclusion without a word—we decided to go into Goof's.

Luckily, it turned out those soldiers weren't looking for young men; they were just thirsty for Dutch beer. They went into the kroeg. There's a common wall between the shops, and through it we heard them singing a drinking song in German:

> *Ein prosit, ein prosit, ein prosit,*
> *Ein, zwei, drie, saufen!*

When they got to 'saufen' I visualized them raising their glasses to drink. They must have been celebrating. German soldiers should drink beer more often. It makes them happy and keeps them out of mischief.

Hitler doesn't drink beer or any alcohol. Maybe if he did he could relax, enjoy himself and forget about power and conquering the world.

My friend, Louis van der Wal, is eighteen and out of school so he's supposed to register with the Labor Service, but since he's afraid they'll send him to a labor camp, he's living on our farm, hiding and helping Dad. A man can hide better on a farm than in a neighborhood where houses are close together. He's afraid a neighbor might tell on him and police would take him to a camp.

When I'm eighteen and out of school, I'll hide, too—maybe even before. The Germans aren't too particular about the exact ages of young men they need for work. Seventeen seems old enough to work to them but I don't want go to a labor camp, freeze in winter and work fourteen hour days without pay and live on starvation rations.

Some time ago, Dad and Rinus built a fake wall in the warehouse to hide behind. We can go there if the police are searching, but we don't stay long. Louis works around the place keeping an eye out for razzias so if they come looking for young men, he can hide. And when I'm at work on the farm, so do I.

Last night a neighbor called to say the green police were looking around our area. Gerard came to tell us to hide. We were in the field, far from the warehouse. There wasn't time to go there so we ducked into a hollow side of a haystack. Our nosy cow ambled over to see what we were doing, curious as a cat looking in a mouse hole. She pulled a big mouthful of hay off the stack next to me. I was afraid the soldiers would notice and come to investigate. But they didn't. Probably they thought cows acted like that. The men looked around the buildings for ten or fifteen minutes and then went into the house. We waited in the hollowed out haystack until they disappeared inside. Then we ran into the woods and waited until they got in their truck and left.

Mother said they went into the kitchen, and she offered them a cup of ersatz. She said it was funny to see them lean their guns in a corner in the kitchen and drink their coffee at the table. They asked Dad how many sons he had and their ages. Dad said Jan, his oldest son, was 20 and working in Germany, and Frans, his second son was 19, studying at the Brother House in Belgium. He told them the twins, Gerard and Ton, are only fourteen, still in school. He forgot to mention me.

They didn't do an all-out search of the farm. That's a full-scale operation with more soldiers and trucks. The soldiers are afraid of being attacked so they never go into barns alone. They just poke their bayonets up under the eaves to see if someone is hiding there. Lou and I hide in the woods if we are working near the trees. Trucks can't drive there.

Rinus, Dad's foreman, looks to see if any German trucks are in Bennebroek when he comes to work and warns us if he sees one. Lou and I work around the farm, feeding potato peelings to the pigs and grain to the chickens. The cow eats grass and hay. She's going to have a calf. We water the animals, milk the cow, gather eggs and clean the warehouse. Sometimes we plant some tulip and hyacinth bulbs. There is still a little market for them.

We eat plain food—potatoes and onions and big winter carrots. Louis likes *hutspot*—potatoes and carrots mashed together with bacon grease on them. Hungry people come looking for food every day. Mother keeps a pan of potatoes on the kitchen stove to give them something to eat, even if it's only potatoes and gravy. She likes to feed people. Our pantry is empty. The fruit and vegetables mother and Jo canned last summer are gone.

Hitler's priority is feeding his army. Before the war Holland exported food of all kinds—vegetables, fruit, milk, butter, cheese and meat. Now with all the soldiers living here, the Germans are taking so much there isn't enough food. Dad was wise to plant more food crops instead of flower bulbs. We always have something to share.

Uncle Cor believed he didn't need to plant vegetables because he had money and he believed he could always buy food. But money isn't worth anything to starving people. Dad gives him potatoes. They say tulip bulbs are edible but don't taste good.

Dad told the farmer who works his farm in Koegras to raise more wheat and rye and vegetables. The farmer has no problem getting his share of the crop. Dad needs to hire a truck to bring his share home. Trucks are scarce—dearer than gold. He took some food home on his bike but it didn't last long with so many people. So he went back to get more.

In the middle of last night, a truck came into our yard. The twins and Lou and I woke from the noise it made. We peeked through the window and saw in the moonlight it was a German truck—or at least it had a German license. Two men got out and began carrying bags from the truck into the warehouse. We were afraid to go out for fear the Germans might put us in the truck and take us to Vught, where they're building a work camp. So we went back to bed and slept. This morning I asked Dad who it was. He didn't tell how he managed to get a German truck to bring grain from Koegras. He must have paid the man by giving him some food. The Germans don't have too much grain to feed their troops either.

Now we had plenty of grain but we needed a mill to turn it into flour. In the barn on the farm where he works, Ton found an ancient hand-powered mill. The farmer traded it for a bag of potatoes. You turn a handle to grind the wheat into a coarse flour that Jo makes into pancakes. We eat them with syrup made from sugar beets cut in pieces and boiled until the juice thickens. Pancakes and syrup are our only sweet treat. We love to eat them whenever Jo makes them.

Alice has many friends. Some are from rich families. A boy whose father owns a department store came home with her one afternoon. When he saw the cat's dish in the kitchen entry, with food the cat left, he picked it up. "Don't eat that," Alice said. "It's scraps for the cat."

"I don't care," he said. "I'm hungry." And he showed us how desperately hungry he was by eating everything in the dish.

Spring of 1944
Rommel's Asparagus

We were eating breakfast this morning when German trucks surprised us by driving down a little dirt road to our field and parking in front of the barn. A crew of Dutch workers got out of the truck. Two German soldiers stood by, guarding them.

"What on earth is going on?" Mother asked.

Dad said. "They're digging holes for the trees they are going to plant."

"Who said they could plant trees in our field?" Ton asked.

"They're not real trees, just tree trunks—to stop gliders from landing."

The men dug holes about half a meter deep and a good distance apart. When they finished digging, they lifted the poles from the back of the truck. The poles were sharpened on one end like a giant's pencil.

It was comical to see how the men carried them. Three of them were tall, husky guys. They balanced the heavy pole on their shoulders. The fourth guy was too short to help lift it. He ran along behind, reaching up his hand to touch the pole, pretending he was helping to lift it.

They stood the poles in the field with the sharp end up and shoveled dirt around the bases to support them. They look a little like giant asparagus plants. The Germans plant them in fields to keep parachutists and gliders from landing. People call them 'Rommel's asparagus' after General Rommel, who ordered them. Hitler is afraid the Allies will attack.

We must protect them because we'll be blamed if they are missing.

Dad said "They stole those trees from the park in Groenendaal." But he thought a minute and added "They'll make good firewood when they dry out."

Chapter 35

Normandy Invasion

June 6, 1944

The Allies have landed. A fake newspaper put out to imitate The *Haarlemse Courant* described the promises made by the Nazis and the way things really are. Rauter thought the Dutch Resistance knew the invasion was coming and had printed it to coincide with the invasion. It made him furious.

The German fighter planes did not attack the allied bombers. Their air forces are too depleted. People are being forced to leave the coast. There are thousands of people who have no place to go.

The RAF attacked the railways so the Nazis couldn't deport Dutch workers to Germany. We think the Germans will surrender soon and the war will be over.

Dad says Hitler has taken everything he can take from Holland. All our railroad cars have been taken to Germany except the ones they use to transport troops and to take the Jews to concentration camps.

There was a cartoon in a paper that said when Hitler made people promise to be loyal to death, he meant they would die. He can't live forever himself. Maybe he will see some of the millions he killed when he meets St. Peter!

June 7, 1944
Anticipation

The Germans announced the invasion yesterday before the BBC did. Leaflets dropped on Holland with Prime Minister Gerbrandy's address to the Dutch and Eisenhower's speech. We heard that there were going to be more landings on other parts of the coast. It was quiet. The German troops did not seem to be active. Men are still working on building the Atlantic Wall.

June 14, 1944
Rumors

Allied landings have been reported on different parts of the Dutch coast. People say there will be another attack closer to Dover. They are going to evacuate Scheveningen prison called the *Oranje Hotel* and transfer the prisoners to Vught. That is a worse place.

The underground is becoming more active. They assassinated a Mr. van Dalen in Rotterdam. The Germans executed more prisoners and had a big funeral for the traitor, van Dalen. He had turned in Dutch people to the Gestapo. People who showed they didn't like him were taken to prison.

Gerrit van der Veen was executed for an attack on the Germans. He was a famous sculptor and was a leader in the underground. Although he was wounded and paralyzed they killed him. He asked other men to hold him up so he would be standing while he was shot. Everyone is angry that they shot such a brave man—a dying Dutch patriot.

Chapter 36

Hitler's Escape

July 25, 1944

Hitler has been attacked many times but always escapes. The men who try to kill him get caught. He has the luck of the devil.

There is a story going around that another attempt has been made on him by his own Generals. A briefcase with a bomb in it was left in a room where he was in a meeting. Someone who did not know the briefcase contained a bomb, moved it inadvertently. So Adolf didn't get the blast of the explosion. It was absorbed by a wall.

The Generals behind the attack know the war is lost and wanted to end the fighting before their country is destroyed. Hitler won't realize that defeat is inevitable. He'll never give in. He thinks his will can't be frustrated. We're waiting for the Allies to end his lawless invasion.

The Germans are taking everything out of Holland now they did not get before. Dad says it is outright robbery. They took the machinery out of the factories, the pictures from museums, the furniture from people's homes, and our bicycles and cars and trains. They are taking food from starving people and taking every man they can find to work for him.

I'd like to show him frustration! He sits in safety, guarded by his soldiers. He orders them to keep on fighting till death and never give in. But he doesn't lead them in the war. He doesn't care for danger, personally. That's for his followers. He has no friends. They all died.

August 30, 1944
Mother's Birthday

There was a time when we celebrated Mother's birthday with food, drinks and flowers. Our relatives came and congratulated each other on her birthday. The feelings of well-being and delicacies and little presents made her birthday a wonderful party. But this year is not like that. The food is meager. There are no drinks except ersatz coffee and weak tea. The relatives who were too weak to walk here or ride a bicycle did not come. The men still talk but it is about how the war is going and speculation about when it will end. They repeat rumors of possible surrender. They talk about losses suffered in the past year and illnesses. The guests left early because the curfew was now changed to 7 o'clock. Everybody took home a little food in a napkin. Jo made a little cake. But this party was not like parties that used to be.

Uncle Nick asked, "Who would have believed this war could go on so long?

Uncle Cor remembered, "I thought the British and the French would beat Hitler and it would be over in a year. It seems endless but since the Allies are invading from the West and Russia is winning in the East I believe it will end.

Mother asked, "The Germans will soon be going and we can get things back together."

Dad said, "If the Allies move up through Holland it will soon be over. But if they go through Germany to Berlin, it will take a while. Hitler is very determined. Even though he realizes he lost, he won't surrender."

The Russians are moving through Romania. Bulgaria declared neutrality. Finland asked for an armistice. The poor Finns! After fighting Russia for so many years, they end up in Hitler's camp.

The Reich is losing. The Allies are in France and moving toward Belgium. The war will soon be over. Then we'll celebrate!

Chapter 37

❀

Dolle Dinsdag
(Mad Tuesday)

September 5, 1944

The war is going well for the Allies in France and Belgium. Antwerp collapsed and the people in Brussels were happy to welcome the British tanks. The Germans are still in North Holland, though.

Last night the BBC broadcast that Breda, Holland had been liberated. We are filled with hope that Holland will soon be free. Paris has been freed. The Allies will come up from Belgium and into Holland. Just the rumor that the Allies are invading filled our enemies with fright. All the German officials and Dutch traitors left their offices, burned their papers and got out of town. They are afraid of being punished by the Allies and the Dutch people.

Today is a big day. The Germans are afraid the Allies will soon be invading so they took everything they could steal and left. We laughed because we are so happy they are gone. We listen to the radio and wait for the Allied armies to come marching in. But nothing is happening.

Dad and I climbed up into the warehouse and listened to the radio. But there was nothing on the news about liberation coming today. So we are going to bed, not knowing what is happening.

In Bennebroek, we heard Rotterdam was liberated and the British were on the way to free Den Hague. Some people stopped working and waited to see the Allied troops. The Germans and members of the NSB had departed east to Utrecht. We were relieved to be rid of them. Now we could breathe freely. We were ready to welcome the Allies.

September 6, 1944

But the rumors were false. The British stopped at the Maas River. We didn't get much news from the BBC. We were hopeful. We thought we would soon be free.

Seyss Inquart declared martial law—he posted signs saying—any offender against the occupying power would automatically receive the death penalty.

Yesterday the Germans left. Today they all came back. They must feel foolish but they act like nothing happened—just business as usual. They don't even mention yesterday's exodus.

We call yesterday "dolle dinsdag" or "Crazy Tuesday." Our Germans And Dutch Nazis are back again and meaner than ever—furious they have been Tricked into showing their cowardice.

They lost the war and they know it or they wouldn't be so scared. You would think it would make them act nicer. But it didn't. What kind of government is this? They marched into a neutral country without any excuse—stole our land and everything in it, made themselves our rulers, killed some people and made others slaves, grabbed our food and machinery, and terrorized everybody. They had no mercy and no justice.

Before the war we were neighbors. They did it all in the name of a madman. How can they be so blind?

Everybody is praying to see them go. The people are hungry in Amsterdam. They need to go out in the country to buy food. The Germans have made it illegal for farmers to sell food. They call it black marketing. You have to wonder about this bunch of thieves and murderers. They stole our land, killed our people, and then have the nerve to call themselves the master race!

Chapter 38

Hiding Place

September 8, 1944

Since I graduated from Saint Henry ULO (high school) Louis and I are living in hiding. This is only partial hiding. As long as there are no trucks cruising around, we can stay around the farm helping with the work.

When Rinus Otte comes to work he tells us how things seem in town. If there are German trucks around we hide behind the potatoes in a little room in the warehouse.

The entrance is behind crates of tools and equipment looking like organized chaos. The crates can be shifted to reveal an opening in the house wall covered by leaning boards. Behind them is a door in the floor that lifts and a person can drop into a hiding place. We stay until someone comes to tell us the danger is past. It's dark and damp. A little light comes through the crack in the floor. When we come out we go to the kitchen and drink something hot.

Chapter 39

❦

Market Garden

September 17, 1944

It was a sunny day. We were having our after-church coffee on the terrace when we saw a huge wave of planes and gliders overhead. They were flying so low so we could see details on the bellies of the planes and under the wings. They were C-47's pulling gliders and they didn't seem to be going very fast.

Our first reaction was excitement. We asked "What's happening?" It must be something big.

It took a long time for hundreds of planes to fly over.

Gerard and Ton and I climbed the trees in front of the house to see if there was any action on the highway. There was nothing to see. There wasn't any news on the BBC, either. It wasn't until the 9 o'clock news that we heard about the paratroopers being dropped near Arnhem and Nijmegen.

No details were given, but everyone was happy. "The war will be over in a week," we said.

The Poles and the Canadians could come up the Western part of the country with no resistance, we thought. There were few German troops anymore.

We were so happy sitting in the sunlight. Our ordeal was ending. The Germans would slink back to Germany. Our prisoners would be free. No longer would we see the hated Swastika flying over our public buildings. We could tear down the pictures of Hitler. German boots would not stamp on our walks. We wouldn't have to sneak around and hide what we were doing. There would be plenty of food, plenty of fun. We could sing our Dutch songs, listen to the free radio, salute our own flag and never hear "Heil Hitler" again.

Chapter 40

❧

The Railroad Strike

September 18, 1944

Dutch railroads have always insisted on their independence although they were forced to obey German orders which helped the Nazis. Now the Dutch government in London instructed Dutch railroad workers to walk off their jobs and go underground. So on September 18, the railroad workers stopped operating Dutch railroads and went into hiding. The strike is devastating to Hitler's war effort in Holland. We hope a shortage of transportation will keep the Germans from moving Jewish prisoners to camps in Poland.

The Germans can't find the missing railroad men in hiding. If they did, they would execute them. They must bring in their own railroad workers to keep at least some trains running.

Seyss Inquart is angry at the Dutch for defying him. To punish us, he's declared a blockade. No coal or oil will be allowed to come in on the trains. And food from farms in eastern Holland won't be brought to the cities in the western part. But people in Amsterdam and Rotterdam will starve if they can't bring in food because the houses there are so close together they don't have room for growing gardens. So the people from cities go out in the country and trade whatever they have for food. It is strictly a barter operation. Guilders can't get you anything. But when the city people come back to Amsterdam on their bicycles, the Germans take the food away if they catch them. The Germans call barter black marketing and made it illegal. So the people must try to smuggle food in.

When the authorities shut off shipments of oil and coal to the whole country, we can't make electricity. When the fuel is gone—there is no way to generate power for cooking or heating or lights. We have to use candles at night or stay in the dark. Winter is coming. It's getting cold and with no food or heat, many people will freeze and starve.

Dad's sister, Corrie and her husband, Wim lived in Amsterdam with their two little children. But now they moved in with us. Our house is crowded but at least we have food because Dad grew grain and vegetables to eat instead of tulips and daffodils and hyacinths.

Chapter 41

The Putten Affair

October 2, 1944

Hitler is losing the war. Dad predicted he would when his army marched into Russia. When Hitler brought huge forces against small countries like Austria, and Czechoslovakia and Denmark and Norway, he always won. In 1940 he attacked Denmark and Norway. A week later he brought the blitzkrieg to France, Belgium and the Netherlands. He was victorious in Greece and Yugoslavia.

Then he did the unbelievable! He marched into Russia, his former ally, without warning. Part of Hitler's pattern is to take his victims by surprise. It's easier to defeat people when they don't expect what is coming. He was already fighting in Africa and defending against the British. When he went into Russia, he was fighting on three fronts.

The German army went swiftly through the Ukraine toward Moscow, Stalin's capital, winning everywhere like a knife cutting through cheese. Then Stalin's armies began their counter-offensive. They surprised the Germans by coming around behind them. They trapped the German army between the Volga and the Don rivers.

The German Army then besieged Stalingrad. General Paulus told Hitler the army was doomed by lack of food, ammunition and supplies. The Russian winter froze the poorly clad soldiers. He asked Hitler to let him retreat until the army received replacements and supplies. But Hitler did not listen. He ordered General Paulus to fight on to the last man. He had no pity for his army. But, like Napoleon before him, Hitler is unable to conquer Russia.

The tide turned. The inevitable is coming.

In Holland, we wait for liberation, praying the war will soon end. When we heard the troops landed at Normandy, we expected the Allied armies to come quickly and liberate us.

Allied planes flew over, dropping leaflets asking us to help the invasion saying "The long awaited moment has arrived." When that happened, we counted the days until liberation.

Broadcasts from the Dutch government in London asked railroad personnel to quit. The Dutch railroad workers quit and went into hiding. The Germans did not have the manpower to operate the Dutch railways as well as their own. Many trains had to stop running. Hitler was not in a good mood. He wanted to punish Holland. So he decreed no food or fuel could be moved into or around Holland. Electricity is cut off. People in Amsterdam eat pigeons, rats, cats, mice—anything they can find--they call the creatures 'roof rabbits.' Without food or electricity or heat people die.

On the night of September 30, in a little farming town of Putten, somebody shot at a German staff car. There were four officers in the car. One was killed, one wounded and two escaped. The captors let the wounded man go.

Nobody knows who fired at the German car, but we presume it was men from the Dutch Resistance. When General Christiansen heard about it, he was furious. He said the town should be destroyed and "the whole bunch put up against the wall."

General von Wuehlisch ordered the commander of the place, "Shoot the people who did this. Burn the whole village but evacuate women and children. Arrest all men aged 18 to 50 and send them to the S.S. to be deported."

The commanding officer was baffled. Apparently he did not want to be an executioner but he obeyed and burned 87 houses in the small hamlet. He spared the rest of the houses but imprisoned all the people in the town.

After a few days, he let women and children go. But he turned all the men over to the S.S. The S.S. took them to a concentration camp in Amersfoort. Then they sent them east to another camp at Neuengamme. The men he sent to prison were farmers. They hadn't done anything against the Germans.

They had no weapons. But they had the bad luck to live in Putten and are sure to be executed.

Nobody knows what happened that night in Putten. But a man who ambushed a staff car wouldn't be inclined to stick around. Would you?

The German commanders were at their wits' ends. Lacking human kindness they rounded up the people in Putten and burned their houses. Everyone in Netherlands is outraged. What good did killing Dutch farmers do? Their childish tantrum will cause more sabotage and more attacks on the innocent residents while the real shooters got away.

Chapter 42

❧

A Windmill of Our Own

November 4, 1944

There is no coal, oil, gas or electricity. Germany cut all shipments to Holland off after the Railroad Strike. The Dutch government in London ordered our railroad workers to quit working and go into hiding. They said our railroads were helping prolong the war.

It made the Nazis furious. They are short of railroad workers themselves. But they can't hunt down the men who quit, they sent Germans to replace the workers and keep some the trains running. To get even, the Germans stopped bringing food and supplies to Western Holland. Our farmlands are in eastern part of Holland but most Dutch people live in the big cities. When the trains quit bringing food and coal, there was nothing to eat and no way to keep warm.

After Normandy, we thought the war would soon be over. But it is still going on and to make it worse, it is the coldest winter anybody can remember. And without coal or enough food, people starve and freeze. Tuberculosis kills many more.

Our kitchen stove with gas burners on one side and coal on the other, is useless without gas and coal. In summer we cooked with gas and in winter we burned coal. Dad took it out and installed a little pot-belly heater made from a pipe on which a blacksmith welded a flat sheet-iron top with holes to set pans. We burn twigs we pick up in the woods and shipping boxes from the warehouse. It's not easy to cook over a fire of paper and twigs. But we're

265

thankful for this makeshift contraption. It can't get the kitchen warm but it tries!

We used candles for light. Then Ton brought home a carbide lamp from the barn of a dairy farmer where he works after school. When he asked, the farmer said it was a carbide lamp. He had one in his house but he let Ton take the other because cows go to sleep when it's dark.

A carbide lamp has two compartments; you put a chunk of carbide in the one on the bottom and water in the top one. The water drips on the carbide giving off a gas that burns brightly.

Dad needed carbide. He knew where where he could get it. The seller wouldn't sell it for money, but he traded it for food—potatoes and beans. But barter is illegal in Holland. The Germans call it black marketing. Farmers may sell food to the Germans, but not to anyone else. Somebody had to go secretly to the place where it was available to get carbide. That was a shop in Sandpoort, a long way from Bennebroek.

So Jo and Alice took our old baby carriage and put vegetables in the bottom. They covered them up with a big doll wrapped in blankets. It looked like they were wheeling a baby with a blanket over its face to keep warm. They brought it to the store and exchanged the food for carbide in the back room. They put the package under the doll. The soldiers don't usually look in baby carriages pushed by young women. There was nothing unusual in a mother taking her baby to shop. So they brought the carbide safely home.

Carbide is a hard rock made of limestone and coal. It comes in big pieces which you break with a hammer until the pieces are small enough to put in the lamp. You fill the top with water, and light the gas it gives off. It wasn't as good as our old lights but it was a lot better than nothing.

Mother and Jo use the lamp in the kitchen when they cook and in the dining room when we eat. Afterward we sit around the table to read and play games. But one lamp is not enough. We need another because Grandmother goes to bed early and she can't go upstairs in the dark.

Our house has four rooms and a WC downstairs and four bedrooms and another bathroom upstairs. It was built of brick in the late 1800's. The builder made the stairs almost vertical, like a ladder, to save space. The steps are only deep enough for half your foot so it's hard to climb and even harder to come down if you're not used to it.

When the twins were babies, Mother could run up and down with a child on each arm. Grandmother can still climb but she can't carry a candlestick and her big purse. I bring her purse upstairs for her and leave the lighted candle so she can get ready for bed.

The house is dark at night. When the sky is not too hazy there is moonlight outside. But we can't see it. Because of the blackout our shutters must be closed and we have to stay inside because of a curfew. We miss our electric lights.

The day they turned off the electricity we were all sitting at the table. The light dimmed. I thought it wasn't too bad—we could live with that. Then it became dimmer. You could still see enough to walk around, but there wasn't enough light to read. If we could keep that much though, I thought we could get used to it. Gradually the light faded until it was almost completely gone. And then it went out. We knew it was going to happen so we had a candle handy and lit it. We don't have many candles. We thought we'd have to live in the dark when they were gone.

We know the Germans are not going to restore the power. Hitler was furious at the Railroad Strike. We don't know how to get around losing our lights. But we couldn't complain. Everybody was in the same leaky boat.

Then, Saturday morning, Uncle Bert, Mother's youngest brother, came over for coffee and a piece of Mother's bread.

"How are you getting along without lights?" he asked.

"It's not too bad. We are getting a carbide lamp," Mother said.

"Well, I have a great idea," Uncle Bert said.

Grandmother Heemskerk was sitting at the dining room table playing solitaire while we talked. She is so funny. She looked around to see if anyone was watching. When she thought nobody saw, she peeked under the piles of cards until she found the card she wanted, slid it out from under the pile and played it. When she finished the game, she proudly announced, "I won! And *no cheating*, mind you!"

Uncle Bert saw the way she was playing and smiled. He's seen her play before but he pretended to believe her and said "I don't know how you do it! You win so often!"

He's friendly and good natured and handy at making things. His face shone when he told us his bright idea "If you put a windmill on the roof, you could make your own electricity. It's not too hard. Electricity is cheap and ordinarily it would be more bother than it's worth. But now that the power is shut off, it makes sense. To make a windmill, all it takes is a propeller and a generator from an old car. It wouldn't give much power—but enough for a light."

He warmed up to the subject as he always did when there was something he planned to make. "I know where I can get a Buick generator for an apple and an egg. Once you have the generator all you need is a big board to make a propeller. I'll put it on a post, attach the generator, and put the windmill on the roof. You can run a wire into the house and voila, free electricity!"

Dad said, "How can we put a windmill on the roof? The house is too high and the roof is too steep. It would be very expensive to put it on the house."

Bert said, "Oh, I didn't mean the house roof. Put it on the warehouse. That has a flat roof so it would be easy to install."

Dad had an old church pew in the warehouse. A few years ago this pew was taken out to put in a bigger, newer one. This was one of the free benches in the back of the church, behind the pews people had to pay for. They were poor people's seats. You didn't have to pay pew rent to sit there. So to add to the church income, the church took out one of these old benches and replaced it with a padded pew. The board Dad saved was just a long piece of wood with no padding.

I don't know how Dad got it. He probably picked it up when the church discarded it. He likes wood and doesn't believe in throwing it away. So he kept it in the warehouse. Now he remembered it.

When his brothers told him he should clean out the old boards in the warehouse, he'd say, "I don't know. It might come in handy. Every time I get rid of something, I need it the next day." There are no building materials for sale because of the war, so his old lumber is coming in handy.

That old board was just the ticket. He had a workman carve it in the shape of a propeller. When it was finished, Bert mounted it on a long pole, attached the generator, and fastened it on the roof. That took a long time because he had to make it secure so the wind couldn't blow it away. When he was satisfied with his work, he turned it into the wind and it began to turn around fast with a whirring sound.

His little mill made electricity—but not enough for the regular bulbs. He soldered two automobile light bulbs to the lamp socket in the dining room chandelier. The propeller turned the generator and sent electricity to the bulbs. "Let there be light," he quoted. The windmill was not quiet, though.

"Purrs like a kitten," Bert said, smiling. Then he was so tickled with his toy, he just stood there laughing like a kid.

That light worked fine so he made another one for the hall light. Now we don't need a candle to go upstairs. Then he got carried away and made a light for the kitchen. It's not terribly bright but any light is better than none. We gave the carbide lamp to a friend who didn't have one.

The wind blows most of the time, making the propeller spin. It's not musical, it sounds like the noisy motorcycle he had before the war. He rode like the wind, his cheeks red and his straight brown hair plastered to his head. He doesn't have his motorcycle anymore. He couldn't get gas for it now anyway. But Bert attached a bicycle to the invention and set it up indoors. If the wind is not blowing the boys can pedal and get electricity that way.

It's a good thing you can't hear the mill in the house, only in the warehouse or outdoors. The only way to silence it would be to go up on the roof and turn the propeller out of the wind. We wouldn't mind a little inconvenience, though if we had to climb and fix it. We're lucky we have light! In the old days we turned on bright lights all over and never gave a thought to electricity. Now we're grateful for a little gleam.

Holland is dark at night with no streetlights. But when the moon is full and clear of clouds we have a 'bomber's moon'. It helps pilots find their way to bomb Berlin.

Chapter 43

❦

Raising Hyacinths

December 30, 1944

Dad was forcing hyacinth bulbs for Uncle Pete to take to a flower show. He does this every year and he always wins the blue ribbon. Dad was proud his flowers were judged the best. It also means he gets more for them when they are sold.

As usual, we potted hyacinths in the fall of '44 so they would bloom early. This is called forcing. The pots were buried in soil and covered with straw to get the roots started growing. In December we dig them up and put them in the greenhouse so the warmth would start them growing leaves and flowers. When we put them in the ground we still had coal to keep the greenhouse at an even temperature. When we needed to put them in the greenhouse, there wasn't any coal. The Germans had cut off our supply. Dad was going to toss them but the twins, Ton and Gerard, and I saved them.

We moved a crazy contraption into the greenhouse—a 'stove' made from a stovepipe with an elbow on it. We can put wood in the lower end to burn. The other end of the pipe we put through the greenhouse roof. We scrounged some wood to burn in our makeshift stove. We got the wood from the tree trunks the Germans had sharpened and stuck in our fields. Actually the Germans had stolen them from cutting trees in a nearby forest. So they were not the property of the Germans at all. They belonged to Holland. The Germans had warned us not to cut or remove them. But when all coal was gone, the Dutch were desperate for fuel so they were disappearing like magic, at night. We knew we could get in trouble for taking them but the logs were tempting. Other people were taking them, too. We tried to thin them out—not taking them all from one place and hoped they wouldn't be missed. We chopped them into little pieces too small to be recognizable. We mixed the pieces with our own wood we got from cutting ornamental trees growing around the place.

It is hard to regulate the temperature in the greenhouse with such a primitive stove, but we worked at it. We kept a small fire going all the time. When we saw little buds poking out between the leaves we were overjoyed. In a few weeks the hyacinths bloomed. However the flowers had black tips because it was too cold. They were only half as tall as they should have been. They would never win any prizes. We nipped off the ruined tips of the flowers. Then we brought them to a florist who was happy to get them just in time for Christmas. There isn't anything we want to buy with the money he paid us for the flowers. We're saving it. Dad is pleased with what we achieved. He didn't expect anything to come of our project. But he had helped, staying up till midnight to check the thermometer and keep the temperature up. We are proud of our accomplishment.

Chapter 44

Dad Sees Abraham

January 28, 1945

I don't know if any other country besides ours has this saying that when you are fifty, you have seen Abraham. But in the Netherlands, everybody understands what this means…for instance, if you want to tell your age in general terms and you don't want to say exactly how old you are, when somebody asks you and if you are over fifty, you might merely say, "Well, I have seen Abraham."

This comes from the Bible where the Pharisees couldn't understand Jesus when he said, "Before Abraham, I am."

They asked "How can he know Abraham? He is not even fifty years old?"

Tonight, January 28, 1945, my father will have his fiftieth birthday. So Jo and I planned a surprise for him, without his knowing about it, of course. Jo and her friend Lou, who was staying overnight on account of the curfew, and I quietly went to my parent's bedroom door one o'clock in the night. I dressed up in a bed sheet and a gray wig and a mustache and the three of us crept down to their bedroom. I held a lighted candle in one hand and a wooden staff in the other. Jo and Lou were in the background, watching. I knocked on their door and when Dad asked "Who is there?" I, as the self-appointed spokesman, answered "Bart Heemskerk, you are now fifty years old. I am Abraham. So now you have seen me."

Dad's reaction was typical—a mixture of stern father and a man trying to keep from laughing. Mother burst into giggles. We all had a lot of fun. We were cold, there was only a candle for light and there wasn't a lot of food in the house. But we thought this was hilarious.

Today Alice and the twins said, "Why didn't you call us? We wanted to see Abraham, too." So I re-enacted the scene and we laughed together. My father laughed ruefully, realizing he had had a good joke played on him. And mother told the story to everyone who came to his birthday celebration, which was very lean. We have no Dutch gin anymore, no butter cookies, and no little cups of real coffee. Only ersatz to drink a toast to Dad, but we all got a howl about last night—the night when father saw Abraham.

Chapter 45

Our Big Parade

May 6, 1945

The war is over. The Canadian army came to liberate us. All the people of Bennebroek seemed to be congregating in town. They said they were going to have a parade. It seemed like a good idea to the twins and Louis and me so we decided to join it.

In the basement of the convent there was an old green car. I asked Meneer Vermeys, the caretaker if we could borrow it for the parade and he said we were welcome to it. There were 4 wheels on the car that somebody had taken from decrepit bicycles. They weren't good but we thought they would last for the length of the parade, at least. We made a sign from cardboard. It said **"The Big Three got Hitler under the knee."**

I dressed like Roosevelt and waved a cigarette holder in the air. Louis was Stalin wearing a uniform borrowed from a policeman with a Russian emblem on it, and "Dikke" Vos was Churchill with a derby hat and a big fat cigar. Gerard was Hitler wearing a little black toothbrush mustache and he was pushing the car. Ton was the driver of the ancient vehicle. It was a wonderful parade. Everybody was laughing and pointing at our official car! We went along feeling like the stars of the parade until we had to make a turn around the corner and the wheels on our car collapsed sideways causing an uproar of laughter because the car fell down!

I wish I had a picture of our great parade.

Alice's Diary
(Translated from Dutch)

New Year's Day
January 1, 1945

At 7:30 we went to church and afterward we had breakfast with ersatz coffee. Annie van der Berg and Aunt Agnes came to visit. We had an early meal so that we could finish by 5:00. Louis van der Wal and Lou van Emmerik and Aunt Annie and Uncle Nol came and we made sandwiches.

When they left we sat and talked by the light of a carbide lamp until we went to bed. The carbide lamp was a godsend. This is how we got it. Ton works for a dairy farmer, Leen Kortekaas. He saw the lamp in a window of the barn. He had never seen anything like it so he asked what it was. Leen said it was a carbide lamp. The way it worked was you put a piece of carbide in the bottom chamber and filled the top with water. The water drips on the carbide, so it gives off a gas that burns with a bright light.

Ton said we needed a lamp and asked where he could get one. The Germans had shut off the electricity in Holland after the railroad workers' strike. Mr. Kortekaas gave it to Ton. He said he already had one in the house and the cows couldn't use it.

Later somebody rigged up more of these lamps from tin cans and metal tubes so we got another one. We kept both of them in the living room where we sat together. If you had to leave the living room after dark you could take one with you.

We know where we can buy carbide in Bennebroek, but you aren't allowed to. Jo and I wrapped up blankets to look like a baby and put it in a carriage. We pushed it to the store and put the carbide under the bundle of blankets and went right by the guards. The Germans never bother women pushing a baby carriage. So now we have light.

January 3, 1945

This morning the sky was clear and blue. Then at eleven the wind blew dark clouds in and covered the sun. It looked like rain so I stayed in and practiced piano.

Dad cut down the big chestnut tree by the house. We hated to see it go, but we had to have firewood.

At the bakery there was no bread. The baker couldn't get flour. We still had some at home so Jo made pancakes of flour, milk and eggs for dinner.

Later a man came to the house and asked for something to eat. Mother gave him some cooked potatoes and carrots and added a lump of butter. He thanked her and said he wished he could pay but he didn't have anything to give her.

Mother told him it was nothing. She enjoys feeding people and can't stand to think of people going hungry.

January 7, 1945

This is Sunday. I went to church at 7:30 and planned to visit Rietje afterward but Cok van Empelen invited me over for her birthday. After that Lou, Rein, and Cor Kievert came over. We had supper. We told Dad it was his turn to do the dishes but he said "I did them last week." It is a family joke and we laughed at that.

So Jo and I cleaned up, read our books and went to bed.

January 9, 1945

This morning there were frost flowers on the windows. This afternoon it started to snow.

Gre (pronounced Kray) came over to sew She made a pair of gray slacks from an old coat in the attic. You can't see where it's worn because she turned the fabric.

The snow stopped and the sidewalks were slippery where we walked on the snow, but drifts stayed in corners around the buildings.

I went to church. It was cold because there is no heat there. The motor of the organ won't work without electricity so when the organist uses it, a young man has to stand on a beam connected to the organ and pump it to put air in the bellows so the organist can play.

January 12, 1945

I'm looking for a purse I thought might have some stamps in it. I need them to buy food if any becomes available. If there's no food in stores, stamps aren't worth anything.

January 14, 1945

Sunday. We walked to church. Our church is on one end of Bennebroek and the Gereformerde church is at the opposite end so we pass them walking the other way.

Afterward we did chores. Louis came for dinner. Later Lou came to see Jo. I went to see Rietje. The icy wind blew against my face. It feels like Siberia. Lou stayed for sandwiches. He had to leave before 8: 00 PM because of the curfew.

January 15, 1945

Ton and Gerard were trying to fix the bike. It didn't go too well because they were nervous. But now it works and we have transportation.

Dad is going to the farm up north. He packed everything he needed to take. Then he went to sit down but he didn't turn around to see where his chair was. Somebody had moved the chair a little. So he didn't sit *in* the chair; he just sat *next* to it. It was so funny. We laughed uproariously. Why does somebody falling make us laugh?

Jo and I tried to bake bread. We mixed the dough and put it in a pan and set it in a warm place to rise. Then we put it in our little oven. The oven was not hot enough so we had to leave it for hours. The top of the loaf was light brown, but the bottom was burned black. But we were hungry so we ate it hot. It was delicious.

January 16, 1945

Dad left for the north early this morning. He had to take care of business on his farm and pick up some food for us. He can't carry much on a bicycle with bags over the back wheel.

January 17, 1945

There was no bread at the bakery. We had pancakes again. We ate them with syrup we made from boiling sugar beets and had milk to drink. We're thankful Dad grows vegetables.

The people in Amsterdam are hungry. When there is nothing in the stores they go out to find food in the country. They have to smuggle it in or the Germans take it away from them when they come back to town.

January 18, 1945

I walked five miles to Haarlem to buy a present for Cok. Sometimes I go on roller skates. But it was too windy and rainy to skate, so I walked. I got soaked right through my raincoat. It was hard to find anything to buy. The stores are almost empty.

January 19, 1945

There were Razzias again today. The Germans collected a bunch of young men and put them in van Engel's Garage with soldiers standing guard outside. After a while one of the boys went to the WC in the back. He discovered a window high up and climbed out. When he didn't come back, another went to the rest room, too. He found the window, too and climbed out into a neighbor's yard behind the building. Lou was one of those who escaped through the W.C. window. But when the neighbor saw them running through her yard she started yelling. That alerted the guards. They ran after them but it was too late. The guards kept the ones who were still inside. But they hadn't bothered to get the names and addresses of the ones they picked up so they didn't know where they lived and couldn't find them.

January 20, 1945

Dad is back again from the north, tired and wet. He came through rain and snow squalls and bad weather. Mother is happy to see him. She worries when he's gone.

January 21, 1945

It's freezing hard. The snow is deep and crusted. I just stayed home and worked around the house. It's cold but not freezing. There's a little fire burning in the kitchen stove.

January 22 and 23, 1945

I worked in the apothecary (pharmacy) today. When I came home I played the piano.

January 24, 1945

There were Razzias again today to find men to work in Germany. The German men have all been drafted into the army. Germany needs to find workers in Holland. They are picking up young Dutch men and sending them to Germany.

The Germans benefit in two ways: they get free laborers and have fewer men in the resistance. Many young men are active in the underground.

January 27, 1945

This morning I worked in the apothecary and bought a present for Rita. This afternoon we had another snow storm. At 6:45 I started to go to Rita's birthday party. She was surprised I came in the bad weather. We played charades and danced until 2 AM and then went to bed.

We slept until 7 and I went home at 8:30 AM. Jan, Rita's brother, stood on the balcony in his pajamas. I guess he wanted to show us he didn't mind the cold.

January 28, 1945

Today is Dad's fiftieth birthday and relatives came over. We served ersatz coffee. We didn't have any cake or cookies but they enjoyed talking and went home before 8 PM curfew.

Last night Pim played a trick on Dad. There is a saying in Holland that when a man is fifty years old, he has seen Abraham. It comes from a verse in the Bible where the Pharisees were talking about Jesus. They said Jesus claimed He saw Abraham but He couldn't have since he was not even fifty years old.

So, since Dad turned fifty, we wanted him to see Abraham.

Pim put on a gray wig, a false beard and a white alb. He carried a lighted candle. Jo and Lou followed him. As the clock struck twelve, Pim knocked on the bedroom door and said in a spooky, ghostly voice, "Bart Heemskerk, I am Abraham. You turned fifty years old and you shall see me." Then Pim opened the door and said "Behold."

Dad woke up and mumbled something that sounded like an expletive. We laughed and ran out of the room.

This was a night I'll always remember—the night Dad saw Abraham!

January 31, 1945

The Russians are marching toward Berlin. They defeated Hitler's army with help from the winter weather. The Allied Armies are advancing from the West. It is a lot like what Poland went through when the Russians attacked from the East and the Nazis attacked from the West. Only this time the Germans are getting a taste of their own medicine. When they marched against Russia, it was a change from attacking little countries with their big army.

We follow the news to find out—when will Holland be liberated?

February 4, 1945

It's Sunday. At 7:30 we walked to church—only a short distance. There were terrible torrents of rain. I got a black spot on my raincoat from my missal.

This afternoon we had visitors again—Louis, Rietje, Rein, Aunt Annie, Jan, Lou, and Uncle Bert.

The Russians stopped at the Oder River.

February 5, 1945

It was dark and raining this morning when Dad left on his bike to get food from the farm up north. He said it was no use stopping for the weather; "It was miserable but it could get worse."

February 6, 1945

We had an adventure. Some time ago the Germans planted tree trunks, sharpened to a point like a pencil on the fields behind the house to guard against gliders and paratroopers that Hitler feared would land in Holland.

Louis and Jan wanted to take them down and burn them for fuel. But it's too dangerous. If they are missing we'll be blamed. But at night other people are cutting them down for firewood.

Last night around eleven, Pim heard the sound of someone cutting one down. So he called out *"Was ist los?"* (Who is there?) to make them think the Germans were around. The woodcutters ran away.

February 7, 1945

Lou came to stay last night because Mother is frightened. Dad isn't back from the north. She was afraid thieves would break in and steal everything during the night.

For supper we had a mixture of beets and potatoes. At midnight we were hungry. We ate a slice of bread with an egg.

February 8, 1945

A lot of bombers are flying over. Bombs fell on Ijmuiden and the railroad bridge at Halfweg and between Leiden and Warmond. Ijmuiden has been bombed many times lately by the British and the Americans. It happens so often I'm getting used to it.

Dad came back bringing some grain and vegetables. Some people have tulip bulbs to eat. They are lucky if they get one a day.

We went to church. It was cold. There is nothing to warm it.

February 9, 1945

The weather is stormy. Yet the sky is filled with planes. The British bomb us to destroy the railroad tracks so the Germans can't bring in more V-I's. The planes have rockets on their wings. The rockets fall next to the tracks but never on them. The planes can't hit the targets but you have to give them credit. They keep trying, acting out the saying "If at first you don't succeed, try, try again!"

February 11, 1945

Sunday morning. Church was over early. This afternoon we played Monopoly with Riet and Ali.

February 13, 1945

Today is Shrove Tuesday, the day before Ash Wednesday. We can't do much to celebrate. We used to eat Olie Bollen. (A Dutch treat made of dough fried in deep fat.) But we did have pancakes.

Dick of Uncle Piet's, Piet Spruyt and Agnes of Aunt Annie apparently smelled them from far away and came to visit.

February 14, 1945

A room with no heat is terribly cold. I wonder if I will ever be warm again. I worked at the apothecary filling prescriptions until my fingers were numb. I came home and had tea. Holding my hand around the cup, it thawed out enough to play the piano.

February 17, 1945

I couldn't go to Haarlem because there was no bicycle available. It takes too long to walk five miles in the cold wind.

February 19, 1945

I studied my chemistry but couldn't concentrate so I went to bed and snuggled up in my blankets.

February 21, 1945

Today we baked banket from sugar beet pulp. (Banket is a Dutch pastry made with marzipan in a butter crust. It is pronounced 'bon ket'.) It didn't taste too bad. Everybody talks about the new recipes made from tulips and sugar beets.

February 22, 1945

Today is Ton and Gerard's birthday. We had poffertjes and banket made in the shape of letters. They taste good. Almond cookies would have tasted better. (Poffertjes are little puffs dipped in butter and sprinkled with powdered sugar. They are made in a special pan like a muffin tin but round on the bottom, not flat.) We sang the birthday song and enjoyed the special treats.

Fighter planes are continually flying overhead.

February 25, 1945

This afternoon we went to Lenten meditations. While we were there the English started dropping bombs. Mother is very nervous, but I'm used to the bombing so it doesn't bother me. A bomb can land anywhere. I'm not afraid it will hit the church.

February 26, 1945

A boiled potato sells for 1.50 guilders in Amsterdam. And tulip bulbs are in great demand for food. They taste awful but any food is better than nothing.

February 28, 1945

Nothing unusual happened. People keep coming here for food. Mother keeps a pan of potatoes on the stove to give them.

March 1, 1945

We got a new little cooking stove to replace the gas stove. It's just a round drum on feet with a cover the blacksmith rigged up. He crafted a top for it with three holes and room for the smoke pipe. The hole in the front is hottest because the fire burns under it. The back is heated by smoke going to the pipe. It is about 30 inches high with its legs. It burns wood. There is no more coal, but we can get wood from the tree Dad cut.

March 2, 1945

It takes forever to cook on the new stove. Supper took forever. Jo made pancakes one at a time. We took turns getting a pancake and were still eating at 8 PM.

March 3, 1945

Church is terribly busy because you have to make confession for Easter. I waited for a long time.

March 7, 1945

This afternoon between 1 and 2 we can pick up Swedish bread. A few weeks ago we turned in stamps for 800 grams of bread, 1-1/4 grams of margarine and for children under 14, half a pound of barley from the Swedish Red Cross. This was given for the hungry provinces of North and South Holland and Utrecht. Jo and I went with pillow cases and got 9 loaves of bread, some margarine and barley. We are very happy. White bread is so delicious! There are 12 people living here. And there are always hungry visitors.

March 10, 1945

We have been eating Swedish bread with barley soup and homemade beet sugar on pancakes. You can make sugar by boiling sugar beets. It's rough and brown, not like cane sugar.

We're always hungry although we're getting more food. We seem to be eating day and night. The tax collector came to ask Dad for his taxes. Dad didn't have enough money but he promised to pay as soon as he could. He gave the collector a bag of potatoes and he went away happy.

March 14, 1945

A couple of days ago Jo and I decided to go to Alkmaar to pick up the beans that were supposed to be delivered from the farm in Koegras. We got up early and Mother made 8 sandwiches each.

Jo took the bicycle with a rack over the back wheel. It has a bag hanging down on each side.

I rode to Haarlem on the back of her bike. We borrowed another bike in Haarlem from Mrs. Sueters. In exchange we promised to give her beans. Her bike had side bags too. We took along some bike tools and some tobacco to pay someone to fix it if we had a flat.

Since the Velsen ferry had no fuel, it stopped operating. To get from Haarlem to Buitenhuisen we had to go via Spaarndam. We didn't have to ask directions because we saw a lot of other people with side bags on their bikes, and followed them. People in Amsterdam have to cross the North Sea Canal to get out into the country to find food.

It was a real race to the ferry. That was quite a trip. When we arrived in Buitenhuisen, crowds of people were waiting. We found out the ferry was out of service there, as well. To take the ferry's place, they had rowboats which arrived at three places. We got into the shortest line. They had two boats there. When one boat left, the other boat would arrive. We waited for a while. Then, suddenly a lot of people from another line came and got in front of us. Our line was pushed back. The rowboat those people were waiting for had changed. They would only transport bicycles and carts. The people from the bicycles were sent over to our line in front of us.

After a long time it was our turn. They loaded our bikes on the boat but we had to take the baggage off and carry it. Seven bicycles were stacked in front of the boat and then more were loaded on leaning against them. The oarsmen sat in the center and the passengers crowded in back. We got across, put our bags back on our bikes and took the road to Zaandijk, Purmerend. This was a long blacktop road.

When we came to the water tower there, we turned left toward Alkmaar.

We rode straight ahead until we had to turn by a railroad crossing. Direction: Uitgeest, a left turn at Uitgeest station and then straight for a long way. This road ran into the road for Alkmaar through Heiloo.

When we came to Heiloo, they warned us that the Germans were confiscating bicycles there. Nobody could stand to lose their bicycles so they all turned around and went back. But Jo said "That won't get us anywhere."

There was no way to take a detour around Heiloo. It was impossible. A boy about fourteen offered to hide our bikes beside his house. We were 3 kilometers from Alkmaar. So we decided to chance it. We took the bags off our bikes. We had to carry them.

Finally we got to Alkmaar, found the street we needed, and asked for the man who knew where we could pick up the beans. They said he was away for the day. That really did it!

His wife said she didn't know anything about the beans. We waited for the son to come. But when he came, he said he didn't know anything about them either. We had to go home. There was nothing left for us to do.

So we walked back to pick up our bikes. Fortunately they were still hidden and the boy gave them to us. Meanwhile a stiff wind came up and we had to ride into it. We ate most of our sandwiches along a country road.

Then we returned to Haarlem, gave Mrs. Sueter back her borrowed bike and went home. We were very cold, extremely tired, no-end frustrated, completely empty handed. What a miserable day that was! We had traveled 100 kilometers through water, wind and rain. And all our trouble brought was disappointment!

March 14, 1945

This morning we had a house search by two German soldiers. Mother offered them ersatz coffee and they stood their guns up against the corner of the kitchen to drink it. They didn't think we would take their guns. They acted like we were friends.

Dad can talk German fluently. He acts friendly even though he hates Nazis. He doesn't want them snooping. They knew he had sons who might be useful for the German war effort. So they asked about them. Dad said, "I have four sons. The oldest one is Jan. He is working in Germany. My second son, Franz is studying in Belgium at the Brother House. I have twin boys, Gerard and Ton who are fifteen.

They saw the stein Dad got in Heidelberg. So they talked about that. They think Germany is the greatest. Much better than Holland. They should be grateful to be here, not fighting in Russia.

Pim was hiding. When the men left Dad went to look for him. He was in the air vent on top of the warehouse. He couldn't get out because he had climbed up into it and closed the door of the vent and he was standing on it. But at least the Germans didn't find him.

When they left at about 5 o'clock, four British fighters surprised us. They aimed at the bridge at Leidse Vaart (Leiden Canal), but they missed it. There were a lot of explosions which made us lie on the ground. The glass in the dining room window shattered. But we weren't hurt. Three homes were completely demolished. Two children were killed and many wounded.

March 15, 1945

People are moving out of the area of Leidse Vaart because the British and Americans are bombing the railroad tracks. Every fighter has two rockets attached to their wings. They shoot them at the tracks but they miss the target every time. How can they do this so often and not change their tactics?

The Brits are bombing there because the Germans are making a launching track for V-1 missiles in the Bekslaan.

The van Emmerik family and their neighbors have to move out. The Germans have decided to occupy their homes because they are putting up the launch track there. Most people are moving out anyway because they can't stand the noise.

March 17, 1945

Today I went to Amsterdam. Bombardments continue. It's hopeless. The explosions hit houses and break windows in nearby homes. Then it's impossible to keep the windowless houses warm. There are many casualties at the RR tracks. But they don't hurt the tracks, just everything around them.

March 18, 1945

It was a beautiful day and Rietje came over. The fighters are at it again.

March 19, 1945

I visited the doctor to see why my leg was so sore. He told me to rest it. This afternoon Alie de Vroomen stopped to see me. There's a lot of bombing in Warmond. The bombs miss targets there, too.

March 20, 1945

The sun is shining through my bedroom window so I sit there to keep warm. When I hear planes, I hobble downstairs as quick as a hungry cat chases a mouse

March 22, 1945

They bombed us continually all day. This evening around 6 they dove down so close I thought they would hit us.

March 23, 1945

There was a rumor going around that between 5 and 6 o'clock, 500 planes would bomb our area. It wasn't true but 7 or 8 women were upset. But there's no point in panic if there is nothing you can do.

I went to the doctor. While I sat in the waiting room, there was a terrific explosion. People were scared. A V-1 rocket must have blown up.

Last night they shot one off successfully. It sounds like trying to start a car with an engine that won't catch. It's like a big engine, first soft and then really loud as if it's heading straight for you.

They launched missiles at midnight and early in the morning. Many missiles misfire, making big explosions and scaring everybody.

March 24, 1945

This week the weather has been beautiful. The fighter planes had plenty of opportunities to shoot off the rockets on their wings.

March 25, 1945

It's Sunday. We had visitors for dinner. It sounds like they were on the menu. I meant they ate with us.

March 26, 1945

The doctor told me my ankle had healed enough so I can walk. So I went to Haarlem. We celebrated Mrs. Hoff's birthday in her parlor with a bundt cake made of tulip flour. There is no sugar to make frosting so she covered it with fruit juice.

March 27, 1945

V-1 Launchings and bombings continue. The Allies invasion of Germany is going well, they say. We hope the war will end by Easter.

March 28, 1945

The Allies are advancing fast! That's the good news. The bombardments are continuing. That's the bad news!

It's impossible to ignore explosions when they're so close.

March 29, 1945

Maundy Thursday. While the church services were going on the Germans launched V-1 rockets. This is unusual because they never launched them in the daytime before.

Dad says they are trying to get rid of what they have left. They were heavy explosions. We hear the V-1 track is destroyed. Our dining room window is gone, frame and all. There is no glass and no lumber. We can't replace it. The explosions were so loud they hurt your ears.

March 31, 1945

Today is Easter so we went to church. After church we walked to Haarlem to find a birthday present for Jo. We couldn't find anything. We saw nothing nice in the stores. They are practically empty.

We were hoping the war would be over by Easter. But it isn't although things are going fast in the Netherlands. Three Provinces: Gelderland, Drente and Overijsel have been liberated.

This afternoon I went to Vespers. The priest delivered a beautiful sermon.

April 4, 1945

We went to Bekslaan to see the launch track that blew up. Many homes and trees in the area were destroyed. Not much remains of the track. The concrete road was cracked and covered with pieces of metal that had fallen on it. There are huge holes in the road and a large ball full of water was in one hole.

In Vogelenzang there was a lot of wreckage. The meadow was plowed under by an errant V-1. Every window was broken.

It's quiet now since the Germans left.

April 5, 1945

April weather is here—cold, windy and rainy. I worked in the pharmacy. Rein gave Jo a bar of soap for her birthday and that's a luxury now.

For dinner, Pim made waffles. They were delicious.

April 6, 1945

Jo had a birthday party. She got a mosaic box with three tiles and a pretty blooming plant from Lou, and a letter from Ferdi, who is not here. Louis van der Wal gave her a photo album and Mrs. van der Meer brought her a book. Tante Co's gift was a tiny bottle of perfume. Aunt To gave her two small paintings and a bouquet. Later Mr. and Mrs. van Emmerik came and presented her a silver spoon.

There was no cake but we had sandwiches for a treat. After eating, they all left except for Lou and Louis who stayed overnight. Gerard Assendelft dropped in and we danced until the victrola's spring broke and the music stopped.

It was late after twelve-thirty then. So we made some ersatz and drank it, pretending it was good. Everyone went to bed around 1:30. Lou and Louis had to sleep on the floor because there were no beds.

We didn't have the food and drinks we had before the war but it was a *gezellig* (happy, cozy, enjoyable) day.

April 24, 1945

So much is happening there isn't time to keep up with my diary. Everything is going fast. One place after another in Germany has been captured. Now Russians occupy 2/3 of Berlin. With all the fighting going on the city must be in ruins.

This morning they announced on the radio food packages would be dropped in the three hungry Provinces. (North and South Holland). All the other provinces have been liberated.

April 25, 1945

Things changed. Food will not be dropped but will be brought in by boat instead.

April 26, 1945

They changed it again. Packages will be dropped by American bombers after negotiations between the Allies and the Germans. The Germans promise to cooperate.

April 28, 1945

This morning I worked in the pharmacy. We hear rumors that the Germans have offered to surrender to the Americans and British but they have not accepted this because the Russians were excluded. The Nazis do not want to surrender to the Russian army. The battle for Berlin continues. The end is not far.

April 29, 1945

Today around 1 o'clock we saw bombers flying low. They dropped tins of food on the airport Ypenburg near Delft and Leiden and Rotterdam. Everybody is optimistic again. They say Hitler is near death. It's only a rumor—how could anybody here know?

April 30, 1945

This is Princess Juliana's birthday. A camp with Dutch prisoners in Germany was liberated. The prisoners sent Juliana a birthday card.

We heard this morning that the Germans would surrender at 10 o'clock. But it is not at all certain. Meanwhile we're waiting for the food packages. That is the talk of the day.

I walked home from Haarlem because the bicycle had a flat tire. Before the war everybody over ten had his own bike. Now they are mostly gone but I have an old decrepit one. The Germans have taken every bicycle they could lay their hands on. And the ones we have left need tires and repairs.

May 1, 1945

The official confirmation of Hitler's death has been announced. His successor is Doenitz.

Rumors of surrender are flying but we don't know when it will be. One says it will happen at noon. Another says it will be at 8 this evening. These are just guesses. Jo and I went to Haarlem to deliver potatoes. The sack kept falling off my bicycle.

I borrowed rope from the family van Emmerik and tied the sack and we were on our way. In Heemstede we were warned that the Germans were confiscating bicycles everywhere but we didn't see them doing it. Maybe they want them to go back to Germany. Anyway they left before we got there. The curfew started this evening at 9.

May 2, 1945

Looking out the window, suddenly we saw large bombers in the distance. They were flying toward Schiphol or Utrecht. We ran outdoors to see where they were going. As we watched, more planes joined them.

It was cold so we went inside. A half hour later Mother called "Come quick. They are flying right over." So we went out again and saw all the bombers flying over our house. They were American Flying Fortresses. We stood there yelling and waving our arms. We climbed up on the warehouse roof because there were so many of them. They were still coming. When we got on the roof, a second flight arrived and they dropped packages on the soccer field and the Jamboree field. (In 1937 the Boy Scouts had a jamboree in Vogelzang and afterward we called it the Jamboree Field.)

It was a tremendous show! When the bombers went, Pim went to town and told us that a lot of tins had been dropped on the soccer field and on the Zwartweg. Quite a few people stole some food and were caught. Several tins had broken open and condensed milk was running out of them.

The ones that fell in Leidse Vaart were fished out of the canal. People took cigarettes and chocolate bars and jars of jam from the broken tins. There were matches, cookies, flour, ham, soap, shaving cream, butter, milk, dried eggs, and plenty of other goodies.

May 3, 1945

Two black marketers who stole food from the packages were caught and made to stand in front of the police station wearing signs saying "I stole food from the packages.

When I left the pharmacy at 4 o'clock I heard they were taken to the big market place. A lot of people were there. When the first black marketer came out between two policemen, the second one hung his head. He was between two policemen, too.

Everybody yelled remarks at them. They had to climb steps so everybody could see them. Photographers took pictures of them and policemen took them away.

May 5, 1945

The Germans surrendered! I can hardly believe it. I know it's true because huge crowds gathered on the main street, standing around and not knowing what to do. I decided to go to Haarlem. Four beautiful Dutch flags were flying on the outskirts of town—what a wonderful sight! We hadn't been allowed to fly them for five years!

As I went along I saw more and more flags. But the Germans didn't like it. People were wearing orange ribbons and children had little flags and were blowing whistles. The Market place was crowded. But in Union Square the Germans threw hand grenades and shot off their rifles because they couldn't stand to see people celebrating their defeat. I went home to avoid being shot. On the way people were celebrating everywhere.

This afternoon Jo and I went to the van Emmerik's and drank lemonade to celebrate our liberation.

May 6, 1945

This afternoon we visited Rietje and spent our time cycling. We expect the Canadians to come tomorrow. We made headscarves with red, white, and blue borders.

May 7, 1945

We waited all day but we didn't see any Canadian troops. We went into Bennebroek and a record was playing good music. They say the Canadians will be here tomorrow.

May 8, 1945

At ten o'clock we went to the main crossroads. All you could do was just walk around. This afternoon Rietje and I sold buttons for the Dutch People's Restoration. We sold quite a few. Today we only saw one Canadian. I wonder where the rest are.

This evening we paraded around town and decided to rest. It was late. Then another parade came with people yelling at the van Wijk family. They were Nazis and the only official Nazi Dutchmen in Bennebroek.

We followed the parade to town hall and waited while the police put them in cells.

May 9, 1945

We sold all our Dutch Restoration pins and afterward went for a bike ride. We wanted to be in Haarlem but the militia wouldn't let us in so we went home. The Canadians rounded up the Germans and sent them out of town. They didn't leave happily. Somebody had rigged up a loudspeaker at the tavern '*The Oude Geleerde Man*' and played records of Hitler's speeches and German music to speed them out of town. Some of them defiantly yelled "We'll be back!"

May 10, 1945
Ascension Day.

We went to church and Rein and Louis came over. There was going to be a big celebration this evening. Jo, Lou, Rietje, Pim, Louis and I went to the crossroads. The record player was broken so we went for a walk while they fixed it. The Canadians set up lights and we danced until 11:00.

May 11, 1945

The war is over. The parades and celebrations are all done. The *Uebermensch* are gone and nobody will miss them. We hope we've seen the last German soldier goose stepping down our quiet streets.

The war caused nothing but grief. And what did Hitler accomplish? Everybody was as poor and miserable now as they were in the years before they listened to his promises and believed his lies. Europe is in shambles because of one man who was obsessed with his lust for power.

Wartime Memories

John, the oldest son of Bart and Marie Heemskerk, was born June 6, 1923. He liked working with his father in the flower bulb business. The Germans were taking unemployed young men to work in Germany. His father, Bart did not want John to be taken into a labor camp so in 1943 he sent John to work for a Dutch friend, Kees Mantel, who had a farm in Germany. John wanted to visit his home in Bennebroek so when the Dutch farmer traveled to Holland, John would hide in the back of the truck under the plants they were transporting, before they reached the border, because he did not have permission to leave Germany.

Once Germans stopped the truck before he had time to hide. They asked John for his papers. John did not have any, but he had a quick mind. He told the guards that his papers had been destroyed during a bombing raid a short time before. The guard accepted the explanation but said he should get new papers in Holland before he crossed the border again.

Kees had two sons who also worked on his farm in Germany. There was a bottling plant on the farm and the young men knew the Germans wanted liquor, so they invented and bottled a brew they sold to the Germans. It was not genuine liquor, but better than nothing, which was the only alternative at the time.

During the war they lived with constant bombing. Once the house he lived in was almost hit in a raid. The Allies were attempting to hit railroads, but missed the target and hit a house across the road, which disintegrated and caught on fire.

He lived through the war and later went to America where he worked for his Uncle Eddie Heemskerk raising flower bulbs in North

Carolina. Later he went into landscaping in Massachusetts with another uncle, Bill Lommerse.

He married Rika Verzaal and brought up a family, George and Charles, and twins, Jean and Judy in Needham, Massachusetts.

Jean and Judy with their Uncle Bill at the
Boston Flower Show in 1955 or 1966.

NOTE: There is another article about John T. Heemskerk on the Internet written by his grandson, Chris Wellington, which tells more about John's life. This was written by Judy Heemskerk-McDonald.

Wartime Memories
Henriette Dekker-Heemskerk

I was eight when the Germans invaded, so I didn't understand what the war was or what it meant but I do remember noticing the impact it had on my parents. The pressure on them was immense and it was very clear they were behaving differently. My father couldn't work, as the bulb trade effectively came to a halt from 1940 to 1945. My mother, meanwhile had to look after seven of us with what were increasingly meager supplies by the end of the war, and there was the constant worry over my brother Jan, who had been sent to work on a nursery in Germany before the war broke out. Once, he came all the way home by himself through sheer homesickness. My father was so angry with him.

Part of the reason for the increased tension was the clandestine things going on around the house. We were lucky we had land and could grow food –indeed we must have had more than enough because my mother and father always gave food—like potatoes and bread to people who came and asked for something to eat. But we would also make (and occasionally smoke) cigarettes and cigars with the tobacco we grew. Selling cigars and tobacco was illegal.

And we had more than two pigs, which was all that were allowed. The Germans would have confiscated them if they'd known. We had a cow that had a calf, but even though there was a family of NSBers at the end of our street and the Germans themselves were based across the field in a village school, somehow we managed to keep the Germans from finding out.

The same went for the radio we kept in a ventilation shaft in the roof. I can still remember my father going up there to listen to the BBC. Anyway, this secret activity meant that I could never have friends over. They might talk about what they saw.

I remember my 10th birthday party. The house was full of people and the main room had decorations Pim made. He played the piano, my father played violin and everyone sang. At the time we had a student friend of Pim's staying with us. He'd been bombed out of his home in Rotterdam.

We couldn't go to school very much because the German soldiers occupied the school building. From time to time there were makeshift schools at various places around the village. Children's education was haphazard then.

Allied and German planes flew over often—both day and night. Mother would call us together with the cry 'zij vliegen weer' – 'they're flying again' – and we would shelter together under the table. Once, incendiary bombs landed all around the house. I think the planes must have been after the school building. Our warehouse was hit by an incendiary bomb and damaged in a fire. My father and Pim soaked the wood around the incendiary to keep it from burning down the warehouse. The bombs burned until they went out leaving craters where they landed in the fields.

A German soldier came to the house looking for young men to take to Germany for labor. I can still see him in his green uniform, kicking in the back door with his boots, his rifle slung over his shoulder. He went through the downstairs rooms and then upstairs but didn't find Pim, who was hiding in an air vent in the warehouse. Mother was beside herself with worry. I wasn't scared myself. Seeing mother upset was worse.

By the end of the war, food became scarce, especially in the cities. We never went hungry because Dad grew food on our land. There was no sugar but we made syrup from boiled and pulped beets, a kind of liquid sugar. We made our own butter in a churn somebody found and bread in a two-foot long tin. We ran out of coal and had to drag the tin to the baker who cooked it in his oven. We used the food we grew and the cigarettes and cigars for barter for things we needed, like clothes. When fuel was gone and electricity was turned off, my uncle installed a small windmill on top of the warehouse's flat roof. This gave us a little light at night. We also used a bicycle to turn the generator when the wind was not blowing. My brothers, Ton and Gerard would turn it by hand.

We were lucky to get something to eat but we got sick of liver sausage and brown bread! Towards the end of the war, Red Cross food parcels from Sweden were dropped by the RAF. They were granted permission to fly over and drop food packages because Dutch people were starving. The contents were gathered at a bakery and divided up among different families. You had to prove how many people were in your household. There were biscuits and white bread, which was really something.

In the last winter of the war, we took in an aunt and uncle from Amsterdam because there was no food at all there. They took over one room of the house. They were real city dwellers – they didn't know how to use our makeshift contraptions—they even needed help to turn on the stove. After a few months they moved into a house that became vacant when the mother of Dad's worker died.

We also took in a cousin of ours called Aad Vaasen, who lived in Heemstede but had no food that last winter. She lived with us for months. I remember she and I brought the Red Cross food home in pillow cases, which we dragged along between us.

Ton's Memories of World War II

Dad was always nervous when our illegal pigs were being slaughtered, illegally of course. He prowled up and down like a polar bear and was impatient with the family.

Cock Vernooy, a first class butcher and Piet Spruyt, Dad's manager, did the work. Once when they were out of ammunition for the humane killer they needed to stun the pig, they had to substitute a rope to kill him.

After butchering the pig, they cut it up and moved the pieces to the smoke house to be cured. Afterward they hid them in a section of the warehouse behind a closed door. Dad took the knob off the door and it was so dark in there the 'moffen' (a derogatory word used for German soldiers during the war) didn't dare to go in and didn't find the hams and bacon stored there.

Once a flight of British bombers flew toward the Amsterdam airport to bomb the runways so the Germans could not use them. But the Germans knew they were coming and a flight of Messerschmidts were waiting. They shot down most of the British planes. We were working in the field and were frightened to see the planes fighting overhead. We tried to hide in a drainage ditch. Part of the wing fell within feet from our house. The rest of the wing with the engine attached fell on Uncle Frans' house and took down one wall. A Jewish couple was living in the attic, but they didn't happen to be in the room at the time so they were not killed. Relatives and neighbors came and repaired the wall and covered up the hiding place which could be plainly seen. But nobody reported it to the police. The couple hid in another place for a while but the Germans did not find out about the couple. So they came back and kept on living there. They survived the war.

We called the winter of 1945 'the hunger winter'. The Germans were so angered by the Railroad Strike they cut off all supplies of food and coal and oil to Western Holland. People were dying from cold and starvation. The Germans finally agreed to let food be dropped to feed the Dutch. So on a day late in March, 1945, American B17's flew over to drop parcels of food. One of the drops was in Vogelzang, a town next to Bennebroek. Gerard, Ton and Mr. Otte climbed up on the flat roof of the warehouse to see the drop. When they wanted to go down, Mr. Otte was afraid because there was a big hole in the roof. So Gerard and Ton helped him down safely.

Stien, Ton's wife, worked with Mr. and Mrs. Gravenstein during the war. He was the headmaster of a school in Amsterdam. The Americans were bombing the bridge over a canal that connected Bennebroek and Vogelzang.

Toward the end of the war there was a Railroad strike in Holland so the Germans were not allowing coal to be delivered by rail. There was no coal or oil or electricity in the country for sale. The people went out into the fields to find twigs and sticks to burn to warm their homes. Mr. Gravenstein was gathering firewood when the bombers flew over. He was killed and his body brought home in a box. His head was torn off by the explosion.

Mr. Gravenstein did not need to be picking up wood because he had enough coal hidden in the attic. Stien found this out when she moved into the apartment Mrs. Gravenstein had given her for working without pay during the war.

A Letter from Gerard and Ellen

In 1943 you needed coupons to buy practically everything. But there was not enough food in the stores.

We grew our own potatoes and vegetables. We had a cow to give us milk and raised pigs to give us meat. There was no bread in the bakery. So we needed flour to make bread ourselves. We had a little old hand mill to grind grain into flour, but nothing to put in it.

Dad raised wheat, rye and barley on the farm in Koegras. The farmer stored his crop but the farm was fifty miles away and we couldn't hire a truck. We didn't have transportation except for a bicycle, so getting the crop home was out of the question.

Then, late one night, I heard a noisy truck. It seemed close, right in the yard. This was very unusual. The Dutch weren't allowed to go out after curfew and only Germans had trucks. I went down to see what was going on. I cracked open the kitchen door and saw a rickety old bus parked by the end of the warehouse, wearing a German license. A couple of men were carrying bags into the open door. I didn't want to be seen so I closed the door and got back in bed.

The next morning when Mother was cooking breakfast, I asked her about it. She told me Piet Spruyt, Dad's manager, went to Koegras and brought our grain home. This was a risky undertaking. It had to be kept secret. I don't know how Dad did it but now we had wheat, barley and rye in the warehouse. Dad must have paid for bringing it with part of the crop. Money was worth nothing; food was like gold.

I don't know where Dad was that night, but he was not at breakfast in the morning. Later that day he came home on his bike. Nobody mentioned the bags hidden in the warehouse.

When the Germans cut off our electricity we got a carbide lamp. For a long time it was the only source of light. We needed carbide or we would be in the dark. Dad found a place in Bloemendaal where he could get some in exchange for beans. Bloemendaal was two towns over, on the other side of Heemstede which was next to Bennebroek, not exactly next door. To carry the goods, Jo and Alice filled our old baby carriage with beans, put the mattress on top and wrapped a doll in a blanket to cover the mattress. It was about eight miles each way so the trip took the best part of a day. The girls had to make the trip. The Germans usually didn't bother women pushing a baby carriage. But if the Germans found out they were hiding beans or carbide, they would take it away.

Once Jo and Alice went to Amsterdam to get material to make clothes. You could still buy things with goods. Bartering was the way to get things; if you offered money, the store keeper would say "*uitverkocht*" meaning they were out. People traded things for food they desperately needed; money was worthless.

In 1944, British planes flew over in the daytime to bomb Schiphol, the airport at Amsterdam. But the Germans had been warned. They knew the Lancasters were coming and Messerschmidts were waiting. The small fast fighters attacked the big bombers like a swarm of mosquitoes. The RAF and Luftwaffe fought in the air right over Bennebroek. Planes and parts of broken planes fell from the sky. Ton and Pim were working in our field right under a dogfight. I was walking on the street nearby. The boys jumped into a drainage ditch for safety and lay there, covering their eyes with their hands. A wing fell in the field a few feet away but it did not hit them. I was covered in dust and hit by small broken pieces of metal, but I was not hurt. When the dogfight was over we were keenly conscious of our narrow escape. We thanked God for protecting us, glad to be alive!

Acknowledgements

We thank our many friends and relatives for their letters and contributions to this book. We thank the Heemskerk brothers and sisters for their letters that bring up forgotten incidents. Alice Dekker, for her diary, written at the end of the war. Pim's brother Anthony and his wife, Stien, Gerard, his twin and Ellen, Gerard's wife, the letter Monique Nachtegeller, daughter of Jo and Harry Meyer sent written by Harry about his brothers' being taken to Vught to work at the prison camp, John's memories of living on a farm in Germany. John was unemployed and by law he had to register for the labor draft. Instead, his father arranged for him to work for a Dutch friend who had a farm in Germany.

And thanks to my sister, Elizabeth Doll, her daughter Nancy Carter, and our children Heidi Gordon, Jill Owens, Laura and Bart and sons Jimmy and Will Heemskerk, and Marilyn Heemskerk.

Our Dutch relatives who sent letters about the war: Monique Nachtegeller, daughter of Jo and Harry Meyer, Anthony and Stien Heemskerk, Ellen and Gerard Heemskerk, Robert and Brigitte Heemskerk, John Heemskerk, Alice Dekker and Henriette Dekker, for their contributions.

Augustine and Linda Calvo, for their many hours of help and encouragement with technical problems.

Members of the Writer's Group in Bradenton for help and suggestions: Annice Cutler, John Garzone, Barbara Goff, Faye Henderson, Bob Marvin, Cindy Miller, Andrew Parker, Kathleen Pasquariello, Thelma Ryan, Nancy Sheriff, Blair Sterling, Bea Tharp, Edna Tiemann, George and Joann Tuttle, Fred Weiss, JoAnn Glim and especially Al Musitano, who designed the cover and wrote a characterization of the story. Thank you!

How This Book Was Written

This is Bill's story about the German occupation of Holland that began May 10, 1940 and ended May 5, 1945. Bill was born in the Province of North Holland on September 10, 1926 to Bart and Marie Heemskerk in Bennebroek, a small town in the bulb district. His father raised tulips, hyacinths and other flowering bulbs to sell to growers in Holland and other countries in Europe and America.

They lived in a white brick house on a farm of about ten acres. This was not enough land for Bart so he bought a farm in Koegras, about 50 miles on the North Sea where he raised crops with the help of a farmer he hired to work the land.

Bart Heemskerk was elected to the Town Council in Bennebroek, so he knew just about everybody in the small town, which was about half Catholic and half Protestant.

The family were Catholics. Their children attended Catholic schools. Protestants and Catholic homes were interspersed but the people associated mainly with others of their own religions, shopped in stores owned by people of their religion. There was a Catholic bakery and a Protestant bakery, Catholic and Protestant butcher shops, and so forth. A Catholic had to get permission from his priest to attend a funeral held in a Protestant Church.

There were eight children in the Heemskerk family, five boys and three girls. Bill, called Pim was a middle child, between his sisters, Jo and Alice. His brothers Jan and Frans were older. His twin brothers, Gerard and Ton and little sister Henriette, called Jet, were younger.

Pim did not have a brother close to his own age. His father didn't want him to bring friends home during the war. He said there were plenty of children already. Also, he didn't want people to see what they were doing during the war. Friends might tell others what they were doing on their farm and the authorities might discover they were not strictly keeping the rules. Pim didn't have a friend at home but he was devoted to his pets—three pigeons, four rabbits, a big German shepherd and two bossy geese.

Before the war Germany and Holland were friendly neighbors. Holland produced plenty of milk, cheese, meat. They brought fish from the North Sea. Their ships carried goods to trade across the world. The Dutch manufactured electronics, ceramics and all kinds of goods. Germany was a customer for their food and flowers and products of their factories. In summer, Germans vacationed on their beaches. Until Hitler rose to power the countries were at peace without guards at the borders.

The Dutch thought Hitler was a comic figure. They were unimpressed by his ranting and raving. They wanted nothing to do with the Nazis. When he began to persecute the Jews, many of them left Germany to live in Holland, a neutral country where they believed they would be safe.

For centuries, people persecuted in their homelands escaped to Holland. The Huguenots came from France. The Pilgrims came from England and lived in Holland before they sailed to America.

Holland was a tiny country. It did not maintain a big army. They did not have the men or equipment to fight Hitler's immense war machine. When they saw Hitler arming, they thought that France with its massive military system would keep Germany from going too far.

When Pim was four he said he wanted to be a priest. He loved the church and its music. So, when he was thirteen he entered Hageveld, a minor seminary where he would study to become a priest.

Later the Germans closed Hageveld and took over the building for administration offices. Then Pim lived at home and attended a high school, called a ULO in Heemstede, the town next to Bennebroek. The Germans were taking young men to work in labor camps. When he was 17 he had to hide to avoid being sent to work in Germany.

Food became scarce. But since Bart raised more food and fewer flower bulbs, the family did not starve. Many people in the cities had to eat pigeons and small varmints they called 'roof rabbit'. They ate anything they could find, including tulip bulbs. After the railroad strike, the Germans would not let them import coal or oil so they had no electricity. In Amsterdam and other cities, people died of hunger, cold and disease.

Near their home, the Germans installed equipment and were firing V-I rockets at England. These were frightfully noisy and dangerous.

In daytime the British flew bombers over Holland on the way to attack Germany. At night, the Americans flew over. It was seldom quiet.

The Allies invaded France and Belgium but their armies stayed below the big rivers and bypassed North Holland, where the Heemskerks lived. The winter of 44 and 45 was extremely cold. The Allies were bombing the railroads and rockets were launched day and night. The Dutch hoped and prayed the war would end.

Germany finally surrendered in 1945. Then Pim was drafted into the Dutch Air Force. It had very few planes. He became a 'medic' for his year of service.

When he was released, his father sent him to America to sell tulips and other flower bulbs. From November until March he traveled up and down the East Coast. Then he went back to Holland to help dig the bulbs and clean and pack them for shipping. He traveled by ship, mostly on the Holland American Line.

We met on the old Ryndam, of the Holland American Line. My friend Dorothy and I were traveling back to America after a three month vacation in Europe. We were students traveling on Eurail passes and staying in *pensiones*. Rooms at the time cost a dollar or two a night and included a big breakfast.

We traveled very cheaply on a Eurail pass bought in America. With this pass we traveled all over Europe for three months. We visited England, Holland, Germany, Switzerland, Italy and France. We would have liked to stay longer in Italy but in November we had to go back home.

Bill was on the Ryndam, assigned to the same table as we were. He was an interesting talker and entertained us the first night at dinner with a story about Dutch customs officers. He said when Dutch passengers returned home the customs opened their suitcases and searched for cigarettes, coffee and tea. But the officers chalked a big X on an American's case and let them go without even opening their luggage.

Dorothy and I sat across the table from Bill. We liked his stories and when dinner was over we felt like old friends. He invited us to the lounge for a drink with him and the friend he traveled with. We talked until eleven. Then Dorothy and I went to our cabin planning to meet Bill at breakfast. But he did not come to breakfast. Neither did he appear at lunch. I asked the table steward why Bill was not there and the man said he would show us. He took us to Bill's cabin. When Bill opened the door, there was a red line on the bridge of his nose. He had bumped it climbing into his top bunk.

And we learned why. After Dorothy and I left, the bartender filled a small round table top with glasses of beer. He invited him and his friend to drink, saying if they could finish it all, it would be free. The men accepted the challenge and won the bet. So Bill did not get up in the morning for breakfast.

It was November and the Ryndam took the northern route to the States. The trip took ten days and we traveled together while the ship fought its way across the stormy Atlantic. On a ship that small we were constantly together.

When we got to Hoboken, New Jersey, Bill was met by the salesman for a car he had bought when he was in New Jersey. We had breakfast together and then we had to part. Bill and the car salesman brought us to the Greyhound station because Dorothy and I had tickets to Grand Rapids where we were going. Dorothy went back to Calvin College and I went to Chicago to teach children at Elim, a school for exceptional children.

We stayed in touch. Bill on his sales trip and after a few months we decided we would marry. Bill went back to Holland and petitioned to immigrate to the United States. The immigration authorities had to look into his background and be sure he was not a Nazi. When they looked into his background they admitted him. He came to this country with a ticket on the ship and $100, that had been given to him by his father.

So Bill came to this country and we married in Grand Rapids, Michigan. Then went to Massachusetts, where his brother John lived. He found a job selling storm windows. This led to a job selling copy machines and then he found his niche—selling encyclopedias to schools and libraries in Maine, New Hampshire, Vermont and later, Massachusetts.

When we retired we moved to Florida. Bill had become a citizen of the United States, but we sometimes returned to Bennebroek, to visit Holland and our Dutch relatives.

We have four children, three daughters, Marilyn Heemskerk, and Jill who married Dave Owens, and Heidi who married Frank Gordon.

Our son Bart, named for his grandfather, married Laura Eden and they have two sons. The oldest, William is in college. Their second son, James, will soon be going there.

Our granddaughter, Kyra, the daughter of Jill and Dave Owens, is in high school. In a few years, she will attend college.